D0873986

# The Afro-American Jeremiad

# The
# Afro-American
# Jeremiad
## *Appeals for Justice in America*

DAVID HOWARD-PITNEY

 33991

# Temple University Press
PHILADELPHIA

Temple University Press, Philadelphia 19122
Copyright © 1990 by Temple University. All rights reserved
Published 1990
Printed in the United States of America

The paper used in this publication meets the minimum
requirements of American National Standard for Information
Sciences—Permanence of Paper for Printed Library Materials,
ANSI Z39.48-1984

*Library of Congress Cataloging-in-Publication Data*

Howard-Pitney, David.
    The Afro-American jeremiad : appeals for justice in America / by
David Howard-Pitney.
        p.   cm.
    ISBN 0-87722-673-3
    1. Afro-Americans—History.   2. Messianism, Afro-American—
History.   3. Social reformers—United States—History.
4. Messianism, Political—United States—History.   5. Civil
religion—United States—History.   6. United States—Social
conditions.   7. Jeremiads—United States.   I. Title.
E185.H65   1990
973'.0496073—dc20                                    89-35268
                                                              CIP

# Contents

# Acknowledgments

I wish to thank my parents, Elvan and Barbara Pitney, who bear some responsibility for this book, having raised me with much love and support and encouraged me to pursue my interests wherever they led, and Beth, my wife, for her love, faithfulness, and patient indulgence.

My intellectual debts are too extensive to list comprehensively, so I limit recognition here to those persons whose assistance was most instrumental in bringing together the book at hand. Chief among these is David W. Noble, my graduate mentor in the craft of American cultural and intellectual history, who introduced me to many of the scholarly works and paradigms that have informed my thinking and shaped this book. He gave unstinting help at every juncture of this long-term project from its origin as a doctoral dissertation, through its reformulation and refinement into journal articles, to the final book manuscript. Others who read or commented on parts of this project include: Drs. Russell Menard, Raymond Arsenault, Brenda G. Plummer, Wilson J. Moses, Herbert Aptheker, and Sacvan Bercovitch. Some of the soundest, most astute writing advice came from Dr. Beth Howard-Pitney, to whose expertise I had unlimited privileged access. I alone am responsible for all the book's contents and interpretations.

Financial assistance came from many grants, fellowships, and institutions. These include, at the University of Minnesota: Dissertation Special Grant, 1984; McMillan Travel Grant, 1984; Dissertation Fellowship, 1982–83; and Graduate School Fellowship (financed by the Bush Foundation). Those institutions that employed me during research and writing of this project include San Jose State University, the Martin Luther King Papers Project, Stanford University, the University of Wisconsin–River Falls, and the University of Minnesota.

The following archival centers and their staffs also are due thanks and praise. Without their help my task would have been infinitely harder. Centers include: The Papers of W. E. B. Du Bois, University of Massachusetts, Amherst; Martin Luther King, Jr., Collection, Mugar Library, Boston University; Martin Luther King, Jr., Papers Project, Stanford University; Columbia Oral History Collection, Columbia University; and the Schomburg Center for Research in Black Culture, New York Public Library.

# The Afro-American Jeremiad

# Introduction: Civil Religion and the Anglo- and Afro-American Jeremiads

On August 28, 1963, Dr. Martin Luther King, Jr., addressed a huge crowd of civil rights marchers gathered before the Lincoln Memorial in Washington, D.C. Thanks to the electronic media, he also spoke to a far vaster audience as he attempted to fix America's attention on the urgent need for national political action to end racial segregation. The site for the event had been thoughtfully chosen. Conscious of the occasion's historic symbolism, Dr. King opened his remarks with a reverent glance backward at the national past. "Five score years ago," he intoned, "a great American, in whose symbolic shadow we stand, signed the Emancipation Proclamation." This "momentous decree" came as "a great beacon of hope" to millions of slaves, he declared, and inaugurated the enduring quest of black Americans for the freedom and blessings of American life.

Dr. King pointedly contrasted the nobility of this past act with the present ignominious neglect of the black demand for equality. Americans in 1963 were not finishing the task heroically begun by Lincoln's generation, he reported disapprovingly. One hundred years after the Emancipation Proclamation, King charged, "the colored American is still not free" but rather is "sadly crippled by the manacle of segregation and the chains of discrimination. . . . In a sense we have come to our Nation's Capital to cash a check," he said:

> When the architects of our great public wrote the magnificent words of the Constitution and the Declaration of Independence, they were signing a promissory note to which every American was to fall heir . . . a promise that all men, yes, black men as well as white men, would be guaranteed the inalienable rights of life, liberty, and the pursuit of happiness.

Yet, King lamented, it was obvious today that "instead of honoring this sacred obligation, America has given its colored people a bad check."

King invoked the nation's noble ideals and past as his prelude to demanding current reform on the issue of civil rights. He and a quarter-million marchers had come "to this hallowed spot to remind Americans of the fierce urgency of *Now.*" "*Now* is the time to make real the promise of democracy," he announced. Today, blacks "have come to cash this check," he declared, and receive their birthright of the "riches of freedom" from "the great vaults of opportunity of this nation." It was time, at last, to make real America's promise of liberty and justice.

This was his expectant faith. Yet, he warned, it "would be fatal for the nation" if it chose "to overlook the urgency of the moment." For "there will be neither rest nor tranquility in America until the colored citizen is granted his citizenship rights. The whirlwinds of revolt will continue to shake the foundations of our nation until the bright day of justice emerges." The current deplorable situation, King declared, "somehow . . . can and will be changed."

Beginning the speech by recalling the hallowed national past, then dwelling on the urgent challenge of the present, King turned visionary at the end, describing in unforgettable language and apocalyptic imagery his dream of America's future. "In spite of the difficulties and frustrations of the moment," King proclaimed, "I still have a dream, . . . a dream deeply rooted in the American dream," that "one day this nation will rise up and live out the true meaning of its creed. . . ." "I have a *dream* today," he cried in mesmerizing cadence to a transfixed audience. In his extended inspirational peroration, King painted scene after scene of a future America transformed into a land of interracial freedom and community. In that rapidly approaching time, he declared, America would fulfill its promise "and the glory of the Lord shall be revealed." Dismissing the crowd, he charged them to go home and work to "speed up that day" when this would happen, when all Americans could sing heartily together: "Free at last! Free at last! Thank God Almighty, we are free at last!"[1]

The image of Martin Luther King standing before the Lincoln Memorial orating magnificently about his American dream is etched into the national consciousness. This speech, more than any other single event, legitimized the ongoing black revolution in the eyes of most Americans and came to symbolize a historic national turning point, lifting King into the pantheon of great American heroes.

What was it in King's rhetoric that made it so deeply stirring for millions of Americans? This study will show how King and other national black leaders have artfully employed a rhetoric of social prophecy and criticism known as the American jeremiad, creating a variant that is specifically Afro-American.[2] The American jeremiad and blacks' major contributions to its development will be explicated by examining the thought and rhetoric of these prominent figures. Because rhetoric operates within a culture, it is best to begin by describing basic American myths that Dr. King and other black spokespersons have so skillfully invoked throughout American history.

## American Messianism and Civil Religion

People in the United States have always believed America to be somehow special and uniquely set apart from the rest of the world. "America" is more than an objective geographic or political designation: it is a powerful symbol charged with great cultural meaning. On one level, "America" refers to a particular society and polity; on another, it represents a mythical space of unlimited human potential. It is the setting in which humanity's dreams can and will be finally realized. This was the dream of America originally conceived by Europeans who hoped to escape the history-ridden Old World for a new land of unbounded opportunity and promise.[3]

Americans' belief that their country is exceptional and an exemplar for other nations is as hoary as the Pilgrims and as contemporary as each presidential campaign. Puritan John Winthrop called New England a "City on a Hill," a shining example of socioreligious perfection lighting the way for the coming of God's earthly kingdom. Over a century later, our rationalist Founding Fathers stated their own fervent belief that it was in Americans' power "to begin the world over again," and customarily referred to their republican experiment as "the world's best hope."[4]

In the 1980s, President Ronald Reagan drew on these popular cultural myths as frequently and effectively as any American public figure. The following passage is typical of many in Reagan's speeches, especially on ceremonial occasions: "I have always believed that this land was placed here . . . by some divine plan . . . to be found by a special kind of people—people who had a special love for freedom." References to America as "a shining city on a hill" and "this last, best hope of man on earth" and Americans' purported ability to "begin the world over again" were all stock phrases in Reagan's speeches.[5] These are not just dead phrases of the past, but still words able to make Americans' hearts beat faster and swell with pride.

Many scholars have held that a national "civil religion" comprised of a shared set of myths, symbols, and rituals underpins American society and unifies its diverse polity into one moral-spiritual community.[6] Well developed and institutionalized, this civil religion is replete with founding myths such as those of the Pilgrims' arrival in America and the American Revolution, with patriarchs and saviors such as Washington and Lincoln, and with scriptures such as the Declaration of Independence and the Constitution. It is commemorated on public holidays such as Independence Day and in such public rituals as State of the Union addresses and the Pledge of Allegiance. From the earliest grades, the public school system inculcates civil faith and reverence in every pupil. No belief has been more central to American civil religion than the idea that Americans are in some important sense a chosen people with a historic mission to save and remake the world.[7]

Such a flattering self-image can promote excessive social pride and complacency or, alternatively, an acute sense of failure in completing the transcendent national mission. The American jeremiad is a rhetoric of indignation, expressing deep dissatisfaction and urgently challenging the nation to reform. The term *jeremiad,* meaning a lamentation or doleful complaint, derives from the Old Testament prophet, Jeremiah, who warned of Israel's fall and the destruction of the Jerusalem temple by Babylonia as punishment for the people's failure to keep the Mosaic covenant. Although Jeremiah denounced Israel's wickedness and foresaw tribulation in the near-term, he also looked forward to the nation's repentance and restoration in a future golden age. A uniquely American version of this rhetorical tradition has been identified by cultural historians as a major convention of American culture.[8]

## The Puritan Origins
## of the American Jeremiad

The American jeremiad originated among seventeenth-century New England Puritans as a vital expression of their self-identity as a chosen people. These early Anglo-Americans believed that they had been called by divine plan to flee a hopelessly corrupt European religious and social establishment and found a holy society in the American wilderness. They felt assured of success in this grand venture because they believed God had chosen them as the historic instrument of his will. America was destined to be a beacon to the world, lighting and leading the way to the millennium. The American Puritans thought that they, as God's new Israel, had undergone an Exodus from "Egyptian bondage" in Europe to a wholly new world. In their westward trek they had escaped the limiting, corrupting forces of tradition and, in accord with divine plan, would march inexorably toward the millennium.

John Winthrop, the first governor of the Massachusetts Bay Colony and the one who dubbed New England the city on a hill, also helped found the jeremiad tradition. In the same address that informed the arriving colonists of their exalted status and destiny, the governor stressed an ominous corollary. He warned: "if we shall deal falsely with our god in this worke we have undertaken," then "wee shall be made a story and a by-word through the world," and God would destroy them and wreck their enterprise.[9]

The jeremiad came to be the special province of the all-male clergy and rang down from New England's pulpits with increasing ferocity after 1650. As Puritan society fell short of its goal of civic perfection, the jeremiad became a ubiquitous ritual of self-reproach and exhortation. Puritan ministers deplored a long list of perceived social failings, denounced the people for their sins and social misconduct, and warned of worse tribulations and divine punishments to come if they did not strictly observe once more the terms of their covenant with God. Believing that their "errand into the wilderness" was to accomplish God's will and establish his kingdom, they declared that the people's everyday misbehaviors imperiled the salvation of the world.

Despite its dark surface tones, the American jeremiad was filled with underlying optimism about America's fate and mission. Sacvan

Bercovitch has argued that the essence of the jeremiad was found in "its unshakable optimism," as it invariably ended by affirming American society's uniqueness and heralding its imminent perfection. The jeremiad's dark portrayal of current society never questioned America's promise and destiny. According to Bercovitch, the jeremiad accomplished this by ritualistically inverting "the doctrine of vengeance into a promise of ultimate success." American Puritans saw themselves as a "peculiar" people to whom God had promised success so long as they observed their divine covenant. Unlike other people, therefore, their calamities were proof of their specialness; God chastened them to hasten the completion of their mission. God's vengeance against them, writes Bercovitch, was considered loving, "a father's rod used to improve the errant child. In short, their punishments confirmed their promise."[10]

The complete rhetorical structure of the American jeremiad has three elements: citing the *promise;* criticism of present *declension,* or retrogression from the promise; and a resolving *prophecy* that society will shortly complete its mission and redeem the promise. The jeremiad's unfaltering view is that God will mysteriously use the unhappy present to spur the people to reformation and speedily onward to fulfill their divine destiny. Bercovitch argues persuasively that this basic structure of the American jeremiad survived Puritanism and evolved into a central American rhetorical and literary tradition.[11]

## The American Revolution
## and the Civil Religion

The American Revolution was the great formative event of the civil religion. Every subsequent generation inherited an existent set of primary sacred myths and symbols created by the Founding Fathers. Future Americans, in the words of one scholar, would henceforth "have to add to or lighten the burden of that original package" in order "to transform its contents" and make the myth fit contemporary needs and sensibilities.[12]

In *Sons of the Fathers: The Civil Religion of the American Revolution,* Catherine Albanese analyzes key changes in American civic consciousness accomplished by the Revolution and offers a general model for comprehending the dynamics of change versus continuity in American civil religion.[13] She underscores the Revolution's essentially conservative inspiration; the leaders' initial rationale for their actions was that they sought to preserve America's virtuous *status quo* against illegitimate imperial encroachments upon their rights as Englishmen. Indeed, until very late in the struggle with the British government over new taxes and Royal regulations that began in 1763, Americans claimed to be defending the traditional English Constitution against tyrannical British departures from it. Not until 1776, a year after the outbreak of military hostilities, did America's leaders formally dedicate their cause to the creation of a *new* political system, Republicanism, thereby finally aligning themselves with political innovation over tradition.

Albanese shows how the American colonists gradually transformed their inherited civic faith. The founding settlers of New England, for example, were already mythic heroes well before independence. New England colonists felt a keen duty to honor the traditions of those who had first settled the wilderness to spread religious and political liberty. This was a powerful social tradition, ritualistically recalled in jeremiads. By the eve of Revolution, this colonial myth of origins had merged with the broader secular myth of Anglo-Saxon political liberty. It was widely believed that England had a mission to develop the principles of free government, and this tradition was thought to have originated in a golden age of free political and legal institutions among the eighth-century Anglo-Saxons. This myth had significant political consequences in England as well as British North America. Eighteenth-century English political radicals, or "Real Whigs," whose views were widely read and admired by colonial Americans, claimed to be honoring the ancient Anglo-Saxon heritage of liberty in their parliamentary battles to curb Royal power.[14] Armed with the potent myth of English liberty, which they amalgamated with the myth of America's own God-fearing, freedom-loving founders, the eighteenth-century Anglo-Americans could view their rebellion against tyranny as being, in truth, dutiful obedience to their fathers.[15]

The inner drama of the Revolution, according to Albanese, was the process by which sons, originally seeking only to conserve the past, became conscious creators of something unprecedented.[16] As the Revolutionary events unfolded, they gained an exhilarating self-identity as progenitors of something wholly *new*. The patriots discovered that they had saved the liberty founded by their fathers by changing and expanding it for themselves and were now creating and actualizing themselves in a time and arena of their own making. Albanese finds that, because of the patriots' intoxicating self-discovery, the Revolution was, for them, "a religious experience." Though the patriots began as dutiful sons, she writes, "somewhere in the process of rallying around their past, they discovered the sacrality of the present" and of themselves in it, and "the result was so powerful an hierophany that it became a new mythic center for themselves and for those who would come after."[17]

With the Revolution, the basic paradigm of the civil religion was set. But it would be ahistorical to suppose that all significant innovation ended there. Albanese's thesis that the first generation was transformed from imitative sons to procreative fathers may be fruitfully extended as a general model of the civil religion's historic development. From time to time, responding to great public events and crises, later Americans would similarly transform their inherited understanding of the nation's mission and freshly redefine its promise. As Albanese notes, the Revolutionary myth was an origins story for a history-making people. True sons of the Revolution were themselves called to take heroic action to advance the national mission beyond all past approximations of liberty. The sons best honored the fathers by initiating acts that simultaneously reaffirmed the nation's beginnings and thrust it forward to start a new chapter in the national saga of expanding freedom. In becoming creators of new norms, latter generations could connect themselves to the timeless experience of the founders.

Opportunities for achieving greatness like that offered by the War for Independence would, of course, not be available to most Americans in most times. Possibilities of heroic action and self-creation amid great, stirring events have occurred only as occasional peaks in American cultural history amid long valleys of seeming national declension. A more frequent feature of the cultural landscape has been incessant jeremiads castigating the present sons for infidelity to the fathers' missionary purpose and lamenting America's decline from its sacred beginnings. The Founding Fathers cast a gigantic shadow over future generations, laying on them the burden of measuring up to the fathers' awesome achievements.[18] For post-Revolutionary Americans, as for the post-settlement colonists, everyday experience seemed mundane and profane in contrast. The world seemed to be continually running downhill as it drew further away from the sacred event. This is the sense of the present as declension that the jeremiad customarily expresses.

When Americans, however, *have* faced momentous public events to which they could respond with bold, self-realizing actions, it has proven an exhilarating, overpowering cultural experience. Then could one generation of sons claim the identity of fathers of future American traditions.

Periodically, Americans have believed themselves in the midst of an Exodus in which they cross a threshold from bondage to freedom as did the Puritan and Revolutionary fathers. For Frederick Douglass, Abraham Lincoln, and others of their generation, the Civil War was such an Exodus. It represented a moment of divine intervention in history in which Americans might save the achievement of their fathers—the Union. And, as the national mission was reborn in the war, it was redefined by it.

The American civil religion, then, has evolved historically as has its jeremiadic rhetoric. An early national jeremiad glorified the American Revolution as a political Exodus in which Americans had escaped Old-World tyranny and entered the New World of Republican liberty. This nationalistic jeremiad quickly became pervasive in national discourse and was ornately embellished in countless Fourth of July orations. As it evolved with American society, moreover, the jeremiad's contents grew increasingly secular. By the mid-nineteenth century, America's "Manifest Destiny" was popularly conceived as spreading the blessings of democracy, free enterprise, and Protestantism across the continent. For a frontier people in ceaseless motion, the jeremiad served as an invaluable agent of cultural continuity and cohesion. It was able to relate the frequently unsettling signs of the times with familiar myths that, amid rapid change, preserved Americans' traditional self-image.

## Abolitionist Origins of the Black Jeremiad

In noting the pervasiveness of the Revolutionary myth, Albanese acknowledges that her book leaves unanswered the important question of how various social outgroups, such as blacks and women, either "appropriated or failed to appropriate the myth and how they viewed their own participation" in it. In this book, I hope to give an answer to that question in the case of six major Afro-American leaders.[19]

As a pervasive idiom for expressing sharp social criticism within normative cultural bounds, the American jeremiad has been frequently adapted for the purposes of black protest and propaganda, starting with the abolitionist crusade against slavery in the North. Although there were many instances of violent uprising and rebellion among Southern slaves, slave resistance necessarily took mainly subtler, non-public forms such as plantation theft and sabotage, grudging compliance with authority, or individual escape.[20] Only in the Northern-based free black community was it relatively safe to protest openly against American slavery and racial proscription.

According to Wilson Moses, the jeremiad was the earliest expression of black nationalism and key mode of antebellum Afro-American rhetoric. *Black jeremiad* is Moses' term for "the constant warnings issued by blacks to whites, concerning the judgement that was to come from the sin of slavery." In this ubiquitous rhetorical convention, blacks "revealed a conception of themselves as a chosen people" as well as "a clever ability to play on the belief that America as a whole was a chosen nation with a covenantal duty to deal justly with the blacks."[21]

Messianic themes of coming social liberation and redemption have deep roots in black culture. The biblical motif of the Exodus of the chosen people from Egyptian slavery to a Promised Land of freedom was central to the black socio-religious imagination. Afro-Americans, by virtue of their unjust bondage, felt that they had a messianic role in achieving their own and others' redemption. Similar themes of messianic purpose and identity and of a historical Exodus figured prominently in both black and white antebellum culture. The interconnected development of a strong commitment by Afro-Americans and Anglo-Americans to evangelical Protestantism in the two generations before the Civil War must have encouraged black leaders to believe that Northern whites would respond to their denunciation of the sin of slavery as a declension from the promise of a Christian America.[22]

The abolitionist jeremiad sometimes crossed the color line to appear in the reflections of prominent whites. Proud nationalists of the early Republic hailed their revolution as the greatest advance for humanity in all history. Having so recently resisted a tyrannical plot to enslave free men, Americans were not entirely oblivious to the stark contradiction of the nation's professed ideals involved in the enslavement of American blacks. Thomas Jefferson worried about the fate of liberty in a land that tolerated the systematic denial of the most basic rights to millions of people. Believing that "liberties are the gift of God . . . not violated but with His wrath," Jefferson lamented, "I tremble for my country when I reflect that God is just."[23]

Far stronger were the fierce condemnations of slavery hurled at white Americans by black abolitionist jeremiahs such as David Walker. Walker was born legally free to a slave father and free mother in North Carolina in 1785. At the age of thirty, he left the South vowing to avenge the wrongs against his people and moved to Boston where he became a militant abolitionist journalist. He was among the most socially advantaged Afro-Americans and, while his fiery rhetoric expressed alienation from the land of his birth, his skillful use of jeremiadic rhetoric reflected his active participation in the highest ideals of American society. In his famous 1829 pamphlet, *The Appeal,* Walker bitterly charged "this Republican land" with gross hypocrisy and called down God's wrath on America: "Oh Americans! Americans! I warn you in the name of the Lord . . . to repent and reform, or you are ruined!" Despite the *Appeal*'s rhetorical threats of violent black revenge, it ended with the optimistic prediction that God meant yet to melt the hearts of white Americans and save them from their folly.[24]

It is ironic that this earliest expression of messianic black nationalism in America should have sprung up in such close proximity to Anglo-American nationalism. For leading black spokespersons' use of American jeremiadic rhetoric signals their virtually complete acceptance of and incorporation into the national cultural norm of millennial faith in America's promise. Yet the Afro-American jeremiad also expressed black nationalist faith in the missionary destiny of the black race and was a leading instrument of black social assertion in America.

## Black Nationalism
## and the Two Chosen Peoples

"One ever feels his two-ness—an American, a Negro,"[25] wrote W. E. B. Du Bois, classically stating one of the key paradoxes of black history: blacks' simultaneous integration into an American culture largely created by whites and their social exclusion from white society. This contradictory experience has bred both an American and strong separate group identity among Afro-Americans, a dual identity that has often been reflected in black messianic traditions.

While black Americans most often have chosen a composite nationality that incorporates both their specific experience of race and their general American messianic tendencies, many blacks have embraced exclusive black nationalist myths such as those in Garveyism and Black Islam, which posit a messianic destiny for blacks apart from, or even in opposition to, the national mission imagined by Anglo-Americans. Marcus Garvey in the 1920s led a popular mass movement among American blacks that championed separate black development in America and ultimate reunion of all people of African descent in an independent African fatherland. Garveyism represented a potent black civil religion promulgating the idea that there was no promising future for blacks in America solely as Americans.[26]

Similar separatist ideas appeared in a black nationalist millenarian sect founded in the 1930s, the Nation of Islam.[27] The so-called Black Muslims' views gained national notoriety in the 1950s and 1960s, especially as voiced to the media by the fiery Muslim spokesman, Malcolm X. For him, America was not and never would be blacks' promised land but rather was a white-run jail from which blacks had, physically and psychologically, to escape. America was Hell and whites were constitutionally evil, Malcolm preached. Allah would shortly wipe them from the face of the earth and found a universal golden age under the benign rule of non-white people. The broader chosen people to whom Afro-Americans should attach their peculiar messianic identity and fate was the colored anti-colonial world. To suppose that it was white America was madness, he taught, the result of blacks' brainwashing by whites.[28]

Malcolm X customarily addressed jeremiads to Afro-American audiences, delivering blistering attacks against such signs of black social depravity as drug addiction, family instability, and lack of thrift and enterprise. These denunciations were jeremiadic in purpose: Malcolm called the people to repent so that they might fulfill their divine destiny, and his harsh criticisms were made in the context of unswerving faith in his people's final redemption.

Malcolm's rhetoric to whites represented a profoundly "un-American" jeremiad. He castigated whites for wickedly oppressing blacks and predicted Allah's wrathful vengeance against whites, but he did not do so within a framework of redemptive prophecy and faith in America. He prophesied that blacks would shortly repent and realize Allah's plan for world salvation but whites were not an instrument of Providence. White Americans obstructed God's work by imprisoning his black chosen people and keeping them from fulfilling their mission. Whites' destruction was a necessary step for achieving the millennium. No salvation but eternal damnation awaited America.[29]

Unlike such forms of "hard," or separatist, black nationalism, the dominant black American jeremiad tradition conceives of blacks as a chosen people *within* a chosen people. The Afro-American jeremiad tradition then characteristically addresses *two* American chosen peoples—black and white—whose millennial destinies, while distinct, are also inextricably entwined.

After its inception in the abolitionist crusade, the black jeremiad remained a prime form of black social rhetoric and ideology well into the twentieth century.[30] It is the story of the development of this influential tradition in the rhetoric of national black leaders from the age of the Civil War to the present that this book tells.

The study examines uses and reformulations of the black jeremiad in the speeches and writings of Frederick Douglass, Booker T. Washington, Ida B. Wells, W. E. B. Du Bois, Mary McLeod Bethune, and Martin Luther King, Jr. Of these outstanding national black leaders of the nineteenth and twentieth centuries only Douglass, Du Bois, and King consistently used the jeremiad in its pure form, that is, boldly and unrelentingly to lambaste white Americans for violating the national ideals and covenant by their racism. Although Washington, Wells, and Bethune employed elements of the jeremiad in their rhetoric, they sometimes deviated considerably from its basic pattern. Washington alone omitted the jeremiadic component in his public words to white Americans, but at the same time he confirmed their status as a chosen people. His openly censorious reform rhetoric to blacks, on the other hand, closely followed the jeremiad format. Unlike Washington, Wells and Bethune clearly operated within the black protest tradition, vigorously defending black civil rights and criticizing whites. Yet their relation to the jeremiad remains ambiguous, because they also relied considerably on less aggressive modes of persuasion. Like Washington, they used nonthreatening symbolism in their rhetoric and frequently shied away from the strident demeanor that marks the true jeremiadic style.

The ebb and flow of optimism about American promise and progress is a pervasive motif in this analysis, affording much inner drama behind these figures' public words. Douglass, Du Bois, and King in particular vacillated with regard to America's perfectibility. Their rhetoric reveals that the intractability of white racism could plunge them into profound crises of faith and that they struggled, often at cost of great personal turmoil, to sustain a vision of America's democratic promise.

# 1. Frederick Douglass's Antebellum Jeremiad against Slavery and Racism

Frederick Douglass, the preeminent black jeremiah of the nineteenth century, was born a slave in Tuckahoe, Maryland, in 1817.[1] His mother belonged to a superintendent employed by the area's greatest slave-holding landowner. His father was white. After his mother's death, Douglass spent his earliest years in his maternal grandparents' home. When six years old, he was called to the plantation "big house" where he worked at light household tasks. Then, at the age of eight, he was transferred to the Baltimore home of Thomas Auld, who would be his master for the rest of his life in slavery.

Young Douglass's appetite for knowledge was temporarily indulged by the pious Mrs. Auld who taught him to read the Bible. The master did not approve and admonished his repentant wife that if a slave "learns to read the Bible it will forever unfit him to be a slave." Douglass took this statement to heart and avidly pursued his self-education. To the consternation of local whites, he helped operate sabbath and night schools where blacks learned to read and write. The more Douglass learned about the world, the more he resented racial injustice. So dissatisfied and restless did he become, he recalled, "I almost envied my fellow slaves their stupid indifference."[2]

Douglass's unusual advantages heightened his rebelliousness, supporting Gerald Mullin's observation that the greatest individual resistance to slavery came from the most privileged and acculturated slaves.[3] When he was sixteen, the "insolent" urban house servant was sent to the country to work as a field hand under William Covey, an infamous "Negro breaker" who beat and whipped the slaves under his command. Douglass found life in the field unbearable. He fled to his owner to protest one of Covey's brutal floggings. Unmoved, Auld sent him back. Determined not to endure further beating, Douglass courageously stood up to Covey and defeated the tyrant with his fists.

Auld, hoping to win the cooperation of his unruly slave, recalled Douglass to Baltimore and had him trained in the ship caulking trade. Auld also promised, if Douglass behaved, to free him at age twenty-five. Acquiring a valuable skill, however, only made the youth more resentful that someone else was pocketing his earnings. Working in the Baltimore shipyards also whetted his longing to know the wider world. After a heated confrontation with Auld over his next work assignment, Douglass, fearing being sent to the fields again, executed a well-planned escape.

Equipped with the papers of a retired black sailor, Douglass in 1838 took the train from Baltimore and, after a series of boat rides, arrived in Philadelphia. Shortly, he went to New Bedford, Massachusetts, seeking work in its shipyards as a caulker. There, hostile opposition from white workers forced him to take work as an unskilled manual laborer. Despite encounters with white Northern prejudice, Douglass found life in the North with its new opportunities infinitely preferable to the life of a Southern slave.

In his new Northern life, Douglass gradually became involved in what would be his great calling, abolition. Having frequently attended and addressed black abolitionist meetings, Douglass attended an 1841 American Anti-Slavery Society gathering at which the famous white reformer, William Lloyd Garrison, delivered a powerful anti-slavery message. "His Bible was his textbook," Douglass recalled, and the scriptural lesson drawn was: Prejudice against color is rebellion against God. "You are the man—the Moses raised up by God, to deliver His modern Israel from bondage," Douglass thought while listening to Garrison's militant Christian jeremiad.[4]

Douglass immediately attended another Anti-Slavery convention where Garrison was to speak. During the convention, a white abolitionist who had heard Douglass at a nearby black schoolhouse asked him to give a brief autobiographical talk to a group of whites which included Garrison. Garrison was so impressed that he asked Douglass to repeat his remarks at the convention's evening meeting. Although intended as the warm-up to Garrison's main address, Douglass's moving oration was the hit of the convention.

From that fateful night in 1841 onward, Douglass became one of the leading orators of the Northern abolitionist movement. He spoke against slavery before hundreds of public gatherings through-out the northern United States and in the British Isles. Publication in 1845 of *Narrative of the Life of Frederick Douglass, an American Slave* proved a huge popular success.[5] A loyal Garrison disciple for several years, Douglass eventually separated his activities from the association in 1847 and became a completely independent advocate for abolition when he founded the first of his several abolitionist newspapers, the *North Star,* in Rochester, New York.

## Douglass's Antebellum Jeremiad

So began Frederick Douglass's career as his era's outstanding Afro-American jeremiah. In adopting this mode of rhetoric, he was influenced by two distinct yet interrelated American traditions. First, he was immersed in Afro-American culture and religion. He pat-terned much of his oratorical style after the Southern black preach-ers and storytellers he heard in his days as a slave. He witnessed black ministers swaying revival crowds and was familiar with the style as well as content of popular black religion. In his oratory, he regularly drew on staple black social-religious motifs like the Ex-odus story, Jehovah the deliverer of the weak and oppressed, and assorted messianic symbols and millennial prophecies. Second, as a man of two races and cultures, Douglass also absorbed mainstream American culture and religion, especially of the New England social-reform variety. Once in the North, he sank deep roots in this middle-class Evangelical milieu. His activities brought him into contact with the descendants of American Puritanism and exposed him to Puritan-influenced modes of thought and language. The social meta-phors of the Exodus, the Promised Land, and the Second Coming, of course, also had a major place in Anglo-American Protestantism. Drawing on messianic themes common to both sides of his cultural heritage, the jeremiad offered Douglass a useful tool for appealing to both black and white audiences.

Speaking as a jeremiah to whites, Douglass forthrightly con-demned the practice of slavery as a severe declension from the promise of a fully Christian democratic America. He excoriated his countrymen for their sinful conduct and threatened them with God's just wrath. "We shall not go unpunished," he predicted; "a terrible retribution awaits us." During the 1840s and 1850s Douglass spoke bravely, angrily denouncing slavery as an abomination to God and curse to the nation. He declared that blacks had a patriotic duty "to warn our fellow countrymen" of the impending doom they courted and to dissuade America from "rushing on in her wicked career" along a path "ditched with human blood, and paved with human skulls," so that "our country may yet be saved."[6]

His prophecy concerning America, however, was just as significant as his harsh condemnation of its faults. The civil religion provided the basis for his stubborn optimism about the future for American blacks. In jeremiah fashion, Douglass denounced the multiplying present evils but drew on the nation's sacred promise to announce his undying faith in the eventual liberation of Afro-Americans and, through it, the realization of America's democratic mission.

A typical pre-war jeremiad exemplifying this faith was an 1857 oration protesting the Dred Scott decision by the Supreme Court upholding a master's right to human property throughout the United States. Douglass interpreted this legal victory for slavery, along with other "signs and events," as "omens" signaling a dangerous slide away from the national mission. Yet at the same time, he discerned "that the finger of the Almighty may be . . . bringing good out of evil . . . hastening the triumph of righteousness." Douglass appealed to America's sacred promise to support his mysteriously optimistic conclusion. "The American people, above all others," he declared, "have been called" to abolish slavery and institute a righteous reign of freedom. "Come what will," he still believed that liberty was "destined to become the settled law of this Republic." Viewed through the lens of prophecy, the Dred Scott decision and the public furor it aroused were "another proof that God does not mean we shall go to sleep" but would shortly rouse Americans to save the nation and its mission.[7] The jeremiadic elements of promise, declension, and prophecy were central in this speech as in most of Douglass's antebellum oratory.

Douglass spoke to many kinds of audiences, ranging from large to small, sympathetic to hostile, and from all-white lyceums to all-Negro conventions. A masterful orator, he skillfully tailored his message and delivery to different audiences.[8] He paid special attention to an audience's racial makeup. Once for example, when an unexpectedly large number of whites came to hear him at a black church, he felt compelled to alter his prepared remarks, explaining,

There are some things which ought to be said to colored people in the peculiar circumstances in which they are placed, that can be said more effectively among ourselves, without the presence of white persons. We are the oppressed, the whites are the oppressors, and the language I would address to the one is not always suited to the other.[9]

To blacks, Douglass preached a gospel of racial pride, unity, self-help, and self-reliance, and other nationalist themes that he tended to downplay before white and mixed audiences. He emphasized to his fellow blacks that they held chief responsibility for realizing their own freedom and social elevation. The oppressed themselves, he taught, must strike the first blow for liberty. He urged blacks to remember "THAT OUR ELEVATION AS A RACE IS ALMOST WHOLLY DEPENDENT UPON OUR OWN EXERTIONS."[10] Blacks could not wait on reformation of white attitudes and conduct—important as they were—but had to take determined united action to bring about liberation and advance.

Douglass constantly called on blacks to redeem themselves from slavery, the racial caste system, and their depressed economic condition. The measures for which he pleaded varied somewhat at different times and occasions. He most consistently demanded vigorous support for abolition, but he also advocated protesting white racism and demanding equal rights as well as more specific acts such as supporting black newspapers and, during the later war years, enlisting in the Union army.

Most generally, Douglass called for black behavior that would command respect. He always viewed winning social respect and consideration through achievement a critical factor in the race's progress. This duty to achieve applied particularly to free Northern blacks who had opportunities denied their enslaved Southern compatriots. Free blacks, being the most prominent examples of black ability, Douglass felt, represented "a potent means of changing public opinion" on all racial matters. With their conduct scrutinized by friend and foe, they must "aim at a high standard of morality and self-respect." Working diligently to make concrete social accomplishments, free blacks could "command something more than sympathy" for their race: they could "earn respect." It was not enough for blacks to claim their natural equality with Anglo-Saxons, Douglass held; they "must [also] show practical equality, or in other words, equal attainments." Black deeds, more effectively than words, would dispel racist misconceptions about blacks' supposedly limited capabilities.[11]

Douglass always imagined black self-help and social uplift in terms of American middle-class values. He believed with most Americans that success in the free enterprise system depended directly on personal application and that outward economic success reflected inner moral worth or "character." To succeed economically and rise socially, blacks had to be thrifty, industrious, and frugal; they had to accumulate property, pursue education, and display in every way praiseworthy behavior.

A major reason Douglass championed black economic self-help was his belief that black attainment of middle-class respectability was vital to ending white racism. In phrases foreshadowing Booker T. Washington's gospel of black self-help and wealth, Douglass declared, "if the time shall ever come when we . . . possess . . . a class of men noted for enterprise, industry, economy, and success, we shall no longer have any trouble in the matter of civil and political rights"; the "battle against popular prejudice will have been fought and won." Demonstrated black merit and achievement supplemented by persistent appeals to white reason and morality would pave the way for blacks' full acceptance into society, because white prejudice "will gradually yield to the pressure of wealth, education, and high character."[12] He sternly commanded blacks to do their racial duty by taking advantage of every chance available to rise, through their own enterprise, to middle-class status.

Although always professing faith in their destiny, Douglass often harshly criticized blacks in jeremiads for their dismal failure to do those things necessary to advance. In one stirring appeal to black Americans, he described their wretchedly oppressed condition and declared, "the worst part of all is, that we are contented under these circumstances," a situation that made him "ashamed! ashamed! ashamed!" of his "identity with those who were thus indifferent— with oppressed cowards!" What were most blacks doing to change their condition and treatment, he demanded? His answer, not nearly enough. Blacks did not deserve respect "if, being under the hoof of oppression, we are not manly enough to rise in our own cause and do something to elevate ourselves." "The colored people do not appreciate sufficiently," he complained, the work of abolitionists and other "instrumentalities" of racial progress. Blacks who were not active themselves were critical of those leaders and organiza-

tions who were doing something. Lack of enterprise and organization were among the sources of the race's shocking indifference and
appalling ineffectiveness. "We have no organization among ourselves," he lamented, but were divided by jealousy into petty fac-
tions. The "ignorant colored clergy" were partly responsible "for the
apathy of the colored people to their own cause" because they
preached passive otherworldly social messages to the people, especially the "absurd notion to expect God to deliver us from bondage."
"We must elevate ourselves by our own efforts," Douglass challenged blacks, since God helped them who helped themselves.

The social remonstrations to blacks in this speech conformed to
the jeremiad format with its severe criticism within a context of an
assumed social mission and a prophecy of a glowing future if the
people would heed the jeremiah's call and correct their behavior.
Douglass's scathing attacks were balanced with the assurance that
black people "are now beginning to exercise their gifts" as they
should and "no doubt the time was coming when the colored man
would occupy the same platform with the white man."[13]

In his frequent jeremiads to blacks, Douglass utilized distinctly
Afro-American messianic traditions. He exhorted them to hold firm
to their faith that it was God's will that they be free and to act in
confidence of this destiny and with determination to achieve it. In
one speech, for example, Douglass urged America's slaves "not to
despair of your deliverance." " 'Lift up your heads, for your redemption draws nigh' " he quoted scripture, encouraging them to continue fighting "to escape from slavery."[14]

Afro-Americans, he always contended, were united by both
American prejudice against them and their common glorious destiny. He asserted that "this people, slave and free" shared a social
identity and mission. They were "a nation in the midst of a nation,"
he declared in a speech by that title: "We are one nation then, if not
one in immediate condition at least one in prospects." Racial proscription and, even more, their millennial destiny bound blacks
together; the enslaved and free of the race were "linked . . . by
indissoluble ties" and "their destiny [was] . . . one and the same."
Despite terrible oppression, blacks remained "a hopeful people"
who would militantly seek liberation while invoking the aid "of Him
who came to preach deliverance to the captives, and to set at liberty
them that are bound." He endorsed the declaration of one anti-
slavery meeting that a "just God will fulfill his promises by bringing

them [blacks] out of the 'furnace of affliction' and getting them 'praise and fame in [the] land where they have been put to shame.' " "I am not ashamed to be numbered with this race," he concluded; "I do not despair for my people."[15]

Douglass's support for nationalistic racial endeavor sometimes appeared at odds with his quest for a raceless American national identity and his assimilationist-integrationist goals for his people. At times, for example, he asserted blacks' need for separate organizations. Although he believed that "in a natural state of society, there would be no necessity of separate action," he noted that until this ideal state was attained, blacks had "a right to associate with each other to promote our interests."[16]

At other times, Douglass cautioned blacks, as he often warned whites, against the evil of excessive race consciousness and feeling. Properly considered, no race was better than another; race was an accident of birth and no cause in itself for either pride or shame. The only justifiable reason for pride among individuals or races was achievement. Black achievement, or demonstrated equality, could best be inspired through racial pride and unity, so he endorsed these useful forces among blacks. Yet he saw racial unity only as a necessary transitional means to a higher social end: an egalitarian America without its present racial fixation. Black overemphasis on racial pride, leading to clannishness and provinciality, he warned, would help the enemy by reinforcing racial exclusivism in America. Blacks could never finally succeed by restricting their social activities and interests to narrow racial concerns. "Our policy," Douglass admonished his people, "should be to unite with the great mass of the American people in all their activities, and resolve to fall or flourish with our common country."[17]

Douglass was adamantly opposed to Afro-American separatist schemes such as colonization or emigration; his ideal of an interracial America took precedence over his racial nationalism. During the discouraging antebellum period and again in the post-Reconstruction era, there was considerable black interest in proposals for leaving either the South in particular or the United States in general, and Africa was often mentioned as the most promising site for blacks' future development.

Douglass's hostility to proposals for black removal and separation from white America partly stemmed from his abolitionist hatred of the American Colonization Society, a white antebellum organization that proposed the wholesale resettlement of blacks— beginning with free blacks—to West Africa as the solution to problems of slavery and race. Removal of free blacks would help sustain American slavery, Douglass believed. It also would be ideologically harmful, as it would imply that blacks had no legitimate place in America. Douglass also vigorously attacked African emigration proposals made by black leaders such as Martin Delaney and Bishop Henry Turner before and after the Civil War.

Although Douglass did make many positive statements about Africa's past and achievements, he steadfastly rejected any idea that Africa, not America, was the blacks' true home and best hope for the future.[18] He made his opposition to black expatriation and his commitment to Afro-American rights in America abundantly clear many times between 1841 and 1895. It was an inescapable fact, he argued, that blacks were in America in huge numbers and no amount of wishful thinking, by whites or blacks, could change the fact that their past, present, and future were inextricably tied to America. It was in the New, not the Old World, that black Americans' destiny would be realized. The black struggle for equality in America represented the cutting edge of the "fight for the redemption of the whole race," he claimed; achieving black liberty here would also be "a blow struck for the Negro in Africa." Afro-Americans were a mixed New World race, he asserted; that "this vast people are tending to one point on this continent" he found "not without significance": "All things are possible with God. Let not the colored man despair then. Let him remember that a home, a country, a nationality are all attainable this side of Liberia."[19]

Douglass ever located his black nationalism within the context of his larger Americanism. Blacks' mission and destiny was inseparable from America's own. By elevating themselves, he suggested, blacks would redeem themselves and the nation, allowing both to fulfill their mutual millennial destinies. Progress through self-help would secure blacks their rights and liberties; it would also erode racism and speed the eventual cure of white Americans' debilitating mental and spiritual disease. Finally freed from slavery and racism (in part through black redemptive action), Anglo-Americans could join with blacks and all other American nationalities to realize a truly democratic society.

## American Promise
## versus Anglo-American Racism
## in Douglass's Thought

The national promise and identity and the power of that promise over the discouraging realities of white racial prejudice and discrimination were central to Frederick Douglass's thought and jeremiad. Each Afro-American jeremiah whom this book investigates had to confront the conflict between America's democratic promise and white America's undeniable racism and be able to prophesy confidently that the promise would triumph. As Douglass provides a baseline for comparing later responses to this perennial challenge and paradox, this chapter examines in some detail Douglass's analysis of white racism, his conception of American mission, and his understanding of the relation between these warring factors in American culture and history.

Douglass's jeremiads were based on faith in America's trans-racial promise. He considered the national mission—to found and exemplify the principles of liberty and equality—an essentially universal, raceless endeavor. All Americans were heir to the national promise, and all other peoples might follow their lead in realizing the blessings of self-governing freedom. Douglass's conception of America's universal promise, however, diverged from the increasing movement among white Americans toward equating the national promise and identity with the special traits of Anglo-Americans, the vanguard of the Caucasian race. Historian Reginald Horsman has described a major shift within Anglo-American culture toward a super-emphasis on race and an overtly racial conception of American nationalism, an ideological trend that crystallized between 1830 and 1850.[20] The national political mythology had long stressed the special contributions of Anglo-Saxon England and America to the development of free political institutions. Nevertheless, Horsman contrasts the relatively universalistic conception of America's mission that predominated in the early Republic with the more particular, racially exclusive idea of American mission that became the norm by the 1850s.

America's revolutionary mission had stressed political principles and values that Anglo-Americans had pioneered but could be possessed by everyone. This inclusive political vision reflected the Enlightenment views of human malleability and perfectibility and the universality of natural law. Eighteenth-century scholars tended to attribute observable differences between individuals and civilizations to the environment, which was susceptible to rational control and direction, and not to fixed biological potential. The prevalent scientific theory of human origins was monogenesis, which posited a single line of human ancestry.

By the mid–nineteenth century, however, it was customary to ascribe American national greatness and success to the unique racial gifts of the Anglo-Saxon who, as one scholar has written, "was represented as carrying in his blood a love of liberty, a spirit of individual enterprise and resourcefulness, and a capacity for practical and reasonable behavior, none of which his rivals possessed."[21] America's missionary genius thus was narrowed from a sphere of universal beliefs and principles to a matter of blood with physical qualifications for membership. In a parallel development, intellectual orthodoxy came to stress the primacy of race and heredity in human affairs, and polygenesis, the theory of human origins as distinct and separate species, was ascendant.

By the 1840s, American scholarly and popular writers had taken the lead in a rising trans-Atlantic wave of racialist thinking. While Southern apologists for slavery were the earliest and most ardent champions of polygenesis, with its concept of superior and inferior races, the racial trend in white American thought was eminently national. In fact, the so-called American school of ethnology, which most authoritatively advanced the new thinking, was centered in the North, particularly in Philadelphia. Samuel Morton, the school's foremost spokesman, wrote in *Cranium Americana* that measurement of skulls demonstrated pronounced differences among races in cranial size and capacity. Morton claimed that these measurements proved the greater mental prowess of Caucasians, and he proposed that polygenesis explained whites' advantage. Morton also pointed emphatically to white civilization's historic achievements to support his thesis that Caucasians were innately superior to non-Caucasians and that Anglo-Saxons were the elect branch of that favored race.[22] Such views were voiced in educated Yankee as well as Southern accents in the several decades before the Civil War.

Douglass was acutely aware of his age's racist trends and firmly opposed them. White racial pride and prejudice constantly challenged his faith in America's universal promise and formed the chief obstacle to the realization of his dream for blacks and America. He confessed, "If I could possibly doubt the salvation of this nation," it would be because of its stubborn refusal to acknowledge blacks' full and equal humanity.[23] Although ever repulsed and perplexed by Anglo-American racism, Douglass's overriding commitment to reform led him to believe that racism could and would ultimately be overcome as a shaping power in American life.

A considerable portion of Douglass's public statements, therefore, reflected his attempt to understand and find ways to end white Americans' racial fixation. His main tenets about the nature, causes, and extinction of prejudice were very consistent. Douglass found racism as mystifying as it was unnatural and perverse. It had no place in the progressive moral universe in which he believed and acted. He considered race hatred and prejudice "a moral disorder" and the product of a "diseased imagination." Racism was mentally disabling because it interfered with the apprehension of reality and capacity for sound reasoning and moral judgment: "Few evils are less accessible to the forces of reason, or more tenacious than a long-standing prejudice." He adamantly rejected whites' claim that racial antagonism was a natural phenomenon based on real racial differences. Douglass always disputed any idea of the naturalness or inevitableness of racist attitudes, contending that social condition, not physical color, was both the cause and the perpetuating force behind racial contempt. "There is no prejudice against color," he insisted: "the white child feels nothing on the first sight of a colored man" but natural curiosity. No, "color is innocent enough, but things with which it is coupled make it hated"—the undesirable conditions associated with blackness being "slavery, ignorance, stupidity, servility, poverty, [and] dependence." When these circumstances "shall cease to be coupled with color, there will be no color line," he declared. Learned association of color with social degradation underlay white racism.[24]

Slavery, the root cause of black degradation, was also the underlying source of white prejudice. Slavery provided a powerful economic incentive for racism. The inhumane exploitation of black people could be rationalized only by denying blacks' humanity. Once established, moreover, racist social conventions and habits of thought were self-perpetuating: after slavery had placed blacks in a wretched social condition, those conditions could be cited as proof of black inferiority, which inferiority was used to justify slavery.

Douglass's most systematic rebuttal of white racialist ideas, and of the views of the American school of ethnology in particular, was an address before a college literary society in 1854, "The Claims of the Negro Ethnologically Considered." For this occasion, Douglass took the trouble to prepare a formal paper, out of respect, he said, for scholarship's role in shaping the "public opinion of the land." To debunk the claims of the American school, Douglass began by establishing his cardinal proposition "that the Negro is a man." Second, he contested the fashionable but erroneous polygenesis thesis. He argued that polygenesis ran counter to traditional Christian theology as well as to common sense and science. Reason and morality, he contended, equally supported the time-honored view that Africans were "a part of the human family . . . descended from a common ancestry, with the rest of mankind."

After highlighting the moral and intellectual deficiencies of polygenesis, Douglass examined the anti-black biases underlying American ethnological scholarship. He detected "ethnological unfairness to the Negro" in this work, charging that Anglo-American writers' racist presuppositions warped their judgment and distorted their science. He found Samuel Morton's *Crania Americana,* for example, full of "conspicuous contempt for Negroes" and "pride of race." Refusing to consider blacks capable of civilized achievement, Morton resorted to specious arguments, identifying the ancient Egyptians not with black Africans but with Caucasians. Douglass proudly reclaimed the grand heritage of ancient Egypt as evidence of blacks' past greatness and future potential.

As always, Douglass identified slavery, now lurking behind a respectable scholarly front, as the real agent of blacks' debasement. Observing that " 'the wish is father to the thought,' " he argued that "the temptation . . . to read the Negro out of the human family is exceedingly strong" in America. American whites wished to transfer the evil of slavery "from their system to . . . their victims" and to soothe their conscience by "making the enslaved a character fit only for slavery. . . ."[25] The scholars of the American school were active participants in the national wish to deny white culpability for slavery.

Douglass's ethnology and sociology emphasized the decisive impact of environment on peoples' present and future condition; he counted on cumulative individual and social advance to dispel white belief in black inability to reach the same level of development as whites. Douglass, in his own person, was a powerful refutation of racist dogma concerning blacks' inherent limitations. His impressive bearing and oratorical brilliance testified to black capacities once freed of slavery's stultifying restrictions.

Douglass was always an ardent advocate of black self-help, seeing a collective responsibility for socio-economic advance. While assailing whites for imposing proscriptions that unfairly retarded black progress, he sternly commanded blacks to take every available opportunity to rise through their own enterprise to middle-class status. Demonstrated black achievement and merit, supplemented by persistent appeals to reason and morality, would pave the way for blacks' full acceptance into society, he promised; white prejudice would "gradually yield to the pressure of wealth, education, and high character."[26]

Douglass urged adoption of American middle-class norms as the key to Afro-Americans' future. He felt that once they had fully absorbed America's ideals and adapted to its institutions, blacks would merge with whites into a common American nationality. To underscore the inevitability of this process, Douglass often contrasted the fecundity of blacks after contact with whites in America with the eclipse of the native American. Where the red race had perished or fled before white civilization, he claimed, the black race had conspicuously flourished. More than simply surviving white society, "we adopt it," he predicted, and "we will follow you in your civilization."[27] By absorbing American culture, Douglass believed, Afro-Americans would gradually become less distinct from other Americans and so find their final social salvation.

As a recent student has observed, Douglass was an ardent Anglophile.[28] He readily accepted Western, especially English and Anglo-American, norms as universally valid and urged Afro-Americans to acculturate to them as rapidly as possible. He resolutely contended, however, that Anglo civilization's high traits and tenets were learned and not, as most whites contended, inherited. Underscoring the goal of blacks' full inclusion in white America, Douglass occasionally identified blacks' nationality as "Anglo-African."[29]

A telling indication of the pervasiveness of racialist thought in antebellum America and of Douglass's own Anglophilia was his frequent analogy between contemporary American whites and blacks and between Normans and Saxons in the mythic past. According to Douglass, at the time of their invasion of England, the haughty Normans regarded the conquered Saxons as fit only for slavery and were filled with racial pride and arrogance. Thus, "the Anglo Saxons themselves had once been slaves": nevertheless the Anglo-Saxon was now "giving his learning, his literature, his language, and his laws to the world more successfully than any other people on the globe." Anglo-American prejudice toward blacks was "the same as the Norman felt toward the Saxon" and the early Saxons' once unpromising prospects. "Low as our condition is," Douglass claimed, "it is no lower than was that of the Anglo-Saxons after the conquest of England by William the Conqueror." Douglass teased a white audience: "You have risen since that time. Come along! Come along! We will come up, too, by-and-by."[30]

Douglass envisioned "a composite American nationality" that would emerge as America's different racial stocks indistinguishably fused. This multi-racial conception of American nationality countered the usual white concern for guarding national "purity" against the enervating consequences of interbreeding, or "race-mixing." Douglass set the fear of mongrelization on its head, contending that, historically, nations had been invigorated by additions to their original stock, while "on the other hand . . . those nations freest from foreign elements, present the most evident marks of deterioration." Douglass pointed to the Anglo-Saxons, that greatest of all peoples, as a "conglomerate people" composed of various Norman, Celtic, and Teutonic strands.[31]

Douglass saw white racism as isolated and fading against the inexorable forces of universal progress. He stubbornly expected reason and morality to triumph, a belief that formed the bedrock of his social faith and vision. Racism was unnatural, immoral, and reactionary, and so it must inevitably be swept aside by the providential tide of history.

As proof that white racism was unnatural, hence impermanent, Douglass declared that it did not exist among large and growing numbers of whites. If racism was natural, it would appear invariably in all racial members; but if some individuals had risen above it, this showed that it was a learned condition that could be unlearned. Citing the examples of many of America's "leading great men" of the Civil War era, Douglass proclaimed "that the number of those who rise superior to prejudice is great and increasing." In addition to finding encouraging signs among white Northern social and political elites, Douglass formed a very favorable opinion about European progress toward racial tolerance from his contacts with English abolitionists during his travels through the British Isles. Strange as it may sound to a modern reader, he often contended that racism did not exist in Europe and particularly not in England: there was "no prejudice against color in England," save what was carried there from America "as a moral disease from an infected country." Douglass could say of racism, "It is American, not European; local, not general; limited, not universal, and must be ascribed to artificial conditions, and not to any fixed and universal law of nature."[32]

## Douglass's Jeremiad to the Chosen People of the North

As we have seen, the Afro-American jeremiad, which combines blacks' particular messianic nationalism with their millennial American faith, always carries the potential for addressing *two* American chosen peoples. In his black nationalist rhetoric, Douglass set responsibility for securing emancipation—and, by implication, for rescuing the national mission—squarely on blacks' shoulders.

As a mainstream member of the Northern abolitionist and political anti-slavery movements, however, Douglass spoke most frequently before predominantly white audiences, and the prime targets of his prophetic scorn were the attitudes and deeds of white Northerners regarding slavery. Abolitionists, of course, were not permitted to speak in the antebellum South, and Douglass considered the demonic Southern "Slave Power" beyond the reach of moral suasion and redemption. The North, on the other hand, had already been freed of slavery. The whole nation would become free of prejudice as well, he hoped, once the South and slavery were overthrown. While excoriating the South as the locus of national evil, Douglass held that the sin of slavery was made possible only by the timid acquiescence of the supposedly anti-slavery North. Precisely because he hoped to reach this target and believed that its aroused support for reform offered the most direct route to black liberation and American transformation, Douglass hurled his harshest jeremiads at the cowardice and hypocrisy of the white Northern public and its religious and political institutions that endlessly compromised with slavery.[33] This temporizing with slavery, he charged, constituted shameful betrayal of America's democratic ideals and mission.

Frederick Douglass's abiding dream—his belief in America's universal promise of democratic freedom, his faith that white America would overcome its contradictory racist strand, and his confidence that Afro-Americans had a special role to play in transforming America and realizing its democratic destiny—sustained his civic activism and commitment throughout his adult life. Probably at no time did Douglass have to rely so totally on this faith in America's future as during the discouraging decades before the Civil War when trends and events seemed decidedly inpropitious for black freedom and progress. This was a time of rising white racism in ideology and practice. The reinvigorated slave system spread rapidly from the 1820s through 1850s, filling vast areas from Mississippi to Texas. As the South's commitment to slavery intensified, it devised ever more extensive methods of controlling and dominating all blacks. Especially did the white South address the threat to its order posed by its increasing free black population. Mechanisms for closely monitoring and controlling black behavior by law and custom were increased and refined. Most Southern states also tried to end black manumission and to banish those persons who managed legally to achieve freedom.

While a drastic improvement over life in the South, the status of free blacks in the North was not very encouraging. Indeed, except in a few New England states such as Massachusetts, conditions for Northern blacks were deteriorating in this era. A racial caste system was the universal norm, by custom and often law, throughout the North. Blacks were usually segregated in transportation, education, and other public facilities, and were restricted to menial low-paying employment. The rising influx of free blacks and escaped slaves from the South into the Northeast and Midwest exacerbated popular white racial hostility, which often culminated in violence against blacks. White backlash led to the passage of Black Laws, modeled on Southern legal codes, for circumscribing black freedom in the old Northwestern states. Three states—Illinois, Indiana and Oregon— banned black immigration altogether in the late antebellum era. Northern blacks were denied political rights and legal protection. In only a few states were blacks eligible to vote; nowhere could they testify against whites in court. Ironically, the spread of Jacksonian democracy and the granting of universal white male suffrage in most state constitutions also occasioned the legal adoption, usually for the first time, of racial qualifications for enfranchisement.[34]

In view of the rise of nationwide white racism and hostility, it was

difficult for most antebellum blacks to feel sanguine about their
prospects for success in America. Among the worst blows to the
hopes of antebellum blacks was the Supreme Court's Dred Scott
decision, which extended legal protection to slaveholders throughout the nation while denying it to blacks anywhere. Few blacks
shared Douglass's prophetic ability to transcend the discouraging
implications of this and other obstacles to black progress in America. One important black response to such trends was the rise of the
National Negro Convention movement and other attempts to organize racial self-help and solidarity, which Douglass actively supported. Another response was a surge in serious black interest in
emigrating to Africa or elsewhere, which Douglass vigorously denounced and opposed.

For Douglass, then, despite his heroic efforts, the antebellum era
was one of deep national decline marked by the growth of slavery
and rampant white prejudice. Buffeted by the flow of events in this
period, Douglass had to base his continued hope for blacks largely
on mystic faith in American destiny, unsupported by empirical evidence. His sense of declension first began to be mitigated somewhat
by a sharp rise in Northern anti-slavery political sentiment. It was
the cataclysmic advent of the Civil War, however, that suddenly and
drastically changed the moment for Douglass and led him to breath-
lessly anticipate the imminent achievement of black liberty. During
and following the war, Douglass imagined America's stepping out of
the mundane, everyday flow of history into a timeless new world of
open-ended choice and creative possibility. In the unplanned events
of war, he came to see the hand of providence acting through the
unworthy North which, despite its faults, still carried God's promise
for America. Jehovah, the mighty deliverer, suddenly and mysteriously had chosen to intervene in national history. Douglass believed that, through the divine chastisement of war, America's destiny would be realized and the nation reborn on a higher plane.

# 2. The Brief Life of Douglass's "New Nation": From Emancipation-Reconstruction to Returning Declension, 1861–1895

The Civil War held deep mystical meaning for Frederick Douglass.[1] The war brought abolition and, he believed, the possibility of a racially just, truly democratic America. It was the high point of his life and of his near-term hopes for America; he considered it a unique moment that transcended ordinary history. The War between the States was seen by many as God's terrible swift punishment, oft predicted by jeremiahs, on America for slavery. At the same time, the war was a redemptive act through which God had wrought black emancipation and national regeneration. It was an epiphanic event in which a generation of sons believed that they had rescued the fathers' heritage while creating a new more glorious Union for themselves and their posterity. The war raised in Douglass high hopes for America and for blacks' acceptance by whites as equal citizens. His sense of an era of new creation lasted until he saw the unmistakable return of national declension after a short season of uncompleted Reconstruction.

The Civil War era represented to Douglass a shining interlude of American progress between two sorry times of declension. During that period, unlike the Antebellum Era and Gilded Age, Douglass's faith in America's future was supported by concrete national events. The last half of the nineteenth century saw extreme changes in national climate and conditions; for Frederick Douglass, it brought corresponding swings between millennial expectations and deep disappointment.

## Debate Over Slavery
## and the National Promise

The Antebellum Era that, for Douglass, was fundamentally one of pronounced declension, nevertheless contained some hopeful portents. Dismayed by slavery's expansion and national popularity of racist ideas, he nevertheless saw the advance of universal principles at home and abroad as a countervailing and ultimately more powerful social trend. Abolitionism was on the upswing worldwide, with England taking the lead; the movement was making encouraging inroads into the American North. Douglass was never so blind to Northern white prejudice as he evidently was to European racial bias. Yet, just as he imagined the United States holding out against a swelling abolitionist tide, so he imagined the South as the lone obstacle to abolitionism's domestic progress. Focusing on the South as slavery's last bastion led him to see the North's greater receptiveness to abolitionism as signaling that it was moving, albeit slowly, in the right direction. Consequently, in Douglass's conception, it was mainly the white South that kept America from fulfilling its democratic destiny, and it was blacks' and white Northerners' duty to defeat the slave power, release the nation from its death grip, and free America to fulfill its millennial destiny.

Well into the Civil War, however, abolitionists remained a tiny beleaguered minority even in the North, and Douglass and his associates delivered anti-slavery jeremiads mostly before empty halls or hostile audiences. What began to end the abolitionists' isolation and create the potential for dramatic social improvements for blacks was the growing sense among Americans that the identities and self-interests of the Northern and Southern states were fundamentally divergent, and that these differences revolved around slavery. Slavery had long been central to the economic and social system of the white South and was rapidly becoming more so with the opening of vast new lands to cotton cultivation near mid-century. Slavery, on the other hand, had never proven economically feasible in the northern regions and so had not taken root and flourished there as it had in the South. Most Northern states had legally abolished this dying institution within their borders in the early national period. When large Western territories began to be settled in the late 1840s and 1850s after the war with Mexico, political conflict erupted between North and South over whether slavery might enter these new territories. Both sides became convinced that the black slave and white free labor systems were incompatible and that one or the other must dominate in the West and in the national future.

Douglass's opportunity to challenge the Northern conscience was not presented by intrawhite disagreement on white superiority and black inferiority (little of which existed) but by an intensifying debate in American political culture about the relation of slavery to the national promise. From the beginning, the existence of slavery seemed to many an embarrassing anomaly for a nation officially dedicated to liberty and equality. The universal egalitarianism of the American Revolution cast slavery in a generally unfavorable light in the early Republic, even though the institution was deeply entrenched in the Southern states and was legal everywhere. Also, at this time, Southern slave-based agriculture was stagnant and becoming less financially rewarding.

Yet the attitudes and policies toward slavery of the Revolutionary generation were finally ambiguous. Some of the Republic's greatest leaders, such as George Washington and Thomas Jefferson, were both slave owners and public proponents of the eventual elimination of the practice. The United States Constitution recognized the institution in the "three fifths compromise," which determined how the South's slave population would count in figuring a state's congressional representation. The Constitution also authorized the national government to return fugitive slaves to their masters and forbade Congress, for twenty years, from abolishing the African slave trade. Congress, however, did end the international slave trade in the United States in 1807 and set a crucial precedent by excluding slavery from the first new territories to enter the Union in the 1787 Northwest Ordinance.

The Founding Fathers seemed to regard slavery as a necessary evil. On the one hand, they considered it an undesirable institution that they hoped would disappear of its own accord. Jefferson's generation saw slavery as unbeneficial to whites and blacks and did not encourage its growth but sought to lessen its hold whenever feasible. On the other hand, tolerating slavery in the near term was considered necessary. Slavery was an extensive institution in much of the South and its sudden removal would be highly disruptive. Moreover, as slavery had resulted in a large Afro-American population, it was thought necessary as a system to ensure white social control over many threatening blacks. America's leaders feared, above all, that national political unity, always tenuous, would be gravely endangered by strong federal measures against slavery. Early government policy, therefore, aimed to discourage slavery generally and to undermine it where it was relatively unimportant and safe to attack. On the other hand, the central government countenanced slavery and refrained from actions against it where the system was deeply rooted, where many blacks existed, and where action threatened national unity.[2] The Republic's early leaders settled for a general attitude of disapprobation toward slavery and occasional mild steps against it, a policy that they hoped might put slavery on a path toward gradual painless extinction.

The Founding Fathers' indecisive position on slavery left ample room for disagreement among their increasingly quarrelsome Northern and Southern progeny.[3] For the founding generation, revolutionary idealism combined with declining economic prospects to permit a mild anti-slavery consensus that prevailed even among many leading white Southerners. Around 1800, some highly respected Southern leaders argued that it was in their region's interest to cease adding blacks and to develop away from economic dependence on slave labor. Slavery's minimal existence in the North declined still further after the Revolution, and by the 1820s, as we have seen, most Northern states had legally abolished it. By 1830, moreover, a small but highly militant and visible Northern movement for national abolition had begun to spread. At the same time, however, the opening of fertile tracts of land from Mississippi to Texas and the antebellum cotton boom invigorated the South's staple economy and dramatically stimulated demand for slaves. By the 1830s, slavery was both more exclusively sectional and more integral to the white South's interests and identity than ever before.

After 1830, abolitionists in the North and apologists for slavery in the South represented the two poles of American antebellum attitudes toward slavery. Radical abolitionists such as Douglass and William Garrison condemned slavery as a sinful rebellion against divine and natural law. According to them, slavery transgressed the first principles of Protestantism, democracy, and free enterprise. Moreover, it was an evil with which no compromise was tolerable. They urged their hearers to break with it immediately and unconditionally. Garrison and his colleagues explicitly renounced the Founding Fathers' willingness to compromise on this moral issue for the sake of national unity. Denouncing the U.S. Constitution for its

recognition of slavery, Garrison became infamous for publicly burn-
ing copies of the revered document, calling it "A COVENANT WITH
DEATH, AND AGREEMENT WITH HELL," and urging "NO UNION WITH
SLAVEHOLDERS!"[4]

While Northern abolitionists were aggressively labeling slavery a
mortal sin and deeming it the main cause of contemporary national
declension, white Southerners were extolling slavery for its role
in promoting America's egalitarian promise—for whites only, of
course. From 1830 onward, the South ceased to concede any immorality or undesirability about slavery and publicly lauded slavery as a
positive social good. Slavery, it was claimed, was a healthy system of
social relations conforming to natural distinctions between superior
whites who were ideally suited to be masters and inferior blacks who
needed a firm hand and direction. Blacks supposedly received the
benefits of Christianization and civilization under their white supe-
riors' benevolent tutelage, and whites received blacks' labor which
they put into the service of American free enterprise and democracy.

For the generation of antebellum Southerners, then, slavery was
not a shameful departure from America's democratic aspirations but
a positive means for white realization of the American Dream. The
political ideology of the pro-slavery South has been aptly labeled
"Herrenvolk Democracy."[5] Only the white race, Southerners contended, possessed the biological capacity for self-government. Furthermore, slavery, which was based on "natural" racial inferiority,
actually helped to advance democracy and end "unnatural" class
distinctions among whites. Emphasizing their common superiority
to blacks supposedly reinforced democracy among whites. Interracial hierarchy and intrawhite egalitarianism were complementary.
South Carolina politician John C. Calhoun submitted in 1837 that
"the existing relation between the two races in the South . . . forms
the most solid and durable foundation on which to rear free and
stable political institutions."[6] Similarly, the right to take slaves into
the new western lands was essential to white Southerners' ability to
exploit their economic opportunities. In the South, black slavery
was not seen as retrogression from the national mission but as a
progressive force for realizing America's promise among whites.

The rise of anti-slavery politics in the North led Douglass to hope
that whites there would eventually be moved to help strike down
slavery throughout the nation. For this reason, he gradually shed his
original Garrisonian view that moral persuasion—never coercive or

political means—was the only acceptable way to seek abolition. To radical abolitionists, politics was a realm of sordid compromise and corruption of moral principle. But as Douglass enlarged his intellectual scope and independence, he revised his initial negative view of political activity.[7]

The Wilmot Proviso, a proposal to bar slavery from all territories gained in the Mexican War that twice had passed the House of Representatives in the late 1840s, greatly excited Douglass. Although the Wilmot Proviso would have allowed the indefinite continuation of slavery in the South and failed finally to become law, Douglass considered it an enormous breakthrough, one that indicated "the presence of a great principle in the national heart, which by patient cultivation will one day abolish forever our system of human bondage."[8] The Wilmot Proviso dramatically injected the divisive debate over slavery into national politics and, by proposing to ban its further extension, expressed fundamental disapproval of the institution. As the white "Free Soil" movement subsequently spread through the North as a major political force, Douglass recognized it as too promising a harbinger of change to ignore.

Sectional political polarization increased rapidly in the mid-1850s with the rise of the first successful Northern anti-slavery party, the Republican Party. The Republicans borrowed much from the abolitionists' damning critique of slave society. Especially did their party help advance the belief, first propagated by abolitionists, in a white Southern "Slave Power" that was supposedly in control of the federal government and was secretly manipulating it to advance slave-holding interests throughout the United States. This Slave Power was not content to dominate blacks and poor Southern whites but aimed to spread slavery and undermine liberties everywhere, including the Western territories and eventually even in the free states. Republicans held that, in order to arrest this conspiracy, any further advance of slavery beyond its present borders had to be halted. But the Republican Party, although anti-Southern and anti-slavery, was not an abolitionist party. Its central platform was to prohibit the expansion of slavery into the new Western territories which, it held, should be left open for settlement by free white Northerners. By 1860, the Republicans had succeeded in convincing a majority of the white Northern electorate that it was in their interest to oppose the nefarious designs of the Southern Slave Power by prohibiting slavery in the territories. At the same time, the party firmly opposed the abolition of slavery where it already existed and refused to endorse social-political equality for blacks.[9]

Political anti-slavery spokesmen vigorously countered the view, put forward by pro-slavery advocates and, oddly enough, by radical abolitionists such as Douglass and Garrison, that America's founders had recognized slavery and accepted it. To gain a hearing in American political culture, anti-slavery politicians had to establish the crucial polemical point that they, not the supporters of slavery nor abolitionists, faithfully preserved the founders' intent regarding slavery. They marshalled quotations and other evidence that they insisted demonstrated the founders' pronounced dislike of slavery and strong preference for its gradual elimination. They especially stressed the Northwest Ordinance as the chief precedent for their current effort to ban slavery from new territories and states. Douglass gradually shed his original interpretation of the Constitution as a pro-slavery document and joined in arguing that the Founding Fathers had really abhorred and actively opposed slavery.[10]

By the 1850s Douglass had become a full-fledged political abolitionist, deeply involved in and voicing qualified support for the burgeoning political anti-slavery movement. His approach to anti-slavery politics was two-fold. On the one hand, he roundly criticized the Free Soil and later Republican parties for their inadequate "half-way doctrine" against slavery, which allowed it indefinitely in the South and refused to support equal rights for blacks. Despite raising these objections about the Free Soil and Republican platforms in the campaigns of 1848, 1856, and 1860, he nevertheless pragmatically lined up before Election Day behind the most thoroughgoing anti-slavery party that had some chance of success at the polls. Douglass tried to serve as the leader of an abolitionist pressure group within the Northern anti-slavery political coalition, supporting those acts against slavery that the movement was presently willing to take while continually pushing it toward forthright support of abolitionism and black rights.

## Douglass's War-Time Jeremiad

The conditions under which Douglass's jeremiad to the North became most effective and influential began with the election of Abraham Lincoln, the Republican presidential nominee, in 1860. Within a few years, Lincoln's election had prompted Southern secession, civil war, and emancipation, although this was not his or his party's intent. Believing that their election had rescued the federal government from the grasp of the Slave Power and stopped the growing menace of slavery, Lincoln and the Republicans tried hard to keep the Southern states in the Union by promising federal protection of slavery where it already existed. The new chief executive repeatedly vowed to respect slavery in the states as an inviolable domestic institution. In 1861 Lincoln feared that several slave-holding border states, only precariously still in the Union, would be driven over to the Confederate side by any hostile federal acts against slavery. Consequently, Lincoln initially pledged to put down the Southern rebellion without endangering slavery. Even after the outbreak of war, Lincoln, for pressing political reasons, continued to avoid even the appearance of waging war on slavery.[11] He defined Northern war aims narrowly as defense of the Union from secessionist treason. This was a goal for which a large majority of Northerners at the war's start were willing to fight, whereas there was little popular support for abolition or any significant change in the status of blacks in American society.

Douglass acted during the war as an abolitionist propagandist to Northerners and the Lincoln administration. His chief objectives were to obtain unequivocal endorsement of abolition as a Union war aim and blacks' acceptance as soldiers in the U.S. Army. He urged these goals on both moral and practical grounds. In 1861, he contended that there was "but one easy, short and effectual way to suppress" the rebellion. "*The simple way, then, to put an end to the savage and desolating war . . . is to strike down slavery itself,* the primal cause of that war." "This can be done at once," he continued. "*Let the slaves and free colored people be called into service, and formed into a liberating army,* to march into the South and raise the banner of Emancipation. . . ."[12] This the Northern nation could swiftly do, if it chose.

Douglass's conviction that resolution of the national crisis required black liberation was not shared initially by the Northern government. From the war's onset, Douglass believed that historical forces were operating to actualize God's will of freedom for blacks and America. There was, he thought, a providential power expressing itself in current events, transcending the intentions of the historical actors themselves. He counted on "powers above those of the Government and the army," and "a power behind the throne, greater than the throne itself," to accomplish the war's destined ends. The United States, almost despite itself, would eventually be "borne along on the broad current of events," on a path charted by Providence. Reflecting his wartime faith in the inherently progressive trend of national events, Douglass habitually invested the phrase "the logic of events" with great spiritual meaning.[13]

The dramatic turn of events in 1861 heightened both his anticipation of the imminent end of slavery and his frustration with the white North's disinclination to accomplish this divine end. His early wartime jeremiads, therefore, angrily deplored the timidity of the Lincoln administration and the North in seizing the golden opportunity offered by the national crisis to uproot the curse of slavery. He scathingly denounced "the sneaking cowardice and pitiful imbecility" of the Northern white government and citizenry, charging that the current generation's conduct in this critical hour "will crimson the cheeks of their children's children with shame."[14]

It is a trait of the American jeremiad to worry aloud about the dire danger posed by current misdeeds to the national future and mission. Arousing fears for the future was instrumental for producing that functional anxiety in listeners that would be the motor force for society's ultimate redemption. The purpose of rhetoric was to persuade, and threat was a leading mode of persuasion. Preachers of the jeremiad threatened that unless the people repented immediately, God would increase their sufferings and eventually withdraw his mission from them and forsake them forever. Like a camp revivalist, the jeremiah painted a terrible picture of eternal woe—and then revealed God's happy alternative. The imaginative world of the jeremiad pictured Americans perpetually standing on the edge of time, facing two starkly different foreseeable futures. Either they would continue in their degenerative ways and meet certain doom; or (and this was the prophecy) the people would reform and rededicate themselves to the covenant. If they did so, God promised them swift success in achieving his perfect order. The terms presented by the jeremiad were "either doomsday or millennium."[15]

Thus Douglass held that the wartime acts of white Northerners were crucial in determining the national destiny. He declared that the "fate of the greatest of all modern Republics trembles in the balance," waiting the outcome of Americans' "Decision of the Hour." No other moment in world history, he argued, matched Americans' unparalleled "opportunity of the present." The nation stood poised to abolish slavery, save the Union, and complete the national errand. But he warned, *if* the chosen people persisted in their present "vacillation . . . and hesitation," if "we omit the duty" to make holy unconditional war on slavery, then "your fathers will have fought and bled in vain . . . , and American Republicanism will become a hissing and a byword to a mocking earth." So, during the Civil War, did Douglass revive and paraphrase the admonitions of Puritan Jonathan Winthrop to guide Americans through their darkest hour.[16]

Although Douglass and fellow abolitionists kept their dramatic appeals ever before the public, it was not until late 1862 and early 1863 that the Union began to adopt some of the measures that Douglass had been urging. This decisive policy change, moreover, came not so much from the change of heart called for by Douglass's jeremiads as from pressing practical considerations. As the war dragged on, expediency suggested such steps as ending slavery and accepting black army recruits.[17] Lincoln's call for more volunteers in 1862 went unheeded and a major draft riot occurred in New York City. The growing need for manpower and the unpopularity of conscription helped pave the way for government and white public acceptance of the idea of black soldiers fighting for the Northern cause. With the slave-holding Border States securely in the Union and no longer in danger of joining the Confederacy, much of the political danger of anti-slavery measures had faded by mid-1862. Furthermore, as Northern spirits flagged before the prospect of seemingly unending carnage and sacrifice, abolishing slavery became a more inspiring war aim than mere preservation of the prewar status quo.

Military experience had also taught the great difficulty of defeating the Confederacy without also attacking slavery, the mainstay of the South's economy and war-making powers. Depriving the Confederacy of millions of valuable laborers made sound military sense. By late 1862, moreover, the Confederates' main remaining hope for independence lay in gaining European aid and recognition. But British and French public opinion was decidedly abolitionist. The surest way of precluding European aid to the Confederacy was to align the Union cause openly with abolitionism.

Although expediency undoubtedly played a major role in the North's eventual decision to free the slaves, there was also an important shift in white Northern attitudes toward ending slavery and countenancing some improvements in the status of African-

Americans. Douglass made significant contributions to this major movement in white opinion. The Southern foe was unabashedly ultra-white supremacist and dedicated to racial slavery and subjugation. As the war progressed, therefore, Douglass was able to prick the conscience of white Northerners by pointing out among them many of the racial attitudes and practices that were associated with the reviled enemy. The need to morally distinguish the United States from the pro-slavery South offered an opening wedge into the white Northern conscience. Douglass's wartime jeremiads skillfully manipulated sacred myths to arouse Northern public guilt, then this guilt was harnessed to reform proposals for aiding blacks. Aroused moral sensibilities played an indispensable role in developments leading to emancipation and, temporarily, to black civil rights.

Douglass kept his compelling moral case before the Northern public through a constant stream of speeches and newspaper columns in which he sought to persuade the public and president to acknowledge the moral and practical imperative of granting freedom to blacks. His fame gained him two war-time audiences with President Lincoln. His and others' propaganda efforts began to show results by 1862, as newspapers and other organs of Northern opinion began commenting more favorably on black freedom and equality.[18]

Despite such headway, it came to Douglass as a startling surprise, something nearly too good to be true, when in September 1862 the president dramatically issued the Emancipation Proclamation, scheduled to take effect on January 1, 1863. Lincoln declared free all slaves in areas currently in rebellion against the United States government. He invoked justice for the act, but mainly justified it as a war measure. Abolitionists were deeply concerned that this cautious decree left unaddressed the fate of slaves in loyal states and areas of the Confederacy already recaptured by federal forces. Nevertheless, Douglass rejoiced and publicly thanked God for the Proclamation, correctly perceiving it as a turning point that irrevocably committed the Union to abolition. As Northern military fortunes thereafter improved and invading Union soldiers (many, by this time, black) liberated the Southern slaves, turning the Proclamation's theoretical emancipation into living fact, Douglass's optimism soared. When in 1865 the Thirteenth Amendment abolishing slavery passed nationally, Douglass saw his life-long campaign against slavery fulfilled.

For Douglass, implementation of the Emancipation Proclama-

tion on January 1, 1863, came as a heavenly thunderbolt radically
rearranging the social-political landscape. He called it "the most
memorable day in American Annals." He marvelled over the "vast
and startling" change that had come over America, declaring that
"we can scarcely conceive of a more complete revolution in the
position of a nation." The only date to which the first of January
could be properly compared was the nation's initial creation. But
while "the fourth of July was great, the first of January" was "in-
comparably greater." The former, he asserted, marked a mere political beginning and statement of intent, whereas the latter "concerns
the national life and character" and would determine "whether our
national life shall be to ourselves and the world, a withering curse
or benediction of . . . blessedness for ages to come." He declared,
"there are certain great national acts, which by their relation to
universal principles belong to the whole human family," and the
Proclamation was such an event in American and world history.[19]

Douglass characterized the current revolution, "this amazing
change—this amazing approximation toward the sacred truth of
liberty," as both soundly traditional and radically new. The war and
Emancipation Proclamation "naturally bring us to the consideration
of first principles," he said. "Mr. Lincoln has not exactly discovered
a new truth, but he has dared . . . to apply an old truth, a truth which
carried the American people safely through the war for independence, and . . . will carry us . . . safely through the present terrible"
conflict. "I feel that we are living in a glorious time," he rejoiced. "I
felt so on the first of January, and have been feeling so ever since. . . .
What a glorious day!" January 1, 1863, would henceforth be hailed
as "the date of a new and glorious era in the history of liberty." In
sum, he declared, "I believe in the millennium and hail this Proclamation as one reason for the hope that is in me."[20]

## Continuing the Revolution:
## Reconstruction and
## the New Republic of 1867

Douglass's national leadership and eloquent jeremiads did not
end with the war and emancipation. 1865 opened a new era of rapid
progress for African-Americans, as war-generated momentum for
social change carried into peace time. Douglass aggressively continued his assault on white Northern consciences, seeking to remove

still further barriers to black equality in America. As early as the first issue of the *North Star,* he had pledged not only to "boldly advocate emancipation for our enslaved brethren" but also to "omit no opportunity to gain for the nominally free, complete enfranchisement."[21] Although Douglass's jeremiads had concentrated on slavery until the end of the war, he had consistently denounced all manifestations of racial caste and proscription in America. His jeremiad, therefore, continued into the Reconstruction era, refocused on the urgency of asserting and defending civil rights and equality for all Americans.[22]

Douglass immediately accepted the challenge of convincing white Americans, who might mistakenly think the nation's redemptive work over with emancipation, that merely ending slavery did not confer freedom and equality on Afro-Americans. Indeed, as of 1865, all that had been settled was that black Americans would no longer be legal chattel. Douglass pointed out that, immediately after the war, Southern state legislatures began closely regulating black behavior. State "black codes" typically made it illegal for blacks to leave their former masters' plantation and employ, to own land and certain other forms of property, to assemble in public, to bear arms, vote, or testify against whites. The black codes had the clear intent of maintaining white supremacy and keeping blacks in a condition as near to slavery as possible. Alarmed by this spreading danger to black freedom, Douglass warned Northerners that "the South, by unfriendly legislation, could make our liberty . . . a delusion, a mockery, a snare," and that as long as Southern whites remained free to pass racially discriminatory statutes to ensure perpetual control over blacks, that slavery "by yet another name" would persist. "Slavery is not abolished," he declared, "until the black man has the ballot" and all other constitutional rights with which to defend his freedom. In scores of post-war speeches, he steadfastly identified this political agenda as the unfinished "mission of the war" and asserted that only with its accomplishment would "our glory as a nation . . . be complete."[23]

Douglass anticipated total national Reconstruction, beginning with thorough reform of the South's pre-war social order and eventuating in a nation completely delivered from racism. "The mission of the war is national regeneration," he announced: "I do believe that it is the manifest destiny of this war to unify and reorganize the institutions of this country—and that herein is . . . the sacred significance of the war." To forward the creation of an egalitarian national union, Douglass urged the federal government to protect black civil and political rights in the South. He exhorted Congress in 1866 to override President Andrew Johnson's permissive requirements for the re-entry of the Southern states into the Union and instead to enact a program requiring black participation in forming the new Southern governments. Bold Congressional leadership was necessary, he argued, to ensure that "we shall, as the rightful reward of victory over treason, have a solid nation, entirely delivered from all contradictions and social antagonisms, based upon loyalty, liberty, and equality." Noting the rejection of the president's Reconstruction policy in recent Northern Congressional elections, he urged Congress to disregard "the illegitimate, one-sided, sham governments hurried into existence" by the president and his white Southern allies and replace them with "true and legitimate governments, in the formation of which loyal men, black and white, shall participate." He urged the establishment in the South of "one law, one government, one administration of justice, [and] one condition to the exercise of the elective franchise, for men of all races and colors alike."[24]

The major political goals of Douglass's post-war jeremiad were achieved by amendments to the United States Constitution. The Fourteenth Amendment, adopted in 1868, nationally secured the freedmen's right to citizenship. With the subsequent 1870 ratification of the Fifteenth Amendment, nationally guaranteeing citizens' right to vote, the program advanced by Douglass in his jeremiads seemed, once again, triumphant.

While the centerpiece of Douglass's Reconstruction agenda was suffrage for the Southern freedmen, he also insisted that black economic opportunity was vital for achieving real, lasting freedom. "The Negro must have a right to land," he argued, for without land, blacks would remain overwhelmingly dependent on the old slave-owning class. Although he fundamentally believed in economic self-help, he maintained that it was impossible for the freedmen to obtain land "on any fair terms" because of black poverty and the refusal of whites, who wished to keep the ex-slaves as landless laborers, to sell blacks land. Douglass proposed the establishment of a "National Land and Labor Company," chartered and capitalized by Congress, to supply credit to freedmen for buying land.[25]

National political action was required to accomplish Douglass's objectives. Thanks largely to circumstances flowing from the war, the Republican-dominated federal government temporarily proved willing to commit the necessary power to force the white South to grant the chief political goals of Douglass's agenda. But the U.S. government was never willing to commit its power to the major economic reforms that he advocated. The conditions which made even the partial success of his program possible stemmed from the white North's wartime enmity toward the white South and the continuing belief that Northern and Southern interests were incompatible. The most effective point in the Radical Republicans' arguments for granting Southern blacks' constitutional rights was their claim that the Slave Power remained in *de facto* control of the South and that, therefore, further corrective steps were necessary to finish defeating it.

From about 1863 through 1870, Douglass was highly optimistic about white Americans' growing willingness to recognize black equality and about blacks' prospects in a new united democratic America. Emancipation had opened this new day, and Douglass had immediately interpreted the white government and citizenry's willingness to accept blacks as soldiers as another "hopeful sign of the times": "Can the white and colored people of this country be blended into a common nationality, and enjoy together, in the same country, under the same flag, the inestimable blessings of life, liberty and the pursuit of happiness . . . ? I answer most unhesitatingly, I believe they can." He found proliferating "reasons for the hope that is in me" even while acknowledging that "prejudice largely prevails, and will prevail to some extent" among many whites awhile longer. But, with slavery's end and the South's ongoing thorough reconstruction, he believed that "the power of prejudice will be broken" everywhere soon.[26]

The New Republic of 1867, which emerged from Northern Reconstruction policies, ushered in a new national reality. In 1870, Douglass founded *The New National Era*, a newspaper which he thought "appropriately named, since it signalized a new world and a new existence" for blacks in America.[27] In preserving the nation left them by their forefathers, the defenders of the Union had transformed that inheritance into an even finer, more glorious realization of liberty. In order to survive, the nation had had to recreate itself.

The former Union was gone, surpassed by something far nobler. "The . . . delusion of the hour is the thought of restoring the country to the condition it occupied previous to the war," Douglass said. The old Union, which had tolerated slavery and accepted racist precepts, had been killed by the war and "can never come to life again." "We do not want it," he declared further, "we have outlived the old Union":

> We are fighting for something incomparably better than the old Union. We are fighting for unity; unity of object, unity of institutions, in which there shall be no North, no South, no East, no West, no black, no white, but a solidarity of the nation, making every slave free, and every free man a voter.[28]

The forces and events that encouraged Douglass's expectations gradually halted, however, then reversed direction. C. Vann Woodward, an eminent historian of the South and Reconstruction, has identified three main factors contributing to the passage of the Congressional Reconstruction program: the moral reformist motive, Republican political advantage, and Northern economic interests. Republican party leaders feared losing political power if disloyal white Southerners returned swiftly to political office and reunited with Northern Democrats to wrest control of the federal government from the Party of the Union. Such a prospect also alarmed powerful business interests that feared repeal of high tariffs and other pro-business legislation passed by Congress during the South's wartime absence. The Radical Republicans' proposal temporarily to disenfranchise the South's pre-war elite while enforcing the voting rights of loyal Southern blacks seemed the best way to keep the defeated states and national government safely under Northern control.

Thus, the case from public morality made by Douglass and other Radical Republicans was an important and moving, but in itself insufficient, cause of Reconstruction policies. Indeed, Woodward finds the weakest links in support for Reconstruction to have been white Northern racial attitudes and lack of commitment to racial equality. When the time came, as it did by 1877, that the Republican Party believed its interests would be better served by courting white Southern voters, and when Northern businessmen saw continued social and political strife over Reconstruction as a hindrance to their penetration of the South, the North showed no hesitation in abandoning Southern blacks. Without the complementary support of political and economic self-interest, white Northerners' moral commitment to black equality proved tenuous, and the brief, half-hearted attempt to create racial justice in America swiftly collapsed.[29]

## Douglass's
## Post-Reconstruction Jeremiad

Through the early 1870s, Douglass continued to believe that American history was progressing toward earthly perfection and that America would be shortly reconstructed as a democratic society. But, as the promise of the Civil War and Reconstruction events began to recede before growing white indifference and hostility toward black rights and equality, he could not sustain his optimistic reading of current trends. By the mid-seventies, the national government was no longer willing to support blacks' political rights in the South. "Redeemer" governments began toppling biracial Republican governments in the Southern states. In exchange for white Democratic acceptance of his contested election, Republican president-elect Rutherford Hayes promised to withdraw all Federal troops from the South and restore so-called home rule. This political deal, known as the "Compromise of 1877" was hailed as an act of national reconciliation by a Northern populace weary of protracted strife over "the Negro question."[30]

Douglass returned, therefore, to a harsher criticism of the present as a glaring declension from the national mission and future in statements that closely resembled his antebellum jeremiad. The country was no longer moving toward realizing the promise of that New Republic bought so dearly and recently with patriots' blood, and Douglass angrily condemned Americans' forgetful, unfaithful conduct. A bitter tone of disappointment and distress, muted in the Civil War years, strongly reemerged in his post-Reconstruction jeremiads, as did the frequency of threats of divine punishment and retribution.

Among the bitterest blows to blacks' hopes for equality was the United States Supreme Court 1883 ruling that invalidated the national Civil Rights Act of 1875 passed to enforce black rights in the South. Speaking at a protest rally, Douglass called the overturning of the civil rights bill one of the most momentous "events in our national history" and likened it to the infamous Dred Scott decision of the 1850s. "It has swept over the land like a moral cyclone, leaving moral desolation in its track," he lamented. He saw the overturning of the civil rights bill as one of the "great evils which now stalk abroad in our land" threatening "to undermine and destroy the foundations of our free institutions." He blamed the event on "a hell black and damning prejudice" that still deeply infected white opinion.[31]

Despite his mounting pessimism about the national direction and growing public indifference to his message, Douglass continued courageously for the rest of his life to issue jeremiads and to voice his tenacious social hope. In a heated 1894 pamphlet, "Why Is the Negro Lynched?", for example, he decried a contemporary "decadence of the Spirit of Liberty" which could only "chill the hopes . . . for the cause of American Liberty." Unjust treatment of blacks, culminating in a hateful anti-Negro lynching campaign, he claimed, posed a "peril at once great and increasing" to the American present and future which, if not halted, "would certainly bring a national punishment" that would "cause the earth to shudder." He began by appealing to America to bring about "the redemption of the world from the bondage of ages"; he ended by pleading with all his persuasive powers for white Americans to "put away . . . race prejudice" and expressing his confidence that this would ultimately happen.[32] As time went on, Douglass increasingly relied on faith in the jeremiad's mystic promise, since he could no longer find empirical substance to support his prophecy that the current declension would be overcome and the promise of a fully democratic America fulfilled.

Frederick Douglass remained nationally active as a black spokesman and Republican partisan until his death in 1895.[33] But he was increasingly unable to stem such threatening trends as the spread of Jim Crow laws, black disenfranchisement, and lynchings. Nevertheless, Douglass's commitment and energy never faded. For all the momentous changes he had lived through, he ended remarkably near where he began: doggedly maintaining faith in America's democratic future despite contrary racist acts and anti-democratic tides. The nation had never fully adopted the measures, including economic reforms, that he had identified as necessary to national renewal, and the great political achievements of the war years were deeply eroded by the subsequent national resurgence of white racism. During the last fifteen years of his life, Douglass found that his jeremiad, which called for using national political force to achieve social justice, had lost its white audience. Well before his death in 1895, his moment as a successful national jeremiah had passed.

# 3. The Jeremiad in the Age of Booker T. Washington: Washington versus Ida B. Wells, 1895–1915

The sharp reverses of the late nineteenth century led to the rise of a new type of black national leader and spokesman. The social and political contexts in which Booker T. Washington and Frederick Douglass operated were starkly different. At the height of Douglass's influence during and shortly after the war, rapid strides toward black progress were made with significant white support; but from 1895 through 1915, when Washington was the leader with most national standing, blacks were struggling to save as many recent gains as possible against rising white opposition.

Washington's strategy accepted the apparent failure of Douglass's comprehensive campaign against Anglo-American racism. Racism as a major white cultural convention had not been extinguished or significantly diminished, as Douglass had hoped, but rather was increasing at century's end. Washington, therefore, did not overtly challenge white racism but worked to direct black efforts into educational and economic endeavors that did not openly threaten white social, cultural, and political supremacy and that had a chance of gaining some white support. He considered it crucial for blacks to work to advance themselves in what he saw as the finally determinative field of social endeavor and only one unaffected by racism, the American marketplace. Whereas Douglass vituperatively and publicly denounced white racism, Washington addressed soothing words to whites and turned away from their racist shortcomings. Washington advised blacks to accommodate themselves to the presently unalterable prejudices of the white public while striving for achievement in the private sector.

Booker T. Washington did sometimes use variations of the American jeremiad in his rhetorical strategies, although his approach was quite different from most of the other major jeremiahs examined in this study. Yet the very fact that leaders as distinct as Washington and Frederick Douglass drew on this tradition testifies to its endemic presence in black rhetoric and the flexibility of the specific notions of American promise and declension that characterize it.

Wilson Moses specifically defined the black jeremiad as blacks delivering prophecies *to whites* warning them of slavery and, by extrapolation, racism's dire consequences for America. In this narrow sense, Washington was not a jeremiah. But the black jeremiad, it must be remembered, assumes both a general American and particular black mission and may address more than one chosen people. Although Douglass and other jeremiahs sometimes gave their strongest reform pitches to alternate racial audiences, of the major figures considered here, only Washington consistently refrained almost wholly from denouncing whites. His words to whites studiously avoided the harsh judgmental tones and strident condemnation of misdeeds that are essential elements of the jeremiad. Washington apparently felt he could get better results from whites with honey than vinegar. He often cautioned blacks against complaining about wrongs, since "a crying, whining race" would be pitied but not respected. Producing concrete evidence of black worth, not "finding fault with others," he contended, was the way for blacks to succeed in America.[1] Although he professed belief in the national promise and civil religion, Washington, because of his disinclination to examine and deplore their misdeeds, was *not* a jeremiah to whites.

Washington's statements of faith in the promise of the *black* chosen people, on the other hand, were typically accompanied by stern remonstrations against their current failings, and he steadfastly demanded their socio-economic repentance. Washington's strategy of highlighting black social responsibility while downplaying white culpability reversed Douglass's mode of demanding reform and defining contemporary declension. Douglass had placed the main burden for reform on white Americans whose racist behavior threatened democracy; he portrayed blacks as more nearly fulfilling their covenantal duty by fighting slavery and racism and helping save and perfect the Union. Washington, on the other hand, preached that prosperity was the chief reward for keeping the American covenant, and that all who tried could become prosperous middle-class individuals. Whites, making unprecedented economic progress after the Civil War, were realizing the American Dream, he felt; whereas blacks were mired in poverty, barely progressing, and lagging ever further behind. In an age of burgeoning legalized white racism, Washington focused his jeremiad reform rhetoric on the *black* chosen people, whose socio-economic conduct he deplored and whose progress could be achieved individually through self-help efforts. He based his social strategy on the power of the marketplace, the basic underlying reality of American life. There he placed his hope for transforming American culture and ending racism.

## Up from Slavery—with White Help

Booker T. Washington was an all-American success story. Born a slave, he became a famous educator and renowned racial statesman. He reached dizzying heights of influence for a black man in white-dominated America by skillfully courting and manipulating the support of powerful whites. Indeed, Washington became the most powerful minority group boss in American history.

Slavery was Washington's school in racial power relations. The son of a white man, Washington spent his early childhood with his mother, the plantation "Big House" cook, performing light household tasks. At a young age, he saw his uncle, stripped and tied to a tree, being brutally beaten for a minor infraction. From such never-forgotten lessons, he developed his life-long conviction regarding the foolhardiness of incurring whites' anger. He never saw a slave profit from defying white power, but he did observe how some slaves managed, by wit, guile, and flattery, to avoid punishment and manipulate the master. As he turned the fan at his master's family table, the young Washington was able to listen discreetly to conversations and to study white mannerisms, storing away the knowledge of whites' habits and foibles that often was the slaves' best defense.[2]

Washington was seven when emancipation came. He moved with his mother and brother to West Virginia where his stepfather worked in a salt mine, living in worse conditions than they had as slaves. Washington soon entered the mines, too, doing backbreaking labor that he loathed. He saw education as the key to escaping poverty and immediately displayed that drive and initiative for which he became famous, attending school before and after work.

He benefited, too, from the sympathetic aid of white patrons whose favor he learned to cultivate. He escaped from the salt mine, for example, by becoming houseboy to the Ruffners, the family owning the mine. Ruffner was a former Union general whose wife was a severe Vermont Yankee. His experiences with the Ruffners confirmed for Washington the wisdom of associating with what he habitually called "the better sort" of whites.[3] His service under the demanding Mrs. Ruffner was the start of his continuing rigorous indoctrination in Puritan-derived social ethics and behavior.

The pivotal event in Washington's life was his enrollment in 1872 at Hampton Normal and Agricultural Institute in Virginia. Hampton Institute was part of New England missionaries' post-war attempt to remake the South in the ideal social image of the North. The institute provided "industrial education," a fashionable educational program for blacks stressing manual-trade skills over classical curriculum. Its primary goal was to promote in freedmen a belief in "the dignity of labor," something that Northerners felt slavery had discouraged in blacks but that was vital to their success in the wage labor system. Besides trade skills and rudimentary general education, young blacks at Hampton absorbed the values of industry, thrift, and sobriety that comprised the middle-class Protestant work ethic.

Washington flourished in Hampton's atmosphere of discipline, learning, and enterprise and quickly became a favorite of teachers and administrators, especially of its white principal and patriarch, General Samuel Armstrong. Upon graduation, Armstrong gave Washington a teaching position at Hampton. In 1881, when commissioners planning a normal school for blacks in Tuskegee, Alabama, asked Armstrong to recommend a suitable white teacher as the first principal, he warmly recommended instead "a very competent capable mulatto, clear-headed, modest, sensible, polite. . . ."[4] Washington was hired.

Having reached this point largely by currying the aid of well-positioned whites, Washington continued this strategy as he swiftly built Tuskegee Institute into a large and powerful institution. He faced a daunting task in running the first publicly funded school for blacks in a small deep Southern community, a challenge that required all his highly-honed skills of racial diplomacy. Many local whites initially opposed the educational experiment, fearing it would make blacks "uppity" and dissatisfied with their customary subordinate social place and economic role as manual laborers.

Washington was able to persuade white Alabamans that black public education of the industrial sort was not a radical venture but a sound investment in social order. He required that all Tuskegee students and faculty always scrupulously observe caste proprieties in dealing with whites. He shrewdly advertised the wholesome effect of industrial education on black youth in inculcating diligence, self-discipline, and the values of Christian service and humility—all laudable goals posing no open threat to the established Southern order or to blacks' position in it.

Washington energetically set about mollifying local whites and gaining their moral and financial support for Tuskegee Institute. Always extremely deferential, he solicited advice and aid from leading town citizens. He soon won over the school's white commissioners and community leaders whom he flattered and co-opted by adding their names to a proliferating list of honorary school trustees. Washington never missed a chance to praise and thank whites ostentatiously for their generous deeds toward their humble black neighbors who were trying to improve themselves in order to be of more use to others. He showed similar deftness in relations with Alabama legislators whose appropriations of funds to Tuskegee rose yearly with their mounting satisfaction with the school's remarkable administrator.

Between 1881 and 1895, Washington assiduously cultivated ties among expanding circles of influential whites. Having cemented his base of support among Alabama whites, he began going North more and more frequently to pitch his appeals for Tuskegee to white philanthropists. He soon found that his formula of black economic self-help and interracial cooperation played equally well to wealthy Northerners. He increased his national speaking engagements before educational groups, and his reputation among whites as a serious speaker of uncommon ability spread.

## The Atlanta Address: Black Retreat and Survival in the Gilded Age

In a social climate distinctly chilly for blacks, Washington met with mounting success and favor, finally achieving national fame in 1895 with his address before the Atlanta Industrial Exposition, an international fair designed to showcase material progress in the so-called "New South." To demonstrate that the South had progressed socially as well as economically, an exhibit of black handicrafts was included and a black was invited to speak along with prominent whites. Washington's rising reputation as a "safe" black leader and entertaining orator earned him the honor. Seizing his first great opportunity to address a national interracial audience, he gave a brief masterful summary of his main social themes and ideas.

Washington took the occasion to propose an interracial "compromise" to secure racial amity and progress. He essentially proffered whites a *bargain* in which blacks would tacitly accept white unwillingness to recognize black social and civic equality in exchange for white aid for greater black educational and economic opportunity. Washington tried to convince whites that helping blacks progress in these specified areas was in their interest, since no movement seeking regional economic transformation could succeed while one-third of the South's population was ignorant and impoverished.

Blacks, for their part, he assured whites, were eager to play their humble role in advancing the South's and nation's material progress. Speaking to blacks, he urged them not to despair over current prospects in the South nor to consider moving elsewhere.[5] Rather, they should stay in the South where opportunities for them abounded. They should not, he admonished, "underestimate the importance of cultivating friendly relations with the Southern white man . . . their next door neighbor," for, he claimed, "when it comes to business, pure and simple, it is in the South that the Negro is given a man's chance in the commercial world." Blacks could advance in the South, he insisted, but only if they remembered that for many years they would be performing manual labor and that therefore, "we shall prosper in proportion as we learn to dignify . . . common labor and put brains and skill into the common occupations of life." So that blacks could improve themselves in order to better serve the South, he pleaded with whites for jobs and education. He urged Southern whites to give employment to the most loyal and docile labor force in the world.

Washington taught that blacks must learn to distinguish between "the superficial" (society, culture, and politics—the areas where racism currently prevailed) and "the substantial" (jobs and property earned in the color-blind marketplace) and set their priorities accordingly. Blacks, he reasoned, had to concentrate on the educational and economic foundation of social success before they could worry about less vital matters. Once they had achieved material prosperity, he promised, all rightful privileges would be granted them; until then, concern with inessential (non-economic) issues was unhelpful to black advance and interracial relations.

Denigrating the abolitionist-Reconstruction legacy of political activism, he regretted that blacks, in their first flush of freedom, had begun at "the top instead of at the bottom," and that "a seat in Congress . . . was more sought than real estate or industrial skill." "It is at the bottom of life we must begin and not at the top," he insisted, nor "should we permit our grievances to overshadow our opportunities." "The wisest of my race," he assured whites, "understand that the agitation of questions of social equality is the extremist folly" and that "enjoyment of all the privileges that will come to us" would have to be earned in the long run and not "artificially forced" in the present. Although he declared that blacks should receive all their lawful rights, he stressed that it was "vastly more important that we be prepared for the exercise of those privileges" through ceaseless application and improvement. The opportunity to earn wages in a factory he considered far more vital than the right to spend money in segregated opera houses. For the moment, he implied, segregation was an acceptable feature of American life. "In all things that are purely social, we can be as separate as the fingers," he summarized, "yet one as the hand in all things essential to mutual progress."

Having thus implied that blacks would tolerate segregation and second-class citizenship without rancorous protest in exchange for sympathetic white help in reaching educational and vocational goals, Washington tried to unify all Americans, black and white, Southerner and Northerner, around this settlement and around a nationwide commitment to economic progress. He ended by offering a pious prayer that by adopting his recommendations, Americans would achieve, besides fantastic wealth, a "higher good" consisting of "a blotting out of sectional differences and racial animosities." This, he prophesied, would inaugurate in the South and in the whole nation "a new heaven and a new earth."[6]

Washington's Atlanta address was a smashing success, attracting favorable publicity and comment from around the country. His mostly white audience that day applauded wildly and the governor of Georgia rushed across the stage to shake his hand. President Grover Cleveland was among several hundred well-wishers who sent Washington hearty congratulations. Leading national newspapers hailed the speech as an act of statesmanship offering a just and practical solution to the vexing race problem.[7]

Washington's soothing recipe for national harmony and material progress was well-received in a nation eager to mute sectional controversies and turn single-mindedly to pursuing economic gain. Particularly heartening to whites, Washington did not contest developing trends toward racial segregation and disenfranchisement. Indeed, by stressing the relative unimportance of such matters compared to blacks getting education, jobs, and money, he seemed subtly to justify these trends. The speech's focus on black economic improvement through self-help (with enlightened white encouragement and aid) took the primary responsibility for the nation's race problem off whites, who were tired of contending with it. The materialist success ethos that Washington articulated fit perfectly the private "get ahead" mood of Gilded-Age America.[8]

Nevertheless, the Gilded Age was not a favorable time for Afro-Americans. The Compromise of 1877, which ended Reconstruction, was hailed by most whites as a symbol of national reunion, as the white North and South showed a desire to end their divisions and meet again on common ground. Articulate Southern spokesmen for an industrialized New South avidly wished for their region to share in national prosperity and rejoin the American mainstream.

Sectional reunion was also aided by growing racism in the white North. Massive post-war immigration of non-Protestant southern and eastern Europeans gave impetus to nativist sentiments among northern Anglo-Americans. Middle-class whites in the urban North began to perceive a shared social problem and even to look to Southerners for instruction on how to control millions of racially inferior workers in an Anglo-dominated society. Racism was as widespread and publicly respectable in the late nineteenth and early twentieth centuries as it had ever been. Social Darwinism and other forms of so-called scientific racism were among the reigning contemporary intellectual and social doctrines that allowed the Anglo-American middle class to place itself higher on the social-evolutionary scale than other races and classes.[9]

In the 1870s, 1880s, and 1890s, flurries of Jim Crow laws segregating public facilities and transportation were passed throughout the South and sometimes in the North. Southern states began convening constitutional conventions in the 1890s to frame legal devices to end black voting. The United States Supreme Court legit-

imized these trends in 1883 by overturning the 1875 Civil Rights Act, and then by explicitly sanctioning racial segregation in the 1896 *Plessy* v. *Ferguson* case. These legal developments accompanied a sharp upswing of white lynchings and terrorization of blacks. Economically, meanwhile, most Southern blacks led debt-ridden existences as tenant farmers totally dependent on white landowners and merchants. The era from the end of Reconstruction through the beginning of the twentieth century has been aptly labeled the nadir for blacks in American life.[10]

## Boss of Black America, 1895–1915

Washington thrived in this hostile racial atmosphere and built up an impressive organizational and personal power base. His control over the flow of philanthropic monies to blacks became absolute. After 1901, he also became prime distributor of blacks' remaining patronage in the Republican Party, serving as unofficial race advisor to President Theodore Roosevelt. He expanded his institutional base in the black community by holding annual national Negro Farmer Conferences at Tuskegee and by founding a Negro Business League with chapters across the country. American presidents visited and praised the Tuskegee Institute. Washington attended dinner at the White House, socialized with millionaires, and had tea with the Queen of England.

Washington used means foul and fair to create what became known among his critics as the "Tuskegee Machine." Always the epitome of modest deference before whites, Washington was dictatorial with black subordinates and ruthless in suppressing opponents. So complete was his patronage power that virtually no black school, institution, or individual had much chance of securing financing without the recommendation of Booker T. Washington. Washington readily used this power to control events and crush black resistance to his will. The legendary "Wizard of Tuskegee" employed a battery of covert underhanded methods to punish and ruin his enemies. From the start of his Tuskegee years, Washington had discredited rival black educators with Alabama legislators by fabricating and spreading unfavorable rumors about them. Later, he regularly made quiet contributions to black newspapers to ensure favorable editorial comment and coverage of his activities. Organizations that he deemed disloyal he had infiltrated with spies. These are but some of the means by which he established and maintained himself as the most powerful black person in America.[11]

In his political pursuits, Washington skillfully invoked and manipulated messianic myths dear to both black and white Americans. Indeed, he was his era's most influential source of Afro-American messianic rhetoric.[12]

Washington suggested that blacks possessed the "soft," non-threatening messianic virtues of (1) servanthood and altruism, (2) humility and meekness, and (3) patient suffering under adversity. One of his leading themes was the "gospel of service." He urged blacks to serve others both as a religious obligation ("Christ said he who would become greatest of all must become servant of all") and as a practical way of gaining an economic foothold in society. "The whole problem of the Negro," he claimed, "rests . . . upon . . . whether he makes himself . . . of indispensable service to his neighbor."[13]

He habitually portrayed blacks' lowly temporal conditions in messianic imagery. For example, he noted that the building first used as a classroom at Tuskegee Institute had been a henhouse and a stable. Thus blacks at Tuskegee's birth, like Jesus, had found no room for their needs save a humble stable. When it came time to raise their own buildings, the students and staff had to learn to make bricks, which Washington later compared with the task of "the Children of Israel . . . making bricks without straw" for Pharaoh. Like the Hebrews of the Bible, Afro-Americans faced hard tasks before they would reach the Promised Land.[14]

Washington often invoked the suffering servant motif that associates undeserved suffering and oppression with redemptive power. Like most blacks, Washington discerned redemptive value in the paradoxical ordeal of slavery. Holding that American slavery "was a great curse to both races," he nonetheless believed that Providence had used the experience to provide blacks with what they most needed for social survival and salvation. America had brought Afro-Americans knowledge of Christianity and English and familiarity with the world's greatest civilization, the Anglo-Saxon. Blacks had entered America as heathens and chattel with no language, he contended, yet had left slavery as Christians and American citizens "speaking the proud Anglo-Saxon tongue." Moreover, the "plantation school" had taught blacks just those work skills now needed by the race in order to develop and prosper. Thus Washington could declare that slavery "in the providence of God . . . laid the foundation for the solution of the problem that is now before us."[15]

Washington portrayed blacks as Christlike to disarm whites and reassure them of black nonaggression. He stressed those gentler traits commonly associated with black messianism to counter the dangerous white stereotype of blacks as rapacious beasts, a popular racial image among whites that spread widely after the Civil War. Negrophobes pictured blacks as such a threatening menace that the severest repression and terror was required to subdue it. Against the rising popularity of this white image, Washington appealed to contrary stereotypes of blacks that invested Afro-Americans with submissive "feminine" and Christian virtues. Blacks, like women, were widely thought to possess an innate religious sensibility and were viewed as naturally meek, devout, unselfish, and inclined to serve and nurture others.[16]

In his 1895 Atlanta address, Washington called blacks "the most patient, faithful, law abiding, and unresentful people that the world has ever seen." When later asked by whites whether lynchings might arouse blacks to violent response, he answered, "No . . . God did not put very much combativeness into our race. Perhaps it would have been better for us if we had not gone licking the hand that had beaten us. But that is the way of our race."[17]

Washington skillfully strummed white Southern heartstrings by playing on their nostalgic myth of the faithful, contented slave. "We have proved our loyalty to you in the past, in nursing your children, watching by the sick-bed of your mothers and fathers and often following them with tear-dimmed eyes to their graves," he told whites, adding that blacks were still "ready to lay down our lives, if need be, in defense of yours."[18] He raised a traditional image of blacks, that of "Sambo," a laughable character with incorrigible but petty faults such as theft and laziness but who was essentially good-natured, harmless, and childlike. Washington liberally sprinkled his talks to whites with humorous stories about sly, lazy, chicken-stealing "darkies," evidently hoping that images of blacks as either Christ or Sambo would counter their image as rebellious beasts requiring violent white domination.

Washington, as had Douglass, posited the universal superiority of Anglo-Saxon, especially Anglo-American culture, and firmly fixed blacks' future within it. Anglo-Saxon civilization was continually demonstrating its superiority through vigorous global expansion, he believed. Indeed, Washington differed from his white compatriots only in his insistence on the cultural, not biological, determinants of Anglo-Saxonism. He maintained that all English-speaking people belonged to that civilization and mission; it was slavery's silver lining that Afro-Americans had received the English tongue and been grafted onto Anglo-American culture. Anglo-Americans had a mission to the world, he affirmed, and blacks, by virtue both of their Americanness and distinctiveness, were a specially covenanted people within the American nation.

Washington always professed to believe in "a proud and great future" for blacks, and he urged blacks to keep faith in themselves and their millennial destiny. He spoke of his work "in putting a new spirit into our people," of inspiring them "with the idea that they *can* . . . they *will* make progress, and fulfill their mission *in this great republic*." The key was the more complete adoption of American middle-class values and behavior. The mission of black people was to perfect themselves as Americans, thereby helping America perfect itself. Their qualities of unselfish service and spirituality were widely considered lacking in the overly hard, "masculine" Anglo-Saxon race that was characterized by material acquisitiveness and competitive, ruthless individualism. The spiritual virtues of Afro-Americans were needed for the fuller Christianization and democratization of the nation. Providence had brought blacks to America, he contended, so "that the stronger race may imbibe a lesson from the Negroes, patience, forbearance, and childlike . . . trust in God." "These eight million of my people have been placed here" that the "white man may have a great opportunity to uplift himself" by the unselfish Christlike act of "lifting up this unfortunate race." By cooperating to further each other's moral and material development, black and white Americans would redeem each other, and together found "the new heaven and new earth." By struggling toward economic equality with other Americans, blacks would hasten the day when all Americans would do right by each other "citizen to citizen" and "Christian to Christian." And "if the Negro, who has been oppressed and denied his rights in a Christian land, can help the whites of the North and South to rise, to be the inspiration of their rising," Washington claimed, the Negro "will see in it recompense for all that he has suffered in the past."[19]

Washington's racial nationalism was complementary but subordinate to his general American faith. This can be seen clearly in his attitude regarding Afro-American involvement with Africa. On the one hand, Washington held that Afro-Americans had a duty to assist in elevating Africans. While it was never his main priority, he accepted his responsibility as a black leader to promote worldwide racial progress. He forged important pan-African ties, sending American missionaries to Liberia and Togoland to found schools patterned on Tuskegee and spread the gospel of industrial education. The same program of agricultural and vocational training and self-help that Afro-Americans were starting to follow, he felt, could redeem black people everywhere. In 1906, he advocated founding an organization for social improvement in Africa, declaring, "I believe all the peoples of the earth may hope to find their task and place" in world progress and that each nationality's distinctiveness "should be preserved . . . for the special service they are able to perform." American efforts to spread Christian industrial education in Africa, he believed, would do much "to secure the future of what is, whatever its faults, one of the most useful races the world has ever known."[20]

But despite his peripheral pan-African interests, Washington was foremost an American nationalist. Insofar as he conceived Afro-Americans' messianic duty extending to Africa, it was as advanced bearers of civilization to backward Africans in desperate need of reformation along Western lines. Afro-Americans, in his view, possessed a special destiny as a result of their ties to America, not Africa. Thus, it was those blacks providentially incorporated into America, he stressed, who "are constantly returning to Africa as missionaries to enlighten those who remained in the Fatherland."[21]

Above all, Washington was an inveterate foe of Afro-American emigration to Africa or migration from the South to black enclaves in the American West or elsewhere. Afro-Americans' destiny, he unswervingly held, would one day be realized right where they were, in America and the South. "I see no way out of the Negro's present condition in the South by returning to Africa," Washington said, rejecting Bishop Henry Turner's call for emigration to Africa. To the contrary, it was in the South that "the great body of our people live, and where their salvation is to be worked out."[22] Blacks need not look afar for the Promised Land, Washington asserted; they were already in it if they would but grasp the opportunities around them.

Washington filled the role of a Moses figure, exhorting blacks to keep the American covenant with its promise of economic success and social salvation. "The pillar of fire" that would lead them out of their current economic wilderness was the myth of the self-made individual.[23] In America, he preached, every person rose or fell in direct proportion to individual effort and ability. The measure was the impersonal marketplace. Circumstances of birth were irrelevant, he maintained, since America promised that everyone who worked hard could become a prosperous middle-class individual, and this promise was abundantly available to all.

The self-made hero was mythically recreated in Washington's best-selling 1901 autobiography, *Up from Slavery*. A loose account of his life, it was an artistic arrangement of the facts into a compelling telling of the American myth of the self-made individual. The work descended from a long line of popular American self-help autobiographies, most notably that of Benjamin Franklin. The contemporary dime novels of Horatio Alger were also a great influence. Alger wrote a stream of popular novels in the late nineteenth century around the same "rags-to-riches" plot: A plucky poor boy, through character and determination, rises to a position of wealth and prominence in the fluid American social structure. *Up from Slavery* is strung along the line of an Alger novel. It chronicles Washington's rise from slavery's degrading depths to a pinnacle of fame and success. Washington could even top Alger's heroes, since they had all had the starting advantage of white skins, which deprived them of a rise from the *very* bottom. He rejoiced at having had this additional hurdle in life, declaring that "mere connection with what is known as a superior race will not permanently carry an individual forward unless he has individual worth," just as blackness "will not finally hold an individual back if he possesses intrinsic, individual worth." "It means a great deal," he reflected, "to start off on a foundation which one had made for one's self."

By ceaseless application and self-improvement, Washington rose to wealth and position in America—indeed, anyone who does so *must* rise, he stressed. Although he often acknowledges timely assistance from well-placed people, there is an air of inevitability about his success in this morality play which says, in effect, you can't keep a good man down. The power of right living and positive thinking is invincible, a social metaphysic that Washington made explicit in the book's "Last Words." Here he confessed that "my whole life has largely been one of surprises," but then concluded, "I believe that any man's life will be filled with constant, unexpected encouragements . . . if he makes up his mind to do his level best every day of his life."[24] In Washington's view, the marketplace offered a fair competitive field in which demonstrated merit determined the outcome. In America's marketplace, if not in its social-civil sphere, prejudice had no role or effect.

Booker T. Washington's well-polished image as the black American self-made man confirmed Gilded-Age America's favorite image of itself. A more flattering, comforting picture of American society was scarcely possible. America truly was the land of unlimited promise and opportunity. Here no inherited, artificial social barriers kept individuals from going as far as merit could take them. More than any Alger novel, more than the examples of such self-made white millionaires as Andrew Carnegie, Washington's story proved that the American myth was true. America works, Washington showed in *Up from Slavery*—even for a black man.

## Washington as Jeremiah

The "self-help" ideology espoused by Washington reflected the dominant social-cultural values that the American jeremiad has historically reflected. Sacvan Bercovitch writes that rhetoric operates within a culture, and that the culture in which the American jeremiad functions is predominantly middle-class.[25] Despite the close fit of his rhetoric with dominant American mores, however, Washington did not deliver jeremiads to whites. To them, he unfailingly celebrated American society, both in its abstract ideals and present reality. In his public statements, there was precious little need of correction in this best of all possible worlds.

Washington did, on the other hand, characteristically deliver jeremiads to blacks. He vigorously upbraided them for failing to fulfill the "duties of Christian citizenship" and urged immediate reformation. Unlike whites, blacks were not adequately advancing toward America's promise of success, partly because of slavery's lingering effects, but mainly because of blacks' myriad weaknesses. Blacks were prone toward crime, "ignorance," "idleness," and "immorality": "The Negroes in the United States," he repined, "are in most elements of civilization, weak." He sharply reprimanded blacks for their lack of will and action to reform themselves. "One trouble with us," he complained to a group of Tuskegee students, was inability to stick with anything long enough to succeed at it. There was no substitute for work and perseverance, no short cuts to success in America, he lectured blacks, a lesson they seemed unwilling to learn. He regularly deplored his race's "lack of ability to organize" its efforts 'and resources intelligently to best serve their own interests. Likewise, he criticized blacks for letting expression of their grievances against whites take precedence over efforts to make the most of the chances for self-improvement open to them in America. "We, as a race, have let some golden opportunities slip away from us," Washington complained, and routinely lectured blacks on such topics as "Unimproved Opportunities" and "Neglecting Opportunity."[26]

Black Americans' future was strictly up to them. They could reform their current ways and follow America's guaranteed formula for success or they could continue as they were and fall ever further behind the admirably advancing white middle class. "The important and pressing question," Washington stressed in *The Future of the American Negro,* "is, Will the Negro . . . take advantage of the opportunities now surrounding him?" Work and proven merit, he claimed, were Afro-Americans' "passport" to "all that is good in the life of our Republic." He affirmed that the urge to reward merit was "everlasting and universal" and much more basic in human relations than cultural bias. When there were enough examples of black economic success through individual initiative, just then, he predicted, will "this race question disappear" forever.[27]

Washington's self-help rhetoric was a form of economic black nationalism that appealed powerfully to racial pride and solidarity. "We are a nation within a nation," he declared, whose "vast latent power" could "be awakened only by united action." He urged blacks to show "that faith in the race which makes us patronize its own enterprises" and support black businessmen. Willingness to support fellow blacks flowed ultimately from self-pride. It is "with a race as it is an individual," he taught; "it must respect itself if it would win the respect of others." He taught that if blacks worked privately to gain education and property and lift themselves as a group, there was no limit to what they could accomplish. Afro-Americans need not remain humiliated as a "weak, vacillating race," he promised; if they "think seriously and work seriously," they would shortly "be thought of seriously, and seriously respected."[28]

Washington overwhelmingly placed responsibility both for

blacks' depressed current condition and for changing it on blacks themselves. He frequently quoted from scripture, "Whatsoever a man so[w]eth, that shall he also reap," stating that "these quotations are applicable to man in all the activities of life, both spiritual and material." He proclaimed over and over "the great" and "eternal" law that "merit, no matter under what skin found, is in the long run, recognized and rewarded." He preached: "In the economy of God there is but one standard by which an individual can succeed—there is but one for a race. This country demands that every race shall measure itself by the American standard."[29]

Being truly jeremiadic, Washington's rhetoric stayed imperturbably optimistic in the face of every current calamity. Blacks' position in America would necessarily improve as blacks began observing America's middle-class social covenant. "Progress, progress is the law of God," he declared, and "the Negro's guiding star in this country." Washington urged blacks not to flee oppression in the South but to look upon it as a land overflowing with promise and opportunity. Clinging to his view of inevitable American and Afro-American progress, he dismissed evidence of whites' unyielding determination to strip blacks of legal and social rights as a trend that was "superficial" and "must, in the very nature of things, be short-lived."[30]

Blacks were not to be disheartened by their current suffering in America, for they were being tested. "Perhaps we needed these trying days to prod us on to greater efforts and more conscientious duty," he suggested. "The black race in America at the present time . . . is passing through a season of trial and testing such as has seldom fallen to the lot of any race in the history of the world." To encourage blacks, he noted that "it is in the storm that the vessel is tested and not in the calm."[31]

His faith in America's promise for blacks could even transform the current upswing in lynchings into a disguised blessing: "You have an unusual number of accounts of lynching; it seems to indicate a going backward rather than a going forward. It really indicates progress. There can be no progress without friction. . . ." "Whom the Lord loveth, he chasteneth," Washington reminded blacks.[32] In the jeremiah's optimistic formula, the people's suffering played a necessary role in their final redemption; even the chosen people's punishments confirmed their promise.

## Washington's Two Civil Religious Styles: Priestly to Whites, Prophetic to Blacks

Washington's conservative middle-class jeremiad to blacks was genuinely prophetic; it both severely castigated blacks' current failings and loftily predicted their glorious future. But while Washington's language to white audiences embodied standard messianic themes, his general civil religious persuasion was more celebratory, or priestly, than prophetic.[33] All forms of civil religion affirm America's millennial promise and destiny. Prophetic rhetoric, however, is further distinguished by its criticism and judgment of present society in light of this transcendent ideal. In regard to Anglo-American society, however, Washington virtually collapsed the jeremiad's vital distinction between present declension and future ideal. America was not only destined to become a land of unparalleled opportunity but, in Washington's view, already pretty much was that place, in actuality for whites and potentially for all. Afro-Americans were in the Promised Land but, because of their shortcomings, were temporarily failing to claim its promise. White society did not have to change for the complete realization of the American dream—black conduct in America did.

The surface similarities between Frederick Douglass and Booker T. Washington were substantial. Both were born slaves but became articulate champions and living symbols of the American self-made man. Both were bi-cultural and had white fathers; they were shaped by both Afro-American slave-based and American middle-class culture. They were the foremost black spokesmen of their eras, at once representative race leaders and important molders of white opinion and national policy. Douglass and Washington voiced messianic nationalism, advocating black self-help and envisioning blacks' social mission as activating America's mission. They prophesied an intertwined destiny for black and white America, and neither supported black separatism other than as a provisional means toward a non-separatist end. Finally, each held that white American racism would eventually yield to black socio-economic development and that a key task before Afro-Americans was to elevate themselves to middle-class respectability.

Despite these striking similarities, Washington and Douglass represented fundamentally divergent modes of racial leadership and struggle. Douglass was pre-eminently a protest leader who made his greatest mark taking white America boldly to task for its shameful practice of racial slavery and caste. And while he exhorted blacks to become self-reliant in seeking socio-economic advance, he also pronounced it part of their sacred duty to publicly oppose and protest every manifestation of racial prejudice and injustice. Washington's racial leadership and strategy, on the other hand, aimed to curb black protest at white prejudice and discrimination. His tactic was to "compromise" on (that is, accept) white insistence on segregation and disenfranchisement, while moving Douglass's secondary message of black economic self-help and middle-class development to the forefront of the black agenda. The key difference was that, whereas Douglass uncompromisingly demanded equal rights and opportunity in every sphere, most especially the civil-political, Washington counseled black accommodation to racism in public life for the present and a focus on self-advancement in the private economy.

It is probable that the worsening political climate for blacks accounted for this important change in how the nation's leading black spokesman deployed jeremiadic rhetoric. It is important to remember that Douglass's public effectiveness, if not his courage and determination, had substantially declined in the face of intensified white racism in the late nineteenth century. He fought for equality in an age increasingly indifferent to the state of democracy and preoccupied with private gain. In the post-war environment, his jeremiad proved ineffectual. Washington's public strategy reflected his unblinking recognition of racism's powerful hold on Anglo-American culture and his considerable sycophancy. Washington never shared Douglass's hopeful expectation that white society, spurred by blacks' jeremiadic appeals, could be cleansed of racism. In an age of rampant public racism and predominant concern for private gain, Washington pragmatically minimized the importance of white reform and stressed black self-improvement.

One of the keys to Washington's amazing rise to power in white-dominated America was his close observance and shrewd manipulation of the code of paternalism that required a respectful, deferential demeanor from blacks toward whites. He grasped the potential benefits of this approach and the grave dangers of violating standard racial etiquette. Thus, while it was safe to engage in rigorous social criticism of blacks, complaints against whites had to be made softly and indirectly, if at all. Whereas Douglass's life experiences led him to bold protest and rebellion, Washington's experience taught him different lessons. Faced with growing disenfranchisement, segregation, and hostility toward black social equality, Washington thought it foolhardy and useless to object to these trends, thereby wasting whatever influence he might exert over whites. By bowing to white intransigence, Washington hoped to expand, with white support, opportunities for blacks in what he considered the crucial fields of education and economics.

## Counterpoint in the Age of Booker T. Washington: Ida B. Wells

Even at the height of Booker T. Washington's influence, however, Afro-American protest against white racism never disappeared. Indeed, by the turn of the century growing numbers of blacks were questioning his opposition to protesting white racism. Deepening dissatisfaction with the result of Washington's compromise with whites—a rapid spread of institutionalized racism and a virtual lynching epidemic—and resentment of his dictatorial control over major black institutions led some prominent blacks to resist his leadership and resume open protest against racial injustice. No other issue so galvanized this rising black protest and impatience with Washington's policies as lynching. No individual was more instrumental in insistently raising the issue of lynching as Ida B. Wells, who from 1887 through 1910 led a public crusade against this shameful American practice.[34]

Ida B. Wells (1862–1931) was born in Holly Springs, Mississippi. Her father was a skilled tradesman and prominent local citizen. She received a childhood education and was away at college in 1878 when her parents and a brother died of yellow fever. Seventeen-year-old Ida returned to care for her five younger siblings. The family moved to Memphis, Tennessee, where she supported them by teaching school in the countryside while studying for the teachers' examination for city schools.

Wells gained local notoriety in 1884, when, riding the railroad home from work one day, she refused when asked to exchange her first-class car for the smoking car to comply with a new state segregation law. She sued the railroad and won. In an 1887 church newspaper column, she used her case to encourage blacks to stand up for their rights. She thereafter started working for the Memphis *Free Speech* and soon became an editor and part owner. She continued teaching in Memphis schools until she was fired in 1891 for writing an article exposing the abysmal conditions of Memphis's segregated educational facilities for blacks.

The turning point in Wells's career stemmed from the 1892 lynching of three black Memphis businessmen, one of whom, Thomas Moss, she knew personally. These men had become partners in a flourishing grocery store that threatened the business of a nearby white grocer. When their competitor led an assault on their store, the partners shot and wounded three of the white attackers. After sensational newspaper stories reported that "Negro desperadoes" had shot white policemen who were searching for criminals in "a low dive" of "thieves and thugs," thirty-one blacks were arrested, and a white mob destroyed their store.[35] The three partners were then seized by masked men in a pre-dawn prison raid and brutally lynched, an event which led to no arrests.

Wells and other Memphis blacks knew Thomas Moss in particular as a respected businessman, outstanding citizen, and Sunday School teacher. They were outraged by his and the other men's murder. The realization that such individuals could be murdered in blatant disregard of the law was as horrifying as their actual deaths. "The city of Memphis has demonstrated that neither character nor standing avails the Negro if he dares to protect himself against the white man or becomes his rival," Wells angrily wrote in the *Free Speech*.[36]

The Moss lynching, Wells later recalled, "opened my eyes to what lynching really was. An excuse to get rid of Negroes who were acquiring wealth and property and thus keep the race terrified and 'keep the nigger down.' I then began an investigation of every lynching I read about."[37]

Wells's study of hundreds of lynchings convinced her that white fear of black advance was the true cause and that the public justifications were only convenient fictions. Newly sensitized to this issue, Wells turned her journalistic talents to carefully investigating the crime with which lynch victims were most regularly charged, rape or attempted rape of white women. She first suggested the mendacity of this claim in a *Free Speech* editorial of May 1892. She noted that, in the short time since the last issue, eight more blacks had been lynched in the South, five ostensibly for raping white women. Her comment: "Nobody . . . believes the old thread-bare lie that Negro men assault white women. If Southern white men are not careful . . . a conclusion will be reached which will be very damaging to the moral reputation of their women." Memphis whites were enraged by this none-too-subtle hint that it was the unrestrained sexual appetite of the white, including the white female, and not black brutishness that mainly prompted interracial sex in the South. A mob set fire to the *Free Speech*. A local newspaper demanded the lynching of the "black wretch who had written that foul lie," and a bounty was put on Wells's head.[38]

Fortunately, Wells was on a trip to the East Coast when her editorial appeared. She received news of these events in New York City from T. Thomas Fortune, noted black journalist and editor of the New York *Age*. Not daring to return, she joined the *Age*'s staff in New York. There in 1892 she began her true career as a famous reform journalist and anti-lynching propagandist. She quickly wrote an article in the *Age* systematically treating the issues raised only indirectly in her now infamous *Free Speech* editorial. This exposé of the rape myth in the *Age* aroused national black interest and, in conjunction with the Memphis incident, made her a black celebrity. The *Age* piece was republished later that year as a pamphlet, *Southern Horrors*.

Wells's career took another major turn when she launched national and international anti-lynching speaking tours between 1893 and 1895. She was initially more successful in attracting notice among Afro-Americans than among whites. It was only when she traveled to the British Isles to criticize and embarrass America abroad for its "national crime" that she began to gain wide national and international attention.[39]

Although best known for her anti-lynching crusade of the 1890s and early 1900s, Ida B. Wells was a remarkable person and leader who made substantial contributions in many public areas. In 1895 she moved to Chicago where she married Ferdinand Barnett, a prominent black lawyer, editor, and civil rights advocate. In Chicago Wells edited the journal, the *Conservator*. She was a prominent leader in the nascent women's clubs movement, a suffragette, and a founding member of such black social service organizations as the National Association of Colored Women and the Negro Fellowship League. Ida B. Wells women's clubs were started in her honor in Chicago and other cities nationwide. She was influential in Chicago black civic affairs through the 1920s, and she and Barnett were prominent in national civil rights and protest circles in the 1890s and early 1900s. Finally, Wells helped found such major civil rights organizations as the National Afro-American Council and the National Association for the Advancement of Colored People.

In her many speeches and writings, Wells punctured the myth of black violent criminality generally and of rape in particular. Wells learned from researching hundreds of cases reported in Southern newspapers that rape was the crime most commonly attributed to lynching victims. Newspapers described the lynched men, in barely varying language, as "burly beasts" whose vicious animal passions led them continually to attempt "the unspeakable crime" against white women. Such a threat to society and the virtue of their wives and daughters, it was customarily stated or implied, forced white Southern manhood to the drastic step of lynching. Most whites assumed that lynching was a necessary, if extreme, white response to the rapacious black menace.[40]

Wells's basic method of disproving the black rape myth was the straightforward presentation of facts. With devastating effect, Wells produced her damning statistics on lynchings. She mainly used figures compiled by a well-regarded "objective" source (usually a white newspaper such as the Chicago *Tribune*) and used whites' own accounts and numbers to make her points.[41] By uncovering the actual circumstances surrounding individual cases and by forming aggregate statistics of all cases, Wells effectively used "the record" to refute "the baseless assumption" that whites lynched blacks to defend themselves against black depravity and to show that most victims were not killed because of rape or any other crime but for political and economic reasons.

The most telling figure that she regularly cited was that, of the hundreds of lynching cases reported, less than one-fifth of the victims were even accused (let alone guilty) of rape. Public records indicated, she said, that blacks were really lynched "for anything or nothing." Among the reasons given for blacks being summarily executed without trial were stealing hogs, shooting rabbits, and being noisy. Indeed a majority of the causes cited, she observed, were "offenses, not crimes." Acts that were legal and trivial but severe *caste* offenses, such as blacks being "saucy" or "quarrelsome" to whites, were repeatedly reported as precipitating lynchings. In several cases, no offense whatsoever was cited. Surveying the published accusations against lynch victims, Wells declared that "it must be admitted that the real cause of lynching . . . is race prejudice, and should be so classified."[42]

Wells's own investigative reporting and interviewing revealed chronic inaccuracy in press descriptions of lynch victims and of rape accusations made against them. Sexual relations between black men and white women, she admitted, were frequent but, she insisted, as consensual intercourse, not rape. Most so-called rapes were lovers' rendezvous that, upon discovery, were declared rapes to hide the white woman's culpability and fix all blame—and white fury and punishment—on the black male for his egregious breach of caste. Wells asserted that white women, not black men, initiated most interracial unions; the black man was lynched, she claimed, "not because he is a despoiler of virtue, but because he succumbs to the smiles of white women."[43]

Wells's charges were sensational, treading heavily on white racial sensitivities and sexual taboos. The widespread "rape of helpless Negro girls and women" by white men, she charged, was regarded by Southerners as a "normal" feature of life, although it was rarely openly acknowledged. Wells brought into the open the deeply buried corollary that "there are white women in the South who love the Afro-American's company even as there are white men notorious for their preference for Afro-American women."[44] That white women might desire sexual relations with black males was unspeakable to most white Southerners, so totally did it violate standard social conventions and myths.

Wells's analysis was equally direct in dissecting the political cause of whites' lynching blacks. The untruth of the black rape myth and whites' nonchalant attitude toward white rape of blacks, she argued, proved "that it is not the crime but the class" that motivated lynchings in the South. The key was that "the Southerner had never gotten over his resentment that the Negro was no longer his plaything, his servant, and his source of income," she wrote. The "whole matter" of lynching, she claimed, was "explained by the well-known opposition growing out of slavery to the progress of the race . . . crystallized in the oft-repeated slogan: 'This is a white man's country and the white man must rule.' "[45] Lynching was integral to a white supremacist system enforcing black disenfranchisement, economic dependency, and caste; it was the final, crowning measure needed to

keep blacks "in their place." When blacks were freed and temporarily accorded civil rights during Reconstruction, she noted, Southern whites launched a campaign of political violence spearheaded by
pogroms (called "riots") to resubjugate blacks. The fabrication then
used to justify white terror was blacks' supposed attempt to "rule"
whites. Having succeeded in reducing blacks to collective impotence
after Reconstruction, her analysis continued, the campaign of white
political violence against blacks was gradually transformed into the
practice of lynching individuals to maintain white supremacy.

"Thoughtful Afro-Americans," Wells said in reference to Booker
T. Washington and his ilk, seeing the protective arm of the federal
government withdrawn and hoping "to stop such wholesale mas-
sacres urged the race to sacrifice its political rights for sake of peace.
They honestly believed the race should fit itself for government, and
when that should be done, the objection to race participation in
politics would be removed."

These well-intentioned people were dead wrong, Wells contended. The campaign of white terror continued unabated well after
the political emasculation of Afro-Americans in the South. Nor did
it lessen before the advances in black morals and civilization urged
by the Bookerites. "The race regardless of advancement," she observed, was herded into filthy segregated facilities. Far from diminishing, the "mob spirit has grown with the increasing intelligence of
the Afro-American," since it was black social progress and em-
powerment that lynching was ultimately designed to thwart.[46]

White propaganda effectively defended lynching with the pas-
sion-filled non-issue of rape. "This [rape] cry has had its effect," she
lamented. "It has closed the heart, stifled the conscience . . . and
hushed the voice of press and pulpit on the subject of lynch law
throughout this 'land of liberty.' " It even stifled the full arousal of
black public opinion and action on this subject:

> Even to the better class of Afro-Americans the crime of rape is so
> revolting that they have too often taken the white man's word and given
> lynch law neither the investigation nor condemnation it deserved. . . .
> They have gone on hoping and believing that general education and
> financial strength would solve the difficulty.[47]

But this hope was illusory, based on a fundamental misanalysis of
lynch law. Lynching did not represent an act of white self-defense

against black backwardness, but just the opposite: it expressed whites' aversion and hostility to black advance and their determination to employ any means to keep blacks down.

Wells had stirring messages for both white and black Americans, though she invariably placed the major burden for reform on whites, since their attitudes and criminal behavior, not blacks' misdeeds, were the true cause of the lynching. Her rhetorical aim, she wrote, was to present "an arrayal of facts . . . which it is hoped will stimulate this great American republic to demand that justice be done." By revealing the racist wellsprings of lynching, she sought to "arouse the conscience of the American people" and reform national white attitudes and conduct. On her wide-ranging speaking tours, Wells always raised the lynching issue with such leaders of white opinion as editors, ministers, and civic officials. "I hoped to reach the white people of the country," she recalled, since "after all, it was the white people . . . who had to mold the public sentiment necessary to put a stop to lynching."[48]

Wells urgently summoned blacks to social action as well. "The strong arm of the law" would not be moved against this crime, she argued, "unless a healthy public sentiment demands and sustains such action." While this appeal had to be made mainly to whites, "in the creation of this healthier public sentiment, the Afro-American can do for himself what no one else can." Blacks, she urged, must act by vigorously protesting all forms of racial injustice. She pointed with pride to the black people of Memphis who "left the city by the thousands" rather than submit to gross injustice. Blacks needed to demand their rights boldly and fearlessly, she declared. "The more the Afro-American yields and cringes and begs . . . the more he is insulted, outraged and lynched." It was abundantly clear that "nothing, absolutely nothing is to be gained by a further sacrifice of manhood and self-respect." Blacks must act in collective self-defense, she urged, by aggressively employing "the boycott, emigration and the press." While organization and propaganda were the main lines of defense, she suggested that "a Winchester rifle should have a place of honor in every black home, and it should be used for that protection which the law refuses to give." Above all, bold, plain statement of the truth was necessary to reform national opinion and end racial abuses; for that, "the race must rally as a mighty host to the support of their journals."[49]

Ida Wells's protest aligned her with the public approach of the traditional (if by then declining) black protest champion, Frederick Douglass. Indeed, the two leaders cooperated in public and enjoyed warm personal relations. Upon publication of her first piece in the New York *Age,* Douglass visited her to say "what a revelation of existing conditions this article had been to him." He confessed that he had been troubled by the rising number of lynchings and had even begun to suppose that it was due to "increasing lasciviousness on the part of Negroes." But Wells showed him the truth and also pointed the way by marshalling the evidence and logic for his own subsequent efforts to decry the rising tide of lynchings. He wrote favorable introductions to her major pamphlets, *Southern Horrors* (1892) and *A Red Record* (1895). Wells and Douglass also contributed pieces to and cooperated with others in producing a pamphlet protesting the absence of a black exhibit at the 1893 Chicago world's fair. For her part, Wells thought Douglass "the greatest man our race has produced in this 'land of the free and home of the brave.' "[50] Most significantly, the two leaders firmly agreed that, while blacks should engage in self-help and take independent initiatives, the prejudice and misdeeds of white Americans were chiefly responsible for contemporary racial evils. Consequently, they directed their appeals for moral reform primarily at whites.

When Booker T. Washington swiftly became the most influential black leader after Douglass's death in 1895, Wells did not get on well with him, professionally or personally. Wells was prominent among the anti-Washington (so-called) black "radicals" by the century's close and was a renowned critic of accommodation and advocate of protest. She and her husband Barnett early and permanently figured on Washington's hit list.[51]

Washington was never comfortable with the lynching issue. Raising it violated his social strategy of downplaying the negative and accentuating the positive. He also felt that blacks gained little by continually harping and complaining about whites. "An inch of progress is worth more than a yard of fault-finding," he was prone to say: "a crying, whining race" was not respected.[52] To blame blacks' problems on racism went against his accommodationist political stance and black nationalist economic program. He always put responsibility for their condition squarely on blacks' own shoulders.

As blacks were responsible for their own social status and treatment, it followed that black misconduct caused lynching. He held that "the worst enemies of the Negro race are those Negroes who commit crimes, which are followed by lynching." Those individuals lynched "are invariably vagrants, men without property or standing," he once stated categorically.[53] He assumed that the lynch victims lacked worthwhile social traits and that, by work and application, blacks could graduate from the low class from which lynch victims came.

Despite Washington's reluctance to discuss lynching, political pressure from other blacks sometimes forced him to do so. Anti-lynching sentiment bridged every usual division of opinion among Afro-Americans, and Washington's position of racial leadership demanded that he go on record against it, particularly after the "radicals" began vociferously criticizing his silence. As time went on, Washington gradually took a stronger stand against lynch law. In 1904, Washington reached a short-lived rapprochement with his most prominent critics, including Ida Wells and W. E. B. Du Bois, by promising to stop telling stereotypic "darky" stories in his speeches and, most importantly, to denounce lynching more often and more forcefully.[54]

Shortly thereafter, Washington made his strongest anti-lynching statements to date. He began to deplore "crimes" of "burnings without a trial" for which, he declared, there was "no shadow of excuse" and brought "shame and ridicule upon our Christian land." Americans must stop to consider "where these brutal and inhuman crimes are leading us." He generally used very conservative arguments in his anti-lynching pronouncements. He stressed whites' own self-interest in ending lynching, for example, more than the rights or interests of blacks. These events were "more degrading to the people who inflict the punishment than those who receive it," he typically said, warning that, if the "law was disregarded when a Negro is concerned, it will soon be disregarded when a white man is concerned."[55] The gravest harm of lynching, he emphasized, was that it bred anarchy and promoted disrespect for law and order.

Even when Washington opposed lynching, moreover, he uncritically accepted much of the white mythology sustaining it.[56] He was too circumspect ever to name the unmentionable crime that supposedly prompted lynching. Where Wells asserted that rape charges were fraudulent and racism the cause of lynching, Washington suggested that condoning extra-legal means for punishing one crime and class opened the way to mob rule in all instances. His stance actually reinforced the notion that black criminality and social underdevelopment were at the root of the phenomenon.

In any event, Washington soon quit making regular anti-lynching statements and resumed telling white-pleasing "darky" stories, too. He had found white audiences unreceptive to his recent changes of tone, and losing the support of powerful whites was too high a price for keeping the restless black radicals in house. He complained privately to the liberal white editor, Oswald Garrison Villard, when the militants accused him of cowardice for not denouncing lynching. He defended himself, saying that he did not protest each individual lynching in order that he might preserve his overall effectiveness on this and other issues, and because too much protesting was counterproductive.[57] Protest leaders soon resumed their attacks on him, especially after his deafening silence on the Atlanta, Georgia, and Brownsville, Texas, riots of 1906. Radicals such as Boston editor Monroe Trotter, W. E. B. Du Bois, and Ida Wells organized resistance to his program in a series of organizations that culminated in the NAACP in 1910.

Accepting the full truth and implications of lynching as identified by Wells would have fundamentally threatened Washington's view of society and the logic underlying his program. He preached that economic progress was Afro-Americans' "passport" to the good life in America and that white prejudice would recede, as a matter of course, before black social advance. Nothing was so threatening to this hopeful position as Wells's thesis that lynching was used to keep blacks down and so was especially inflicted on those blacks who were progressing. Blacks who competed with whites and sought economic independence from them, as had Tom Moss, were prime targets of white violence. At bottom, it was their contrary social analyses that most divided Washington and the anti-lynching activists. Wells, unlike Washington, interpreted lynching as an integral feature of a comprehensive and rigid white supremacist system and held that the only real remedy for it was the elimination of caste in all its forms.

## Wells as Jeremiah

To what extent did Ida B. Wells employ the jeremiad in her anti-lynching propaganda? Invariably, her message was blunt and her evidence damning. Her no-nonsense manner and presentation were meant to shock whites with the truth to correct their vision and arouse their conscience. Above all, Wells ultimately aimed to convert white opinion and move the nation to end lynching. Unquestionably, she tried to provoke guilt and shame in Americans over their current misdeeds and directed a moral appeal to their better natures and ideals.

Other features of the American jeremiad—sharp social criticism, condemnation of those violating national ideals, demands for repentance, and professed faith in America's future—did appear in Wells's rhetoric, if somewhat haphazardly and irregularly. Of these distinctly jeremiadic elements, social criticism and discontent were easily the most pronounced in Wells's language. Her essays and speeches bristled with denunciations of America's "national crime," "disgrace," "abominations," and so on. She also tried to arouse white America concerning the damage done by these deeds to its national identity and international reputation: "Equality of the law" had to be a fact, not just theory, she regularly chided her compatriots, "before America is truly the 'land of the free and the home of the brave.'"[58]

Also like a jeremiah, Wells challenged Americans immediately to make a clear, firm moral decision. If white America would only respond with conviction and energy, she asserted, "these problems would soon be solved." The pressing question was: "Will it do so? . . . Eight million of so-called free men and women await the answer," she declared, and the world "waits with them."[59]

Wells sometimes accompanied her catalogue of discouraging facts with hopeful predictions that Americans would respond to their pressing moral challenge. After the first few years of her crusade, Wells found grounds for optimism, saying, "The year 1894 [was] marked by a pronounced awakening of the public conscience." After a decade in which lynching was so unremarkable that "scenes of unusual brutality failed to have any visible effect upon the humane sentiments of the people of our land," she claimed that international publicity had made "the entire American people now feel . . . that they are objects in the gaze of the world" and made them finally begin to examine their atrocious conduct. She declared, "Lynch Law can not flourish in the future as it has in the past." She prefaced a 1900 pamphlet with this bold statement of faith:

> We do not believe that the American people . . . will remain unmoved by these accounts . . . [or] that the moral conscience of the nation—that which is highest and best among us—will always remain silent . . . for God is not dead. . . . When this conscience wakes and speaks out in thunder tones, *as it must* . . .

Then, she was confident, all would be well.[60]

Wells's rhetoric also reflected the jeremiad's paradoxical anxiety and uncertainty about the national present and future. From a transcendent viewpoint, the prophet is serene about the national outcome. From the immediate temporal vantage point, however, the nation's fate appears to hang precariously in the balance. "This crusade will determine," Wells contended, "whether this Nation shall write itself down a success at self-government, or in deepest humiliation, admit its failure complete." On at least one occasion, she looked to America's glorious past for reason to believe in its imminent redemption. In a land that produced such champions of liberty as William Lloyd Garrison and Abraham Lincoln, "there must be those of their descendants who would take hold of their work of inaugurating an era of law and order," she asserted, "and the colored people . . . who have been loyal to the flag believe the same, and strong in that belief have begun this crusade."[61]

Finally, however, Wells's status as a jeremiah is not clear-cut. Jeremiad-like rhetorical elements and strategies surfaced in her public language but not so regularly or uniformly as in the rhetoric of, for example, Frederick Douglass. Overt, well-developed references to America's sacred mission and mythic past, such as those just cited, were not numerous and frequently were lacking. She referred much more often, for example, to white Americans' duty to behave as Christians and members of the civilized world than to any peculiar national mission or uniquely American values. Nor did she customarily threaten the nation with approaching doom or divine punishment for its offenses. She warned of loss of self-respect and moral reputation but never approached Douglass's cry that unless Americans immediately repented, God would smite them with a punishment to make the earth shudder.

Wells's objective, austere journalistic style did not readily lend itself to the jeremiad's moralistic sermonizing and rhetorical flourishes. Her method was to rely on the facts themselves, artfully arrayed, to make and carry her case. Over and over, she asserted the unaided power of "the facts" and "the record" to cure people's "baseless assumptions" and make the truth clear to all. "This table [of lynching statistics] tells its own story," she characteristically stated. She advised individuals wishing to help the cause to "disseminate the facts . . . to the end that public sentiment may be revolutionized" and to "let the facts speak for themselves with you as medium." Wells said that her writing did "not attempt to moralize . . . over the deplorable state of affairs . . . but simply presents the facts in a plain, unvarnished way."[62] Disinclination to moralize over a "deplorable state of affairs" is decidedly not typical of a jeremiah's style.

Wells's consciously unrhetorical style most clearly distinguished her statements from those of Frederick Douglass, despite their substantially similar content. Introducing Wells's first pamphlet, Douglass admired how she set forth "the facts with cool, painstaking fidelity and left those naked and uncontradicted facts to speak for themselves." Even while lauding her manner, Douglass did not restrict himself to such a detached style. Rather, he immediately declared:

> If American conscience were only half alive, if the American church and clergy were only half Christianized, if American moral sensibility were not hardened by persistent infliction of outrage and crime against colored people, a scream of horror, shame and indignation would rise to heaven [from them at their lynching deeds]. . . .[63]

It may be the influence of social gender restrictions that inhibited Wells's adoption of the role of jeremiah in her public persona. She operated within nineteenth-century expectations regarding appropriate behavior for women and men. The reigning ideology of "true womanhood" assigned to women the Christian virtues of piety, moral purity, submission, and nurturance of others. This ideology was usually interpreted as limiting women's activities and interests to the domestic sphere. These same qualities, however, could also justify women's participation in reform movements to work for more wholesome and moral conditions outside the home.[64] Many Victorian American women became very active in wide-ranging social reforms such as temperance, anti-prostitution, woman suffrage, and—in Wells's case—anti-lynching. Middle-class women formed the majority of the ranks in many reform movements and often invoked the ideology of true womanhood to legitimate their expanded civic roles. Their participation in social reform often involved them in such new activities as public organizing, speaking, and leadership. At the same time, the notion that leadership was mainly a man's role continued to influence even many activist women's mode of public participation. Men disproportionately filled leadership positions even in movements with mostly female memberships, and those women who assumed leadership roles still faced public expectations that they act "womanly," that is, morally, modestly, and self-effacingly.

This cultural definition of womanhood in some ways supported the appeal to conscience and attempts to spur moral reformation that are basic to the jeremiadic enterprise; in more ways, however, it worked against women's appropriation of the form. Considered as innately moral beings, women were ideally suited to serve as society's conscience. There was a cultural predilection for women to address moral issues and for men to acknowledge their role as society's moral guardians. Nevertheless, women were expected to prick society's conscience in a soft, gentle, compassionate way incompatible with the jeremiadic style. The social role of the jeremiah as it originated in colonial New England was exercised by the all-male clergy. The jeremiah was a patriarchal authority figure whose hot admonitions and angry warnings reflected the masculine attributes of a jealous, wrathful Jehovah. Social-religious changes had considerably "feminized" American Protestantism by the mid-nineteenth century and softened the harsh masculinity of the Puritan's Old-Testament God by emphasizing the meek, loving, more "feminine" qualities of Jesus.[65] Nevertheless, the stern jeremiah figure peering down disapprovingly at the people and harshly denouncing their conduct continued to be considered a singularly male public role and image.

Ida Wells clearly stretched the usual accepted arenas and boundaries of female social action. Her participation in the black women's club movement and in the anti-lynching crusade were acceptably "feminine" in that it was considered woman's place to elevate society's moral awareness. But her exposé of rape charges and blunt declarations concerning the ubiquity of interracial sex and white lust were utterly unladylike topics for discussion. Taboos on these subjects were particularly meant to protect pure, delicate women from such sordid realities. Wells sided, moreover, with the radicals against Washington's accommodationism and the inoffensive "feminine" stance that he presented to whites. Wells favored a bolder, more "masculine" public stance by blacks. Beyond the many specific disagreements that Washington's critics had with him was a visceral sense that his manner was supine and passive before white mistreatment in a way that sapped the race's self-respect or "manhood." The frequent complaint of black radicals, including Wells, that Washington showed "unmanliness" and lacked "manhood" was nearly always expressed in such gender symbolism.[66]

Wells sided with the "masculine" (aggressive, protest-oriented) camp against the "feminine" (passive, accommodationist) position associated with Washington; and her protest propaganda, which sometimes included elements of the jeremiad, reflected this "masculine" political stand. Yet Wells, like most women of her time, including most activists, did not reject outright the dominant definition of womanhood, a stance that ever conditioned and sometimes hindered her work. She was ambivalent over the tug between mothering and her career upholding public causes. With her first child's birth in 1897, she partially retired for about a year, determined before all else "to do my duty as mother"; nevertheless, she confessed that she "looked forward to the time which I should have completely discharged . . . [and] be emancipated from my duties in that respect."[67] Within eight months of weaning her first born, however, she had her second child and withdrew almost wholly from commitments outside the home until her youngest was eight years old. Altogether, she retired from active public service for nearly a decade.

Thus Wells's self-image and woman's role militated against her using the rhetoric of the black jeremiad. Even in her propaganda, Wells, as a woman, felt pressure to be self-effacing and not push herself forward too obviously. Her journalistic method of "letting the facts speak for themselves" let her step into the background and pose as a passive medium for the truth, which itself did the active accusing. By this literary device, Wells avoided directly denouncing the people in the manner of a jeremiah. Although she advocated the same political positions as male proponents who employed the jeremiad, Wells herself did not specialize as fully in the role and language of a black jeremiah.

## 4. Great Expectations: W. E. B. Du Bois's American Jeremiad in the Progressive Era

Booker T. Washington's judgment that racism was insurmountable in white American culture seemed to be confirmed by national conditions in the late nineteenth century. But between 1910 and 1920, more promising conditions enabled many black leaders like W. E. B. Du Bois to recapture some of Douglass's enthusiasm for prospects for racial reform in America. This chapter describes those factors of analysis that allowed Du Bois to minimize the power of white racism during the Progressive Era but then forced him to confront it increasingly after the First World War.

Some years before Washington's death in 1915, many Afro-Americans had already lost patience with his prescription for racial progress. Mounting dissatisfaction with the apparent fruit of his racial compromise with whites—a rapid increase in institutionalized racism and a lynching epidemic—and resentment of Washington's dictatorial control over many major black institutions led some prominent blacks to begin resisting his leadership and protesting white racism. As the celebrated leader of the anti-Washington radicals in the early twentieth century, W. E. B. Du Bois renewed a Douglass-like jeremiad criticizing white racism and demanding black civil rights. A founder of the National Association for the Advancement of Colored People and activist for black rights throughout his long life, Du Bois was a pioneer of the twentieth-century civil rights movement. It took him years to arrive at this position, and his social thought and prophecy never ceased to evolve.

### A Black Yankee's Search for Social Identity

William Edward Burghardt Du Bois was born in 1868 in Great Barrington, a small rural town in Massachusetts where middle-class values prevailed. "I grew up in the midst of definite ideas as to wealth and poverty, work and character," Du Bois recalled. "My general attitude toward property and income was that those who had property had earned it and deserved it," and "poverty . . . connoted lack of thrift and shiftlessness."[1]

In most ways, Du Bois grew up a typical New England Yankee, and Puritanism was a significant part of his social heritage. Du Bois attended Great Barrington's predominantly white First Congregational Church with his mother. Although he abandoned belief in religious dogma during adolescence, Du Bois keenly felt the continuing inspiration of Puritan social ethics. Indeed, he personally embodied many of Puritanism's behavioral ideals: diligence, discipline, and individual sacrifice for ideal social ends. He deeply internalized Puritan insistence on the responsibility of the individual and community for accomplishing God's ends on earth.[2]

Du Bois's early racial consciousness was slight compared to that of his later years. He derived from mixed African, Dutch, and French ancestry. His father was a very light black of mixed race from out of town who left his wife and child shortly after William's birth. In all his memoirs, Du Bois described his childhood as idyllic and said that he grew up generally feeling himself an accepted member of the community. Most of his youthful playmates were white, and he "took part with no thought of discrimination" in town activities. He was dimly aware of belonging to a small black group of about fifty but did not on this account feel set apart from the general community. "The color line was manifest" in Great Barrington, he later recognized, "and yet not overdrawn," tending to appear mainly in subtle forms. Conscious that most town blacks were poorer than most whites, Du Bois was more aware of poverty than ethnicity. His mother's long-established family in Great Barrington "felt above" recent black immigrants "because of our educational and economic status." Du Bois was taught that

> the secret of life and the loosening of the color bar . . . lay in excellence, in accomplishment. If others . . . of my colored kin, had stayed in school . . . they could have risen to equal whites. Of this my mother quietly insisted. There was no real discrimination on account of color—it was all a matter of ability and hard work.[3]

By adolescence, however, Du Bois began experiencing social discrimination and painful rejection because of race. It had never occurred to him before high school that he was "different from the other boys," except that he was "a matter of curiosity" who "sort of stood out." This was especially true in school where his scholastic brilliance shone and he was frequently asked to recite before astonished parents and visitors. "I sort of had to justify myself," he remembered, and soon made it "a point of honor to excell white students." While in high school, however, a new aloofness spread among his white peers, especially the girls. He started perceiving that he was no longer welcome among the other students outside the classroom. Gradually, he grew accustomed to this and resigned himself to existing outside white social circles.[4]

Du Bois reacted to white rejection by redoubling his efforts to excel academically and by imagining a role for himself as a heroic leader with a great duty to perform toward both blacks and whites. "I very early got the idea," he said, "that what I was going to do was prove to the world that Negroes were just like other people." Du Bois was valedictorian at high school graduation in 1884 and spoke on Wendall Phillips, the white abolitionist and social reformer who sought to change white racial attitudes and to improve conditions for blacks. "I was fascinated by his life and work," Du Bois wrote, and in studying him, "took a long step toward a wider conception of what I was going to do."[5]

To prepare for his grand social vocation, he determined to attend college, preferably at Harvard. Du Bois's academic plans were jeopardized temporarily by his mother's death just before graduation, but family and friends were able to find him a summer job and make financial arrangements for him to attend college in the fall. Eventually a local white secured him a church scholarship to attend Fisk College, a black institution in Tennessee.

Attending Fisk College near Nashville was an exhilarating experience for young Du Bois. He "was thrilled to be for the first time among so many people of my own color" to whom he felt bound "by new and exciting ties." For the first time, Du Bois became immersed in a close-knit black community surrounded by the much larger Afro-American population of the Tennessee countryside. He also had his first glimpse of rural black folklife and culture and observed first-hand the harsh realities of the black masses' extreme poverty and social oppression in the South. From a region where "the status of me and my fellows could be rationalized" as reflecting lack of education and enterprise, Du Bois recalled, "I suddenly came to a region where the world was split into black and white halves, and where the darker half was held back by racial prejudice and legal bonds, as well as by deep ignorance and dire poverty."[6]

Du Bois felt tied to his race both by shared social subordination in the South and by the missionary elan of Fisk's student body and faculty. Fisk students were taught that they were being prepared as an elite vanguard to lead their race forward to freedom and dignity. "The freed slaves," Du Bois grew convinced at Fisk, "if properly led had a great future. . . . Through the leadership of men like me and my fellows, we were going to have these enslaved Israelites out of their still enduring bondage in short order."[7]

Fisk confirmed Du Bois's maturing concern for group development and identity which he had already demonstrated by high school. He recalled thinking that, while "in the long run," he was "going . . . to break down segregation and separateness, yet for the time I was quite willing to be a Negro and to work within a Negro group." At Fisk he first strongly felt himself a member of "a closed racial group" with "rites and loyalties," "art and philosophy," and "a history and a corporate future" all its own.[8]

Simultaneously, Du Bois's faith in the best side of America (especially of New England) was reinforced. Fisk's white faculty came mostly from New England and from Midwestern areas settled largely by New England migrants. The institution descended from the evangelistic abolitionist tradition and was founded as part of the "New England schoolmarm" post-war crusade to educate and uplift the ex-slaves. These white emissaries of Yankee culture meant to train a generation of blacks to lead their people into freedom, a duty they constantly impressed on their charges. Fisk's emphasis on social duty and the transforming potential of education strongly inspired Du Bois.

After graduating from Fisk, Du Bois continued to prepare for his "mighty task" by seeking out the "best in organized learning."[9] Winning a scholarship, he was admitted to Harvard College as a junior in 1888. Intellectually, Du Bois found Harvard rich and inviting. Socially, however, except for the friendly interest of a few faculty, he lived in near-total isolation from whites and found his companionship within Boston's black community.[10]

Du Bois was confident early on that the struggle for black advance and against white prejudice was "mainly a battle of wits, of knowledge," a matter of education, which he would see that both races received.[11] From 1888 to 1894, as a philosophy undergraduate, then history graduate student at Harvard and as a fellow at the University of Berlin, Du Bois got the best possible contemporary education with which to accomplish his mission. His academic credentials were impeccable (although he could not, of course, obtain an academic position at any white college). Steeped in the highest canons of Western scholarship, he felt that the white world would have to listen to him and acknowledge the facts as he presented them, thereby ending their racial ignorance and prejudice and hastening the advance of black people.

During his European student travels, Du Bois, like Frederick Douglass, was favorably impressed and encouraged by the relative mildness of the white prejudice he met in Europe. Among educated and cultured whites in particular, it seemed, racism was an unusual and declining phenomenon. Europe's progress raised his hopes that similar progress in white American racial attitudes was imminent, given the inevitable advance of science and civilization. "I felt myself standing" no longer "against the world," he wrote, "but simply against American narrowness and color prejudice, with the greater, finer world at my back."[12]

Du Bois wished to have the authority of modern science with him in his life work. Sociology gradually became his chosen field. The purpose of rigorous sociological study, he learned in his German seminars, was to accumulate the necessary scientific knowledge for enacting social reform. While vowing to "do the work with scientific accuracy," Du Bois entered the new field of social science "primarily with the utilitarian object of reform and uplift." His ambition was to conduct the first statistical studies "of the conditions and problems of my own group." "I was going to study the facts, any and all facts, concerning the American Negro and his plight," he wrote, believing that he would thereby identify the solutions to America's race problem.[13]

## Du Bois's Initial Strategy for Black Progress: Scientific Research and Washingtonian Rhetoric

Du Bois began his career with great faith in the ability of reason to persuade people and foment reform. For years, his main mode of addressing whites combined a studiously polite, restrained manner with presentation of a logical argument based on solid scientific facts. At Atlanta University and elsewhere, he produced pathbreaking sociological and historical research on blacks of very high quality, much of which still stands as impressive scholarship.

In this period of black thought and leadership dominated by Booker T. Washington, moreover, Du Bois, who became famous as Washington's arch foe, initially concurred with Washington's focus on building an economic foundation for black social progress, as he also echoed Washington's accommodative tone toward whites on other matters There were always between them, of course, substantial ideological and personal differences, especially Washington's admiration for capitalists and hostility toward unions, which were destined to expand. Nevertheless, Du Bois's initial stance toward whites was one of accommodation on such emotionally threatening issues as so-called social equality while attempting to persuade them with polite reason.[14] In contrast, his rhetoric toward blacks was, from the start, sternly disapproving of their failure to strive with sufficient zeal for self-reform.[15]

Du Bois's 1899 book, *The Philadelphia Negro,* presented the results of a sociological survey of black Philadelphians that he conducted on temporary assignment for the University of Pennsylvania. It is an excellent example of Du Bois's early middle-class jeremiad to blacks and accommodative approach to whites. This book, the first methodologically up-to-date statistical study of an American black community, was a landmark in American sociology, and it established him as a major American scholar.

Although *The Philadelphia Negro* was widely praised for its scholarly objectivity, Du Bois was acutely aware of the study's political ramifications. Prevalent racist theory blamed blacks' depressed social condition on an innate biological inferiority and recommended removing them from the public social and political order. Du Bois suspected that the university study was commissioned "to give scientific sanction to the known causes" of Philadelphia's chronic political corruption—that is, black voters—and to justify their disenfranchisement.[16] Du Bois's statistical survey vividly portrayed Philadelphia's black slum as a center of crime and vice, and it documented the prevalence of many of those unflattering social traits commonly ascribed to blacks by whites. His report's explanation for these facts and his accompanying recommendations, however, deviated sharply from conventional white wisdom. Du Bois interpreted the conditions he found not as the result of unchangeable heredity but primarily as the product of blacks' social status and history.

Du Bois organized his findings so as to elicit sympathy from enlightened whites regarding blacks' social problems and struggle for advance. The book was moderate in tone and conservative in ideology. Its middle-class bias was reflected in its exceedingly critical description of lower-class black life. The study's unremittingly dreary portrayal of black social conditions and sharp denunciation of blacks for not changing their deplorable conditions made it a severe middle-class jeremiad. He deplored Afro-Americans' low status "in the scale of civilization" and blamed Philadelphia's black community for the majority's failure to lift themselves out of the urban slum.[17] He attacked widespread black promiscuity, criminality, and laziness and decried the lack of racial purpose and unity and the ineffectuality of black institutions. All segments of black society, from social and political leaders to the deprived masses, were roundly chastised.

White prejudice, he further declared, was not responsible "for all or perhaps the greater part of the Negro problem." Efforts at correction, he insisted, "must commence in the Negro homes" which "must cease to be . . . breeders of idleness and extravagance and complaint." Rather, "the homely virtues of honesty, truth and chastity must be instilled in the cradle." "Work, continuous and extensive; work, although it be menial and poorly rewarded . . . must be . . . impressed upon Negro children as the road to salvation." He advised blacks, meanwhile, as they took these needed measures, to "cultivate a spirit of calm, patient persistence" toward whites and to suggest improvements in white conduct toward blacks with "some finesse," not with "loud and intemperate complaint."[18]

In the book's conclusion, Du Bois recommended ameliorative steps by both blacks and whites. On the one hand, he declared that it was "the duty of the Negro to raise himself by every effort to the standards of modern civilization" and to eliminate "his own social vices and degradation." Whites, he gently but firmly suggested, also had obligations to blacks. It was their duty to be fair and to help, not hinder blacks' social ascent. While whites had a right "to guard their civilization from debauchment," he contended that it was "not necessary to hinder and retard the efforts of an earnest people to rise." He frowned on white prejudice that wrongly assumed that blacks could never lift themselves to the level of whites. Whites should also quit harping on the irrational fear of racial intermarriage and social mingling in every discussion of black social advance. "Natural pride of race," he asserted, "may be trusted to ward off such mingling as might in this stage of development prove disastrous to both races." Such emotional non-issues were a smokescreen justifying racial discrimination of every sort, resulting in a narrowing of "opportunities afforded Negroes for earning a decent living"— blacks' most immediate need. It was the duty of all Americans, he observed, to reward talent and merit in the marketplace without regard to race. White citizens should note and applaud social differentiation among black people and assist those enterprising blacks who, through determined effort, were rising in business, education, and life. "Social sympathy must exist between what is best in both races," he urged. If each race did its duty toward the other in a helpful fashion, mutual progress was assured.[19]

In temperately nudging whites toward improved conduct, *The Philadelphia Negro* followed a rhetorical pattern similar to that of Booker T. Washington. Du Bois's stress on interracial duties and cooperation and on black self-help as the solution to blacks' plight, his muting of demands for social equality, and his calls for sympathy between the "better" sort of both races and for less friction in race relations—in all these respects, Du Bois's advice markedly resembled Washington's proposals for black progress and social harmony. *The Philadelphia Negro,* in its message to blacks, was a Washingtonian middle-class jeremiad bedecked in the latest scholarly attire.

For nearly a decade, Du Bois pursued his conviction that careful accumulation of scientific facts and presentation of reasonable argument would quickly end white prejudice and all other barriers to black progress. It is significant that at the time of Washington's 1895 Atlanta compromise, Du Bois endorsed it as a promising first step toward better conditions for blacks and improved racial relations.[20] At that early date, Du Bois, like Washington, saw few prospects for gaining significant social or political concessions from whites, so was willing to explore the possibilities of seeking greater economic opportunities from them while exhorting blacks to redeem themselves through economic exertion. Du Bois's jeremiadic rhetoric before 1903 largely embraced Washington's contention that blacks were a chosen people who had turned their backs on America's promise.

Reorientation, 1900–1909:
Toward a Jeremiad for Whites

Events gradually led Du Bois to demand political rights for blacks and to issue militant jeremiads against white racial prejudice and discrimination. He grew increasingly impatient with the results of Washington's approach and alarmed by the deterioration of race relations in the early twentieth century. The rapid spread of black disenfranchisement, Jim Crow laws, and lynchings made him begin to doubt that science alone would solve the race problem. The Atlanta Race Riot of 1906 and the grisly lynching of Sam Hose, an Atlanta black man, were key incidents that cast across his beloved plan of science "a red ray of emotion which could not be ignored." It "pulled me off my feet," he wrote, to realize that "one could not be a calm, cool, and detached scientist while Negroes were lynched, murdered and starved."[21]

Du Bois recalled "being swept" by events after 1900 "to a new and different mode of expression."[22] Du Bois's rhetoric to whites between 1900 and 1910 gradually moved toward openly censorious language. In 1903 he published *The Souls of Black Folk,* a collection of essays on topics of black life. The book was a brilliant synthesis of scholarly and imaginative writing styles. It employed a wide variety of literary forms to prick Americans' intellectual and emotional sensibilities. It ranged from restrained reworkings of some of his more accessible scholarly prose to new material including passionate passages, personal narrative, poetry, and fiction. In this literary masterpiece, Du Bois used an expanded repertoire of styles to teach ignorant, and hence unsympathetic, whites something of the oppression and richness, the pain and beauty of Afro-American history and culture. In many pieces, Du Bois's anger and bitterness burst through his calm scholarly *persona.*

*The Souls of Black Folk* also showed substantive ideological and political change in several essays that argued against the adequacy of industrial education for blacks and stressed the need for liberal education, the ballot, and civil rights. These essays vigorously assailed positions associated with Booker T. Washington.

Du Bois began the essay, "Of Mr. Booker T. Washington and Others" respectfully, praising Washington's contributions to black education, professing himself hesitant "to criticize a life which, beginning with so little, has done so much." An unmistakable critical edge quickly became apparent, however, as Du Bois recounted Washington's rise to power on a "programme of industrial education, conciliation of the South, and submission and silence as to civil and political rights." Du Bois credited Washington's great success in "gaining place and consideration in the North" to his intuitive grasp of and identification with the dominant ideals and "spirit of the age"—those "of triumphant commercialism, and . . . material prosperity." But this was a philosophy of unrestrained materialism, or "mammonism," which Du Bois criticized throughout the book. "Mr. Washington," he charged, "represents in Negro thought the old [slave] attitude of adjustment and submission" and "practically accepts the alleged inferiority of the Negro races." In assuming that blacks could survive only by submission, Washington, according to Du Bois, had forced his people to give up three things—political power, civil rights, and higher education—in favor of a single-minded concentration on accumulating property. But, Du Bois asked, after fifteen years, what was the "result of this tender of the palm-branch" to Southern whites? Blacks had experienced complete disenfranchisement, legal ratification of their inferior status, and declining white support for black higher education.

Du Bois pointedly placed blame for these developments on Washington, whose program, he claimed, "without . . . a doubt, helped their speedier accomplishment." He assailed the "triple paradox" of Washington's inadequate program for blacks. First, although Washington minimized the value of higher education for black people, industrial schools such as Tuskegee could not "remain open a day" without college-trained teachers. Second, it "is utterly impossible . . . for workingmen and property-owners" to defend their interests "without the right of suffrage." And third, Washington preached black self-respect and pride yet "counsels a silent submission to civic authority such as is bound to sap the manhood of any race."[23]

For these reasons, Du Bois stated, a class of "educated and thoughtful colored men" felt compelled to criticize Washington and to object openly to white racial prejudice and discrimination. These patriotic dissenters were "conscience bound" to demand equal rights for black Americans, including the vote, civil rights, and equal educational opportunities.[24]

*The Souls of Black Folk* stirred great controversy in the black community and quickly became the virtual Bible of young anti-Washington radicals. The book's general impact was also great, and it is nationally and internationally acknowledged as a literary classic.

Its 1903 publication permanently poisoned Du Bois's relations with Washington and sped his transition from the role of social scientist to black political activist and crusader-journalist. Feeling that the nation's black crisis demanded his full attention and finding that funding for his sociological studies at Atlanta University and for the University itself were evaporating (clearly a result of his incurring Washington's enmity), Du Bois began gradually disengaging from academia and entering a new career as social reformer and crusader-journalist.

## The Niagara Years: Exhorting the Black Elite

Although he did not formally leave Atlanta University until 1910 after the formation of the National Association for the Advancement of Colored People, one of Du Bois's key activities between 1905 and 1909 was organizing and publicizing the aims of a national black protest organization, the Niagara Movement. In 1905, he circulated a letter among black professionals around the country announcing a conference for all those dissatisfied with Washington's program and dictatorial methods. The subsequent meeting of the race's "talented tenth" at Niagara Falls, Canada (the New York side refused them hotel accommodations), resolved to assert blacks' claim to every right possessed by other Americans. An ongoing organization was established with Du Bois as general secretary. Although it disbanded within five years, the Niagara Movement was highly significant as the first militant black protest movement organized against Washington's wishes and as the forerunner of the National Association for the Advancement of Colored People.

Niagara was predominantly a nationalist effort to activate the race's "talented tenth" in a missionary quest for black advance. The bulk of Du Bois's messianic rhetoric was still aimed at black people, therefore, and most particularly at that saving remnant, the educated elite, whose task was to provide bold racial leadership by militantly demanding equal rights for blacks and sharply protesting their unjust denial.

The Niagara years, however, saw an important change in Du Bois's mode of addressing whites. Several speeches explaining the movement's purpose to others indicate how completely Du Bois had shed his former accommodative gloves for a hard-hitting attack on white prejudice. As he emerged as the nation's most recognized and outspoken black protest leader, his rhetoric toward whites hardened into an unqualified jeremiad.

The "Niagara Address to the Nation," delivered at the movement's second annual conference in 1906, was a classic American jeremiad. Standing at Harpers Ferry, West Virginia, the site of abolitionist martyr John Brown's failed attempt to free and arm the slaves, Du Bois solemnly asked America "in the name of ten million the privilege of a hearing." He delivered a litany of wrongs suffered by blacks at white hands, lamenting that "step by step the defenders of the rights of American citizens have retreated." These were shameful times for America. "Against this the Niagara Movement eternally protests," he declared, pledging that "until we get these rights we will never cease to . . . assail the ears of Americans." The battle that he and fellow blacks waged, moreover, was ultimately one "for all true Americans." "It is a fight for ideals, lest this, our common fatherland, false to its founding, become in truth the land of the thief and the home of the slave—a byword and a hissing among the nations for its sounding pretensions and pitiful accomplishment."

Du Bois ended this address on a confident note, staking the Afro-American hope for justice on a revival of the American spirit. He thanked God for inspirational examples like those of the abolitionists of old and appealed "to the young men and women of this nation" to "stand up" for America's democratic principles and "prove yourselves worthy of your heritage." Against this coming revival of the true American spirit, the evil trends of the day were doomed: "Our enemies triumphant for the present, are fighting the stars in their courses." "And we shall win," he declared. "The past promised it, the present foretells it." "All across the skies sit signs of promise," he prophesied: "The morning breaks over blood-stained hills."[25]

Du Bois's reticence to risk offending whites declined and his tone toward whites grew less deferential and more openly censorious. His strong protests against racism and new willingness to speak forthrightly about social equality and interracial marriage were topics taboo to whites.[26]

The all-black Niagara Movement eventually gave way to the interracial National Association for the Advancement of Colored

People (NAACP). The movement had met limited near-term success and encountered formidable obstacles, chief of which was Washington's powerful enmity. The Wizard of Tuskegee orchestrated a campaign to give the fledgling movement the silent treatment in the press. Indeed, Niagara was often ignored, dismissed, or vilified by black newspapers beholden to Tuskegee and, also through Washington's agency, ignored by most of the white press. Most white philanthropists and reformers interested in black problems still supported Washington in the early 1900s and did not welcome the radicals' strident criticisms of him and of the nation. Washington, furthermore, had the movement infiltrated with spies. In historical terms, however, the Niagara Movement was successful. It started the first black movement to break with Washington's power and program, brought a militant public demand for equal rights to the fore among blacks, and gradually attracted enough white support to found an interracial movement built mainly on its program.[27]

## White Progressive Reform and the NAACP

Founding of the interracial National Association for the Advancement of Colored People (NAACP), which absorbed Niagara's membership virtually whole, in 1910 gave Du Bois hope that white America was finally ready to respond to blacks' just demands for equality. Two notorious lynchings and a white pogrom against blacks in Springfield, Illinois—Abraham Lincoln's hometown—led some important white Northern social reformers to conclude that conditions warranted something other than continuing Washington's policies. They issued invitations to white and black reformers, including Du Bois and Ida B. Wells, to discuss what to do. These progressive reformers included a number of socialists, Mary White Ovington, for example, as well as, by 1907, Du Bois himself. The result was the founding of the NAACP as an organization committed to securing blacks' public and legal rights. Du Bois was elated by this powerful infusion of white reformers' support and took a leading role in the association as the editor of its official journal, *The Crisis.*

The NAACP was ideologically rooted in the abolitionist movement and self-consciously looked back to that campaign for methods and inspiration. Some white founders of the NAACP, such as

Oswald Garrison Villard (grandson of William Lloyd Garrison), were descended from abolitionists. Throughout his life Du Bois held abolitionism as his personal ideal of morality in action, and he regarded it as the finest historic moment of the American nation.[28] Since the close of Reconstruction, however, white Americans had slid into a national declension characterized by public racism and indifference to the state of democracy. But now in 1910, the Progressive crusade seemed to him a proto-abolitionist revival of the true American spirit. And when the NAACP came into existence, Du Bois believed that the morally-awakened descendants of the abolitionists were starting the final push to bring justice to blacks and democracy to America.

Du Bois drew a parallel between the alliance of black and white abolitionists in the Civil War era and the current alliance of Northern white reformers with blacks in 1910. The South, in 1910 as in the 1850s, was a reactionary society that stifled all social dissent. Then as now, the South stood alone against rising national and international trends toward democracy and freedom. In leaving Atlanta for New York City as his new operational base, Du Bois was escaping the undemocratic South as Frederick Douglass once had and, like Douglass, he was able to unite with white Northerners who shared his abhorrence of racial caste and injustice. This alliance, he believed, could recreate national conditions of the 1860s and institute reforms to reconstruct the racist undemocratic South.

As the editor of the new association's journal, *The Crisis*, Du Bois directed a jeremiad at the nation that recaptured much of the enthusiasm Frederick Douglass had felt at the end of the Civil War. Like Douglass and unlike Washington, Du Bois persistently leveled his most stinging condemnations at white misdeeds and his definition of declension mainly blamed whites, not blacks, for betraying America's mission. Finding strength and encouragement in the re-energized forces of liberal American reform, Du Bois between 1910 and 1920 predicted the rapid reversal of present declension and the approaching fulfillment of the original promise of a fully democratic America.

## Du Bois and *The Crisis*, 1910–1919

Although Du Bois had many notable activities in a career spanning many decades, he had his greatest impact on black and white

American public opinion through his editorship of *The Crisis*. The bulk of his jeremiadic rhetoric was now directed to whites, as he saw white reform as the most immediately promising instrument for black progress.[29] His tenure with *The Crisis*, particularly between 1910 and 1919, corresponded to the zenith of his faith in America's promise for Afro-Americans.

In brilliant, slashing editorials against American racial prejudice and discrimination, Du Bois penned a torrent of eloquent black jeremiads expressing both harsh condemnation of American racial practices and invincible social optimism based on America's mythic past and future. The first issue of *The Crisis* boldly stated its faith that the world was on the threshold of a new order of democracy and brotherhood. Although the outcome was preordained, the present was uncertain and urgently required people to act. *The Crisis* "took its name," Du Bois wrote, from the belief "that this is a critical juncture in the history of the advance of men." In this pivotal situation, the NAACP had a crucial role: "The function of the Association is to tell the nation the crying evil of race prejudice" so that, alerted, the nation might reform. "It is a hard duty," he asserted, "but a necessary one—a divine one."[30]

With unflagging zeal, Du Bois relentlessly exposed in each issue the glaring racial evils in U.S. society. He used a variety of methods to accomplish this task, ranging from anecdotes about the humiliations routinely experienced by blacks under the American caste system to monthly tables of the latest lynching statistics. Du Bois could be bitter and sarcastic in denouncing American hypocrisy toward its democratic ideals, so much so that he received constant complaints from readers about his tone. But he never wavered in his conviction that by dragging the nation's sins into the open, *The Crisis* performed a necessary function. "It was ever so," he declared; "When the Hebrew prophets cried aloud there were respectable persons who said: 'Unfortunate exaggeration! . . . Ungodly bitterness!' Yet the jeremiads were needed to redeem a people."[31]

His writings in *The Crisis* followed the jeremiad's pattern of interpreting current evils as harbingers of the coming promise. It was strange but true, Du Bois wrote, that black " 'optimists' are largely pessimists, while our 'pessimists' are optimists." There was "a large class of professional optimists" (which obviously included Mr. Washington) who, while really believing that blacks had no chance of receiving equal rights in America, reaped personal reward by presenting "a cheerful, sunny attitude" that pleased whites. Para-doxically, this supposed optimist "does *not* have the slightest faith in the white race, or in the eventual triumph of justice. . . . On the other hand, there is the colored pessimist," Du Bois continued, who "is in reality no pessimist at all" but rather the profoundest optimist. The true optimist believes that "the way to victory is the Truth" and "the Truth may make us free." Unlike the professional optimist, whose pleasantness made him popular, the pessimist tended to be shunned by whites "made uncomfortable by lynching statistics," who ran from the truth of his words. In a phrase that speaks volumes about Du Bois's stubborn hope for white Americans, he concluded, "He [the critic] is so optimistic that he even believes in these runaways and runs after them with the truth."[32] Whereas Washington did not criticize whites because he had no faith in their ability to reform, Du Bois upbraided them precisely because he believed in their potential for change.

Ever underlying Du Bois's unsparing denunciations of American society was faith in the inevitable triumph of its democratic promise. The terrible things that daily "fill our pages," he maintained, "are but the unsubstantial smoke and shadow that hides the Real things." What he saw alone as "real" and final was "the Hope that burned in the breast of Douglass and Garrison . . . and John Brown . . . that never dies." The great moments from America's past, such as Recon-struction when the nation had moved faithfully toward the comple-tion of its democratic mission, outweighed the negative present, foreshadowed the future, and fueled Afro-Americans' continued hope. Thus, in spite of every discouragement, "the Negro has re-fused to believe that the present hesitation and hypocrisy of America is final . . . so firm has been his faith."[33]

Since Progressivism—to Du Bois the symbolic revival of aboli-tionism and the American spirit—provided the main source of pro-phetic confidence in the early years of the century, American Pro-gressivism's last burst of millennial social expectations during the First World War marked the peak of his liberal optimism. As the United States edged toward entry into the global conflict, white Progressives began to define the war as a holy crusade in which the United States, while finishing the perfect democracy at home, would lead the world into a new era of peace and freedom. It became, for them, the historic fulfillment of America's long-awaited destiny.

Du Bois came to support America's war effort enthusiastically, both because he broadly shared the Progressives' understanding of the nature of the war and because he saw it opening dramatic new possibilities for Afro-American progress. "We are facing a new world," Du Bois declared,

> never again are we going to cope with the same conditions and the same social forces that we faced in the last half-century. Never again will darker people of the world occupy just the same place they have had before. Out of this war will rise an American Negro with the right to vote and the right to live without insult.[34]

Inspired by this faith, Du Bois wrote many remarkable jeremiads in these years, but his classic assault on the nation's wartime conscience and self-image was the 1917 editorial "Awake, America." Condemning recent violent racial disturbances, he called on the country to repent of its racism and, with this last act of purification, go on to fulfill its grand destiny. "Let us enter this war for liberty with clean hands," he implored the Chosen: "May no blood-smeared garments bind our feet when we rise to make the world safe for democracy." He continued,

> Rather let us bow our shamed heads and in sackcloth and ashes declare that when in awful war we raise our weapons against the enemies of mankind, so, too, and in the same hour, here at home we raise our hands to heaven and pledge our sacred honor to make our own America a real land of the free.

He urged, as a fitting act of national atonement and rededication, the adoption of equality before the law and recognition of individual merit, and an immediate end to segregation, disenfranchisement, lynching, and all forms of racial discrimination as well. "Awake!" he cried; "Put on thy strength, America—put on thy beautiful robes. Become not a byword and jest among the nations by the hypocrisy of your word and contradiction of your deeds." Reminding whites of blacks' contributions to America in war and peace and of the nation's destiny on the world stage, he declared,

> This is as much our country as yours, and as much the world's as ours. We Americans, black and white, are the servants of all mankind and ministering to a greater, fairer Heaven. Let us be true to our mission. No land that loves to lynch "niggers" can lead the hosts of Almighty God.[35]

The First World War marked the dramatic zenith of Du Bois's immediate expectations for blacks in America. Bloody race riots in

the infamous "Red Summer" of 1919 and the national revival of the
Ku Klux Klan in the 1920s blasted his high hopes for national
reform. During the war he had envisioned the participation of blacks
in the national crusade for liberty as heralding rapid worldwide
democratic advance. Suddenly Du Bois had to urge blacks to redou-
ble their efforts at home to fight the anti-democratic declension of a
segregated America.

> This country of ours is yet a shameful land. It lynches, it disenfranchises,
> it encourages ignorance, it steals from us, it insults us . . . [but] we return.
> We return from fighting. Make way for democracy! We saved it in
> France, and by the Great Jehovah, we will save it in the United States of
> America, or know the reason why.

By 1920, Du Bois could no longer prophesy that the promise of
national and international democracy was about to come true. Most
uncharacteristically, he publicly expressed despair. "We sit back
exhausted," he wrote, "what is the use? We are still in bonds; wages
lag behind the mounting costs of life; lynching flourishes. What's the
use of it all?"[36]

As Du Bois's hopes for Anglo-Americans' imminent redemption
dwindled, his messianic rhetoric addressed to whites declined while
admonitions addressed to the black chosen people once again became predominant. Never again would a liberal jeremiad to whites
be so central in Du Bois's program and propaganda as they were
between 1910 and 1919. After 1920, he increasingly turned his
attention to black nationalism, pan-Africanism, and international
socialism as forms of messianic social prophecy offering more hope
to blacks than did the American civil religion. Still, to the very end of
his life, whenever Du Bois did speak to white Americans, he unfailingly did so as an American jeremiah.

## Black Nationalism between the Wars

Du Bois's keen interest in Africa's welfare and development was
established long before developments after 1920 shattered his liberal belief that the white Western world was evolving rapidly toward
justice and democracy. After the war he moved with fresh vigor to
realize an international pan-African movement. His immediate concern was to protect Africa from rapacious white colonialism, which
he felt had emerged stronger, not weaker from the war, and to

prevent the victorious European nations from incorporating Germany's former colonies into their empires. He organized in Paris a pan-African Congress of black representatives from all African states and colonies as well as from the United States and the West Indies for the purpose of persuading the League of Nations to ready Germany's colonies for independence by placing them temporarily under an international mandate system. Du Bois also played a leading role in organizing subsequent Pan-African Congresses in 1921, 1923, 1927, and again in 1945 after the Second World War.

Du Bois was ecstatic over the success of the 1919 Pan-African Congress and optimistic about the movement's impact on African and world destiny. The rising wave of pan-African sentiment and black independence was destined to swell, he believed, and exert an ever more powerful unifying effect on black people everywhere, emboldening them to break the bonds of white imperial domination. "The world-wide fight for black rights is on!" he cheered. Africa's fight for human rights and justice made it "the Spiritual Frontier of humankind," as it led the way toward universal democracy.[37]

Du Bois's long-standing black cultural nationalism also intensified after 1920. Du Bois himself wrote poems, pageants, and novels, but his greatest contribution to black artistic development was as a leading publicist and critic of black art in *The Crisis*. Du Bois helped introduce many young black writers and artists to the public and otherwise encouraged and contributed to that artistic movement of the 1920s known as the Harlem, or Negro, Renaissance in which black writers and artists drew inspiration from black folklife.

Black artists, Du Bois contended, had a crucial role to play in social advance by nourishing racial pride and distinct black aesthetic values. Black artists had a duty to be true to their race and not simply to conform to the standards and values of Anglo-Americans. Du Bois taught that they should be "inspired with new ideals" for themselves and the world. By being true to black people's own spiritual vision, the black artist "dreams a splendid future" and a "mighty prophecy" that was needed for "that sort of world we want to create for ourselves and for all America" and the world.[38]

During the 1920s, economic nationalism was also becoming a major cause for Du Bois; by the 1930s, it was his dominant goal and consuming passion. He urged blacks to create a self-sufficient separate group economy in the United States as their only hope of immediate survival and eventual salvation. The American economy, then and for the foreseeable future, he believed, would afford blacks no other opportunity. "We see more and more clearly that economic survival for the Negro in America means the building of his own industrial machine," he wrote shortly after the end of the First World War, "and that he must enter American industrial development as a group."[39]

Developing proposals for the establishment of a system of Afro-American consumer and producer cooperatives was therefore one of Du Bois's chief priorities in the 1920s and 1930s. He argued that, since American industry excluded blacks or gave them only the most menial jobs and since labor unions were racially exclusive, blacks had no alternative but to create a group economy independent of whites. With the onset of the Great Depression, Du Bois considered this program more urgent than ever. Amid the collapse of white capitalism, he asserted, blacks must organize themselves and focus their communal resources and energies on making economic advance in which they all could share.

By 1934, Du Bois's support in *The Crisis* for black "voluntary self-segregation" in separate racial institutions prompted a confrontation with the NAACP board of directors which led to his resignation as editor. While always believing in the rightness and value of black civil rights, Du Bois grew increasingly critical of the NAACP's emphasis on securing legal rights through litigation and court challenges to discriminatory laws. He had come to believe Karl Marx's dictum that society's economic base was its primary determinant and that pursuit of little else mattered until blacks "were able to earn a decent, independent living." Blacks' most pressing problems in the economic disaster of the thirties were unemployment and starvation. Therefore, he was not interested in "a program of mere agitation for 'rights,'" such as the NAACP represented. When Du Bois began urging blacks not to concentrate at present on integrating themselves into America but to focus on group economic advance in separate institutions, the association's executive board felt, incorrectly in his view, he had abandoned the NAACP's founding principles.[40] It was his position that group loyalty was not equivalent to segregation.

Whereas most black middle-class leaders continued to pursue white progressive reform during the thirties as the most promising means of promoting racial progress, Du Bois believed, in view of blacks' dire economic straits, that "a further prolongation of looking for salvation from the whites" was untenable.[41] It followed that there was a further diminishment in his jeremiadic rhetoric toward whites and intensification of concern for the decisions and actions of black people.

The most noticeable thing about Du Bois's emphasis on black economic solidarity after the First World War was the increasingly cooperative, socialistic nature of the ventures he advocated. He believed ever more strongly that economic cooperation and collective ownership represented "the new spirit" of the industrial era which was eventually "going to work itself out in the white world." Furthermore blacks, he believed, "can evolve a new and efficient industrial cooperation quicker than any other group." But in developing their internal economy, he warned, blacks must not "try the old paths of individual exploitation, develop a class of rich and grasping brigands of industry," and so "reproduce in our own group all the industrial hell of Old Europe and America." Rather, they should strive to transfer control of capital to the democratic majority.[42]

Planned coordination of resources and equitable distribution of goods in the black community, he said, would both improve blacks' present circumstances and speed the world toward the approaching age of economic justice. He declared, "We who have had least class differentiation in wealth can follow in the new trend and indeed lead it." "Here, then," he concluded, "is the economic ladder by which the American Negro . . . can move . . . with the modern world into a new heaven and a new earth."[43]

Theoretically, Du Bois's commitment to Afro-American progress and to socialism were complementary, for, as he often stated, "The struggle for the liberation of the working classes in general and of the Negro race in America in particular is, of course, at bottom the same struggle." But into the 1940s, whenever one cause conflicted with the other, his greatest commitment was to race. For decades, therefore, Du Bois dissented from orthodox Marxism on several major points. His lingering liberal reformism led him to reject the dogma of inevitable class conflict between workers and every other class (including the progressive middle class) and of the necessity of violent revolution to institute socialism. His racial loyalty, however, posed the biggest obstacle. Du Bois felt that Marxists fundamentally erred in assuming the interracial solidarity of the working class. The irrational prejudice of white workers prevented them from uniting with other workers to end the world's current capitalist declension and fulfill the universal promise of economic democracy. Marxist theory, he wrote, "did not envisage a situation where instead of a horizontal division of classes, there was a vertical fissure, a complete separation of classes by race, cutting square across the economic layers." "In America," he continued, "we have seen a wild and ruthless scramble of labor groups over each other in order to climb to wealth on the backs of black labor and foreign immigrants." Du Bois deplored the pragmatic cooperation between nationalistic white capitalists and white laborers, who seemed to perceive a joint interest in exploitation of colored workers overseas.[44]

He considered Afro-Americans the lone exception to this pattern of capitalist exploitation of labor. In America, he contended, "the colored group is not yet divided into capitalists and laborers" and blacks shared an "interclass sympathy" that would allow them to organize economically in a just and cooperative way. In the United States, he declared, "in the hearts of black laborers alone lie those ideals of democracy in politics and industry which may in time make the workers of the world effective dictators of civilization."[45]

This decisive change from Du Bois's youthful liberal prophecy of swift world progress from racism to justice was expressed poignantly in his book of 1940, *Dusk of Dawn: An Essay toward an Autobiography of a Race Concept.* Written in his early seventies, *Dusk* shows the mellowing effect of age and experience. "Life has its pain and evil—its bitter disappointments," he wrote, although he held that one must never lose faith in the final, eventual triumph of right. Ever the prophet of social progress, Du Bois nevertheless revealed a sharply chastened sense of evil's tenacious presence in human society. Looking back on his life, he admitted that he had initially overestimated the power of science and reason in human affairs. Even after he concluded that scientific research alone could not produce the desired social progress and that "agitation," "boycott," and "organization"—the weapons of protest—were also needed in blacks' struggle, he still expected quick dramatic results. When he "founded . . . the *Crisis*," his "basic theory had been that race prejudice was primarily a matter of ignorance . . . [and] that when the truth was properly presented . . . race hatred must melt and melt quickly before it."[46]

The unanticipated disappointments of the twentieth century undermined his once sanguine view about democracy's swift triumph throughout the world. "Upon this state of mind after a few years of conspicuous progress [during the Progressive Era] fell the horror of World War," the first major blow to his liberal reformist faith in human reasonableness and goodness. There soon followed the Great Depression and its economic misery for Afro-Americans. The "scope of chance and unreason in human action" seemed far greater to him in 1940 than it had at the turn of the century. In the 1920s and 1930s, he realized "that the color line could not be broken by a series of brilliant assaults." Gradually, from contemporary events and his reading of Freud and Marx, he grew to appreciate the existence "of certain more powerful motives" that were "less open to appeal and reason" than simple ignorance. These more intractable evil forces were, first, selfish "economic motives" based on exploitation rationalized by racism, and second, psychological forces ("unconscious acts and irrational reactions") based on inherited, centuries-old social beliefs and habits. To change the world, as he still meant to do, he had come to believe that "not sudden assault but long siege" was called for, and for this, "time was needed."[47] In the meantime, blacks could not afford to wait for the white world's progress but had to focus inward on their own potential and messianic mission.

## 5. Mary McLeod Bethune and W. E. B. Du Bois: Rising and Waning Hopes for America at Midcentury

In the inter-war years, Du Bois advised against seeking immediate racial integration of American society and instead urged blacks to develop independent social power. It is ironic that this founder of the modern civil rights movement was increasingly pessimistic about chances for interracial reform in the 1930s and 1940s just when other black leaders were growing more optimistic about making major improvements in the conditions of black Americans through collaboration with white liberals.

No figure was more representative of this surge of black hope in American liberal reform than the prominent black New Dealer, Mary McLeod Bethune.[1] In 1934, Bethune was already a leading figure in Afro-American women's organizations and president of Bethune-Cookman College when she was appointed special advisor on minority affairs to President Franklin Roosevelt. She became director of the Office of Minority Affairs in the National Youth Administration (NYA) in 1936 and served in both advisory positions through 1944.

Bethune became a person of influence in the federal government. She worked assiduously to promote maximum black participation in planning, distributing, and receiving the educational, health, and recreational benefits that the NYA dispersed to local communities. She was a key member of the informal New Deal "Black Cabinet" of racial advisors in federal departments who met regularly (usually in her home) to share information and form strategy among blacks in government. Bethune cooperated with civil rights organizations such as the NAACP and National Urban League to promote civil rights legislation. She also worked with them to hold a series of high-profile conferences in Washington, under NYA auspices, focusing attention on Afro-Americans' oppressive conditions. Above all, Mary Bethune was a publicly visible and articulate symbol of black Americans' rising aspirations in the New Deal and war years. She was prominent at the start of a black tide of social hope and assertiveness that would continue to swell through the mid-1960s.

One of the most influential black leaders of the New Deal–Second World War era, her political and ideological positions paralleled those of the most typical black jeremiahs in this study: Frederick Douglas, W. E. B. Du Bois (in his liberal-reformist stage), and Martin Luther King, Jr. Bethune championed civil rights and integration and protested national racial inequality and discrimination. She called for greater social-civic responsibility among blacks but assigned to white America major responsibility for obstructing race progress and equality. Bethune was dissatisfied with current American conditions and proposed change, yet she always expressed her abiding faith in blacks' and America's future.

Because she sometimes employed features of the black jeremiad, she seems a strong candidate for the role of female black jeremiah. Yet, like Ida Wells and Booker T. Washington, her reliance on feminine imagery and gentle modes of persuasion significantly diminished the jeremiadic aspects of her rhetoric. Although the substance of her public message recalled the jeremiad as she criticized and warned Americans regarding injustice, her tone was far from jeremiadic; her customary manner was that of a genteel Southern woman. She made her often assertive points in a soft, unoffending way and generally avoided harsh or accusatory tones. Nevertheless, her public message consistently contained some characteristic elements of the jeremiad: faith in the national promise, expressions of dismay at national declension, urgent moral appeals to reform, and a prophecy of the promise's imminent fulfillment and the start of a new age.

Bethune was a devout churchwoman who believed in democracy and progressive reform. Her optimism was based on government-led social reforms and the national changes and unity brought about by the Second World War. Citing the precedent of federal programs in public housing, health, social security, education, relief, and employment, she declared that Afro-Americans, having been "ostracized, segregated, denied wholesome living conditions, underschooled, underpaid and underfed," especially were "in need of every liberal program for the benefit of the masses." "As definitely underprivileged people," she told blacks, "we have everything to gain in a program of social reform." New Deal reform represented what black Americans needed desperately for survival as well as what America needed to become a true democracy. In 1938, she described the "new era of social reform" that made "the problems of the people . . . the problems of the Government" as the modern realization of Lincoln's "government of, for and by the people."[2]

Bethune consistently deplored and decried the economic inequality, educational limitations, social restrictions, and denial of civil rights that stunted life for black Americans. Indeed, her unrelentingly dreary portrayal of current conditions for blacks in America seemed sometimes to justify despair:

> We are beset on every side with heart-rending and fearsome difficulties. Our people cry out all around us like children lost in the wilderness. Hemmed in by a careless world, we are losing our homes and . . . farms and . . . jobs. We see vast numbers . . . sunk into the degradation of peonage and virtual slavery. In the cities, our workers are barred from the unions, forced to "scab" and . . . fight with their very lives for work. About us cling the ever-tightening tentacles of poor wages, economic insecurity . . . broken homes, ill health, delinquency and crime. Our children are choked by denied opportunity for health, for education, for work, for recreation, and thwarted with their ideals and ambitions still a-borning. We are scorned of men; they spit in our faces and laugh. We cry out in this awesome darkness.[3]

In highlighting America's current social shortcomings, Bethune reminded Americans of their neglected duties and warned of the harmful consequences of continuing along the same path. She frequently pointed to the unnecessary costs that the nation paid to keep "the nigger in his place." The money needed to maintain prison facilities in Florida where two-thirds of the inmates were black, she noted, deprived the whole community of funds that could have been "diverted into more constructive channels for the public good." If America continued to discourage black morality and progress and to promote poverty and vice, she contended, the nation would jeopardize its present and future welfare. Declaring that "the price [of discrimination] is too high to be paid in this generation," she predicted, in prophetic Old-Testament style, that it "must be paid by the children unto the third and fourth generation." She identified the "cost of discrimination and segregation to a nation at war" as loss in efficiency and productivity in the armed forces and the civilian war economy. Finally, she called attention to "the implications of American racial attitudes for our relationships with the other United Nations."[4] Failing to enact thoroughgoing racial and social reform would be disastrous, she prophesied, because the world's gathering momentum toward social justice was irresistible.

Bethune developed these themes in her 1944 speech and essay "Certain Unalienable Rights," in which she compared the little people's revolt at the Boston Tea Party to recent outbreaks of racial tension in Harlem, Detroit, and Los Angeles. This "rumbling of anger and resentment," she explained, was fueled by blacks' anger "against restriction and oppression and discrimination." There was, she declared, "a ferment aloose among the oppressed little people everywhere, a groping of the long inert masses" toward freedom. They were determined to bring down "the walls of ghettos" and to end the "economic, social and political restrictions" in which "the forces of tyranny and oppression and race supremacy" held them. All around the world, "the little people want 'out,'" she claimed.

Stirred by democratic liberalism's promise of justice to "the forgotten man" and by "the clarion call of the Four Freedoms" to battle the racist Axis dictatorships, people of color were eager to help realize the great ideal "that all men are created equal." Blacks' mounting determination to hurl down the walls of restriction, however, clashed with the "unwillingness of white America to allow any appreciable breach in this wall." Blacks resented being mistreated at home, segregated in the armed forces, and held back from full participation in war production.

Bethune declared that responsible black leaders "must make plain to America that we have reached a critical stage in assimilation of colored people." White America had to be educated to accept this change, for only by winning white "understanding and support" could "the swelling force among minority racial groups be channeled into creative progress rather than exploded into riots and conflicts . . . [or] hoodlumism." The drive for racial change would not disappear, and so it was critical that America respond "so that we [blacks] may cooperate with orderly social reform . . . rather than turn to the quicksands of revolution or the false promises of communism or fascism."[5]

Bethune often tried to shame America into changing to demonstrate fidelity to its great ideals and mission. "America is disregarding its plain duty," its "moral and spiritual obligations to more than 12,000,000 souls of its population," she charged, when it denied democratic rights to citizens of African descent. White Americans had to honor their sacred heritage by opening the doors of opportunity to all. This moral necessity, moreover, could be accomplished in orderly fashion "without this evolution causing revolution." Bethune pointed proudly to efforts "on the part of our great leader, the President of the United States to open for the Negro some of the doors that have been closed" and to "a determination on the part of the Negro to open, or batter down some of these closed doors." But, she urged, "there must be an equal . . . cooperation on the part of the American public to join in the effort." Here then was "the challenge to America": "Can it? Will it?" If America refused to grant blacks' God-given rights as Americans, "it will be guilty" of betraying its own founding ideals. "*Awake America!*" she pleaded. "*Accept the challenge! Give the Negro a chance!*"[6]

An unshakeable optimism always characterized Bethune's public words and deeds; she always prophesied social progress and perfection for America. Over and over, Bethune announced the arrival of "a new day" of hope and progress. "The progressive program" of the New Deal, she declared enthusiastically in the thirties, "is bringing us a new day, a sense of security we could not have dreamed of yesterday." "These are times of a great awakening and new opportunities for all"; "the spirit of democracy" was finally "being galvanized into realistic action." She asserted, "We stand tonight on the threshold of a new era, of a new vision, of a new world," based on the principle of "one practical democracy for all" and on "the spiritual understanding that all mankind has been created in the image of God" and "is endowed with certain inalienable rights." "It thrills me to think that a dawn of a new day, a new opportunity has come to my people," she exclaimed, and to realize "what God has wrought in the changes which are enveloping us today." "As I look from this veritable mount of transformation down through the valleys of hope for the underprivileged," she wrote, "I cannot help but" be filled with faith, seeing how "our promised land of liberty and equal opportunity is before us." Bethune conveyed the exhilarating sense that the corner had been turned in the trek to democracy. Although she cautioned that "our goal has not been reached," the "doors have not been thrown open widely enough," and "our integration and participation have only just begun," she nevertheless closed many statements with her triumphant refrain: "We are on our way!"[7]

## Bethune on Blacks, Whites, and American Destiny

Although Bethune most stressed the duty of whites to reform their racial attitudes and practices, she also exhorted blacks to fulfill their social duty. As a founder of a black industrial education school, Bethune long advocated black self-help in basic education and economic training. She believed that the emergence of "large and growing numbers of . . . Negroes who have achieved by discipline and training a measure of culture which qualifies them for advanced status in our American life" was absolutely vital for the race's success and future.[8]

The sphere of activity that she most persistently urged for blacks, though, was increased civic and public involvement in the American mainstream, not isolated socio-economic self-development: "We must take a full part in the political life of our community, state and nation. We must learn increasingly about political organization and techniques. We must prepare for and fight for places on the local, state, and national committees of our political parties."[9] Bethune worked to ensure the fullest, most equal participation possible for blacks in the National Youth Administration and in American political life and institutions generally.

In order to benefit from democracy, Bethune taught blacks, they must be in a position to influence their representatives by registering, voting, and organizing. She advocated the development of black political power but always advised its use in an interracial liberal coalition. A partisan New Deal Democrat, she believed that it was in black Americans' immediate as well as long-term interests to support and help extend New Deal reforms. "We must continually educate our people to the great benefits of our national progress," she declared; they must be shown "the need for becoming more and more an integral part of this progressive movement."[10]

It was also blacks' civic duty to criticize white America's racist faults, Bethune asserted:

> We must challenge . . . resolutely every sign of restriction . . . on our full
> American citizenship . . . protest openly everything in the newspapers,
> on the radio, in the movies that smacks of discrimination or slander . . .

take the seat that our ticket calls for . . . and challenge everywhere the principle and practice of enforced racial segregation.

She declared that she "would not be true to my duty as an American" if she did not tell white citizens that the battle to remove obstacles to equal opportunity in the nation was their battle, too—a battle for American democracy.[11]

The development of black self-reliance was, for Bethune, ultimately intended to promote complete integration into American society. "The Negro wants a fair chance to work out his own destiny," she stated significantly, in order "to contribute to the honor and glory of the nation." Blacks sought to help create a new nation, perfected in democracy and freed from racism, she argued. "I hold that blood and color does not define an American citizen," she declared, and that this land was "our land." Denied equal opportunity, "we have protested" and "shall protest and protest again." Yet "our patriotism is a conviction, a consuming impulse, devouring flame," and "we have stood the acid-test." Despite America's disregard of "its plain duty in regard to its black citizens," she believed that "America can [and] . . . will be changed." "Even now the soul of this nation is undergoing a rebirth regarding citizens of Negro blood," she said. "Here and there we see bright signs; stars of hope" to which "we must hitch our wagons." Therefore, "we must resist the implication that we constitute a separate part of this nation, invade every field of activity in America, [and] contribute in every way we can to fostering and perpetuating the honored national ideals."[12]

Black people marched to war for democracy despite the barriers that blocked their full participation in their own country's freedom, she declared; but "march they must, and march they will, because they do understand that every hope they have for full democracy hinges upon the outcome of this war. They understand that the fate of America is the fate of the Negro people; we go up or down together." For what, after all, were all Americans fighting? "We are fighting for the perfection of the democracy of our own beloved America, and the extension of that perfected democracy to the ends of the world."[13]

## Bethune as National Leader

Bethune's reputation reflects her considerable effectiveness and assertiveness in seeking black equality. There was another side to her public manner, though, one not so consonant with her role as a black jeremiah. This important aspect of her approach to whites was conciliatory, unoffending, indeed, deferential. It reflected partly Booker T. Washington's strong influence on her and, more fundamentally, the sentimental Christian and Victorian ideals of "true womanhood." In adhering to these "soft" feminine qualities in her public presentation, her genuine propensity (particularly from the Depression onward) for jeremiadic rhetoric was subdued. Bethune's nonconfrontational public style was formed in her late nineteenth-century and early twentieth-century youth and remained a conditioning force throughout her public career.

Mary McLeod Bethune came up the hard way. She was born in 1875 in South Carolina to poor sharecroppers. As a child, she worked in the fields with her parents and sixteen brother and sisters. Her parents were uneducated but loving and pious. She inherited from them a deep religious outlook and personal faith that was basic to her makeup.

Her parents recognized her early as a precocious child, "different" from the rest, and so encouraged her desire for education. When a Presbyterian missionary board opened a local school for blacks, she enrolled, although she had to walk a long way and her work in the fields prevented very regular attendance. Still, she was a fine student, and when she graduated a white church benefactor from Denver enabled her to attend Scotia Seminary in Concord, North Carolina. Between 1887 and 1894, she studied hard there and supported herself by doing domestic work. She next received a scholarship to Moody Bible Institute in Chicago where her burning ambition was to become a Christian missionary to Africa. Upon graduating, however, she found that there were no openings for black women missionaries to Africa, so turned to teaching.

While teaching school in South Carolina, she married Albertus Bethune; she also taught in Georgia before moving to Palatka, Florida, in 1899. In the early years of her marriage, she bore a child and ran a local mission school. To make ends meet, she also became a part-time life insurance salesperson for which she had the necessary dynamic and persuasive personality. Her husband was skeptical and unsupportive of her ambition, but Mary was the dominant partner in their marriage.[14]

Brimming with energy, charm, and charisma, Mary Bethune doggedly pursued her dream of establishing a school for black girls.

With almost no down payment, she persuaded a local man to sell her a building and in 1904 she opened Daytona Normal and Industrial School for Negro Girls. For several years the tiny Florida school with meager facilities managed to weather successive financial crises; eventually it grew and prospered. All pupils performed work for the school and raised funds by selling food and handicrafts.

Bethune's school was patterned after Tuskegee and Hampton Institutes and followed Booker T. Washington's program of black industrial education. A survivor of rural poverty herself, Bethune was strongly convinced that blacks needed instruction in basic life skills and training directly relevant to their immediate economic opportunities. All her girls were trained in housekeeping and domestic service as well as academic subjects. Holding her students to high moral standards, Bethune taught them to perform common labor uncommonly well. Even when she was accused in church once by the preacher of preparing her pupils only for menial servanthood, she stuck with her industrial education policy.

Booker T. Washington visited her school several times and encouraged her activities. There were many similarities in the careers of the two educators. Both built, largely through their own energetic and inspirational leadership, thriving vocational schools that originally relied on their own students' labor for survival. In describing the heroic self-help efforts needed in its early days to keep her institute alive, Bethune sounded remarkably like Washington: "This was part of the training: to salvage, to reconstruct, to make bricks without straw."[15] This line was taken directly from Washington, who had adapted it from the Bible.

Mary Bethune packaged her own story and her school's story together for public relations nearly as successfully and in much the same fashion as had Washington. Like him, she proved talented at attracting white moral and financial support. She adroitly exploited her school's location in Daytona, a favorite resort of the wealthy of the East Coast. One of her most successful fundraising techniques was bringing her girls to sing and perform for vacationers at beach hotels. After the entertainment, Mrs. Bethune would give an inspirational talk explaining the school's goals, history, and present needs, and then solicit contributions. She initiated contact in this way, for example, with James Gamble of Proctor and Gamble, who became the first chairman of Daytona Institute's board of trustees. Later she used such connections to launch publicity and fundraising campaigns in the North where her audiences included Rockefellers, Carnegies, and Mellons. Wherever she went, she was well-received and rewarded. The sight of her polite, well-scrubbed black girls won audience sympathy, and Bethune's obvious faith in her cause and infectious enthusiasm rubbed off on her audience. She was a folksy but compelling speaker whose basic appeal, according to one biographer, went: "Here I stand, Mrs. Mary Bethune. Let me tell you who I was and what now I am. I am only a humble servant of the Lord. What does He want of us all? With your help other little girls can rise as I have done."[16]

Her school kept growing and in 1923 merged with Cookman Institute, a similar school for black boys, to form Bethune-Cookman College. As a young adult in the early years of the century, she was apparently uninterested in the ideological controversies between Washington and W. E. B. Du Bois and Ida Wells. Such issues simply were not relevant to her immediate consuming educational enterprise, although in practice she supported Washington's social program.

By the mid-1920s, though, Bethune's growing involvement in regional and national black women's organizations began displacing education as her main public pursuit. In 1909, she had attended a meeting of the National Association of Colored Women at Hampton Institute. There she met and took as role models such women as Mrs. Booker T. Washington and Mary Church Terrell. The efforts of women's groups to promote health, morals, and homemaking in black youth and families wonderfully complemented her own educational mission. She eventually become president of that group as well as of the Florida State Federation of Colored Women's Clubs. In 1935, she became founder-president of the influential National Council of Negro Women, a national federation of black women's groups that sought to coordinate women's participation in the broad social and civil life of their communities. Under her leadership, the National Council became increasingly active in social causes like prison reform, black voting, and decent and desegregated public schools for black children. Bethune's prominence in the black women's club movement in the 1920s led to her national political appointments.

Bethune's leading life cause was protecting and advancing the interests of black children and women and, through such activity, of the whole race. According to her, black women had a special social role and duty: "The Negro woman is the torch-bearer of her race," she declared, who "not only points the way, but very often leads the way out of perplexity and despair." "The average Negro wife and mother may not be able to distinguish between a vitamin and a microbe," she said, and "budgets and balanced diets may not yet have entered her vocabulary," but in her most crucial social task, that of keeping "her own spirit and the spirits of those about her, wholesome," she already excelled. The black woman kept a faithful, "cheery philosophy" through everything and always put others above herself. She was "unfailing in her encouragement, inspiration and support to her husband. . . . The Negro man," Bethune observed, "is beset by difficulties no other man has to face and he needs the understanding, love, patience, and help that his mate is capable of giving." Denied chances for social and intellectual development herself, the black woman "possesses ambition for her children" and "welcomes any sacrifice for [their] future."

Black women also served their race in the teaching and other service professions. "The exact synonym for Missionary is Negro teacher," Bethune declared, and "the 'gospel' which she carries is that of successful living." Cleanliness, manners, and morals were the most important things to be taught. These "earnest, zealous, poorly-compensated missionaries" of culture were "consecrated women" answering "a spiritual call" of tremendous social import.

In order to serve others better, black women were also developing their powers and capabilities outside the home. More and more black women, Bethune asserted, were "learning to combine a home with a career," developing into "organizers and promoters," venturing successfully into "the arts, literature, business, politics, education and social service," and "learning the scope and power of the vote . . . as one of the means to betterment." Whatever her endeavor, the black woman's quintessential trait was spiritual faith: "Hers is a spirit of patience, tact, fearlessness, love and forgiveness; hers the spirit of Christ."[17]

Bethune's participation in national politics was largely conducted within the framework of this idealized version of women's social role. Her first trip to the White House was as a member of a 1928 Child Welfare Conference called by President Calvin Coolidge. It was for her work in education and child and women's welfare that the Roosevelt administration sought her as an advisor to the president and in the National Youth Administration (NYA). Bethune's job was generally to promote healthier conditions for black as well as white youth within the programs of the NYA. In her fifties when she came to serve in the New Deal, she was a heavy-set, matronly woman. Since her thirties, she had been called "Mother Bethune," not just by students but by most adults as well. Her appointment and political effectiveness were based on her presentation of her self and causes in a feminine light. On one occasion, however, she was in President Roosevelt's office passionately pleading for executive action against prejudicial policies against blacks in southern NYA offices when she suddenly realized that she was speaking loudly and wagging a finger in the president's face. Bethune immediately apologized. According to her, FDR smiled and said that he was always glad to hear her "because you always come for others and never for yourself."[18]

Even as a chief advocate of equal treatment for blacks during the New Deal, Mary McLeod Bethune's noncombative methods always coexisted with her frank assertiveness and occasional outright militancy. From her earliest public days, she refused to be addressed by whites as anything other than "Mrs. Bethune"; she demanded the title of respect and refused to be called by her first name like a servant. She also consistently disregarded segregation laws in seating arrangements at interracial meetings held at her school or under her auspices. And she was well-known among blacks for her curt retorts to White House personnel foolish enough to mistake her for a servant or question her right to be there. A person of great presence and bearing, Bethune could be emphatic and persuasive, particularly in private. Indeed, one severe critic of Bethune's effectiveness as a New Deal administrator, B. Joyce Ross, called her "a Janus-faced figure who presented a public position to . . . white groups which often differed appreciably from her privately expressed attitudes." Before whites, Ross noted, "her appeals for racial equality often were couched in terms which could only be flattering to white people, while her demeanor was usually that of a supplicant whose primary approach lay in appeals to white people's consciences and sense of fair play."[19]

Bethune avoided seeming abrasive or antagonistic in public. Toward whites generally and especially with Southerners, her manner was so affable, her speeches so laced with religious homilies and folksy "down-home" humor, that she could make comfortable even many who were violently opposed to her views. Asking for more blacks to be appointed to local NYA posts in the South, she jokingly told Southern whites that she would "like to see some more of those darkies dotting around here." Some younger black aides found offensive Bethune's frequent use of the term "darky" to put white audiences at ease. She often used Southern-style stereotypes to cajole whites, such as her frequent line about chicken: "You white folks have long been eating the white meat of the chicken. We Negroes are now ready for some of the white meat instead of the dark meat."[20]

Bethune faced an intractable social situation. As her comment above indicated, she often had difficulty getting Southern NYA offices to appoint black personnel or to deal fairly with the black population in their jurisdiction. She consistently fought for integration of public facilities supported by federal funds, but usually had to settle for segregated access to make them available to blacks at all. By and large, she was unsuccessful in getting the Roosevelt administration to compel Southern compliance with the federal guidelines for racial equality in government programs. FDR and the national NYA usually chose not to risk antagonizing white Southerners and losing support for New Deal programs.

Bethune was especially forgiving toward white liberals like FDR whose hearts, she believed, were in the right place but who found it expedient to temporize on racial issues. When Jessie Daniel Ames, the white president of the Association of Southern Women for the Prevention of Lynching (ASWPL), announced opposition to a proposed federal anti-lynching bill on the grounds that anti-lynching reform had to be accomplished voluntarily by the states, she was attacked by many blacks, but not by Bethune. Bethune wrote Ames, expressing her continuing friendship and support and assuring her that she had "only gratification for what you have done." When the distraught Ames passionately defended her good intent, saying that she feared Northern coercion on the matter would inflame Southern sectionalism, Bethune replied, "Enough said. I understand you thoroughly . . . [and] have unswerving confidence in your interest and cooperation and sincerity."[21]

Bethune's forte was her forceful personality and speaking skills. She was more a government coordinator and advisor than actual decision maker. Her lack of an independent power base forced her to pursue her agenda mainly through persuading her immediate superior in the NYA, Aubrey Williams, or the president himself to implement her recommendations.

"Mother Bethune" effectively masked her militancy with home-spun words and manners, fitting the clenched fist of her demands into a velvety rhetorical glove. In their substantive content—political protest and social criticism, insistence on equal rights for blacks, and demands for white change—Bethune's public themes were markedly similar to the jeremiads of her liberal black male counter-parts, but in her delivery, there was a subtle but important differ-ence. In private and public, Bethune avoided the aggressive, even abrasive demeanor that most authentic delivery of the jeremiad requires. She was never angry or accusatory and never berated audiences. She never threatened whites except in the mildest, most indirect manner. B. Joyce Ross pointedly contrasted "Mrs. Bethune's subdued public approach" with the more assertive stance of Dr. Mordecai Johnson, the president of Howard University who served with her on the NYA National Advisory Committee. Ross observed that although Bethune and Johnson usually agreed on the issues, Johnson, "unlike Mrs. Bethune," presented "a forceful public im-age." The "more publicly forceful Dr. Johnson" spoke more can-didly of blacks' "rights" and "demands" and more bluntly about the dangerous "consequences" and perils to America posed by segrega-tion.[22]

Being less involved in government, Dr. Johnson may have felt freer to speak without regard for the reactions of white officials. But it may also be that Johnson and Bethune merely reflected the gender expectations of their time—his rhetoric masculine and forceful, hers feminine and conciliatory. For whatever reason, there was never a perfect fit between "Mother Bethune" and the role of a black jeremiah.[23]

Mary McLeod Bethune personified the revolutionary hopefulness among blacks in the 1930s and 1940s, when the social-psychological foundations of the post-war civil rights movement were first set. The substantial progress achieved during the New Deal and Second World War whetted black desires for further change. This was true even though the basic position of blacks and whites in America changed very little.

On the positive side, the federal government at this time assumed responsibility for national social welfare and provided new pro-grams that gave tangible aid to many blacks. Moreover, white liberal leaders showed heightened concern for the conditions and issues affecting Afro-Americans. More official attention was fixed on black needs and grievances than in any time since Reconstruction, and the federal government endorsed the principle of racial nondiscrimination as a goal of public policy. The ongoing mass migration of blacks from rural Southern areas to the urban North and Midwest also began to have political consequences by the late thirties. Black voting power in Northern cities grew to the point that white politicians had to consider it. After most black voters left the Republican fold to join the New Deal coalition in the 1936 election, their support became an object of genuine competition between the national parties. Accordingly, black leaders such as Bethune were able to get more concessions, both symbolic and substantial, from the administration. Important victories included getting President Roosevelt to support federal repeal of poll taxes and to issue an executive order denying government contracts to firms practicing racial discrimination in hiring and wages. The latter was achieved only by threatening a protest march on Washington in 1941.[24] Federal relief programs, black inclusion in industrial unions in the 1930s, and above all, the booming war economy after 1941 brought blacks significant economic gains as well.

At the same time, there were definite limits to change. The economic position of blacks remained far worse than that of whites, and this imbalance was never fundamentally addressed or altered. Nor did the federal government directly attack or even regularly denounce customary white racial attitudes and segregation. The Roosevelt administration did not wish to antagonize the white South, calculating that white Southern votes were politically more important than the black vote and outweighed the benefits of promoting racial reform.

Nevertheless, the impact on blacks of this era's changes were important and enduring. If the actual changes in blacks' circumstances were indeed limited, the fact of change itself in a favorable direction was undeniable. Many blacks believed Mary Bethune's hopeful rallying cry, "We are on our way!" The awakening of Afro-Americans to the possibility, indeed expectancy, of major progress was the New Deal's legacy to blacks in the post–Second World War era. The factors of black's later success—rising political power, liberal white sympathy and support, greater government activism in racial affairs, and new international implications of the United States' domestic racial policies—first began to come together at mid-century. One student has observed of these turning-point years: "The soil had been tilled. The seeds that would later bear fruit had been planted. . . . Harvest time would come in the next generation."[25]

Mary Bethune's optimism about interracial liberal reform foreshadowed the hopeful mood of Martin Luther King, Jr., and other blacks of the 1950s and 1960s. Bethune typified the black intellectual trend of her day, which stressed interracial class issues and economic reform as the keys to black progress. Influential black social thinkers such as Charles Johnson and Ralph Bunche minimized race as a factor in blacks' social experience, emphasizing instead economic conditions. Since the effect of economics extended to the entire population, remedying problems in this field would require broad reforms achievable only through interclass and interracial alliances with whites. For this reason, influential black social theorists and political leaders like Bethune opposed any ideology or program of racial separatism. This same emphasis on the transracial economic nature of blacks' social problems would be paramount in Du Bois's post-1940s socialism and in King's thought as well from the mid-1960s onward.[26]

An acute theorist, Du Bois was always sensitive to the importance of class, but in the thirties and early forties, his thought stressing the centrality of racial identity and of racism to blacks' condition ran counter to most contemporary black analyses. By the time of the New Deal, he was long past his youthful liberal hope for America and was growing more deeply cognizant of the systematic place of racism in Western capitalist society. He was significantly older than most of his black scholarly colleagues, who harshly criticized or brusquely dismissed his race-oriented theories and proposals. Although nearer his age, Mary McLeod Bethune had been too absorbed in surviving and building her school in the early years of the century to have entertained such high hopes for liberal reform as had Du Bois. Chastened by earlier disappointment, Du Bois could not share the easy optimism that buoyed most black liberals in the thirties and forties.

## The Decline of Race and Afro-American Mission in Du Bois's Thought

By the mid-forties, Du Bois turned from his proposals for a segregated Afro-American economy and society as he found it increasingly difficult to divorce Afro-Americans' problems from international relationships of race and class. Black nationalist and radical economic thought converged on that topic which had come to command his attention: colonial imperialism.

The Second World War was pivotal in redirecting Du Bois's thinking from internal experiments among Afro-Americans toward a universal socialist vision. "Not from the inner problems of a single social group . . . can the world be guided," he now concluded. After the war, he "began to enter into a World conception of human uplift . . . centering about the work and income of the working class" irrespective of color or nationality.[27]

Du Bois's international interests became increasingly paramount. Temporarily reunited with the NAACP from 1944 to 1948, he directed production of a 155-page NAACP petition to the new United Nations Commission on Human Rights protesting violation of blacks' civil rights in America and seeking international redress. He also participated in lobbying the United Nations to grant representation to African colonies and helped to organize the fifth Pan-African Congress in 1945.

In that same year, Du Bois's book *Color and Democracy: Colonies and Peace* reflected his acutely pessimistic sense of world declension.[28] The fervent hopes of the world's peoples for lasting peace after the Second World War, he concluded, were doomed to disappointment because of the persistent malignant cancer of white racist imperialism. Racism and colonialism, which persistently had led to international injustice and conflict, had emerged from the war more powerful than ever: "It is with great regret that I do not see after this war, or within any reasonable time, the possibility of a world without race conflict." The habits of white racism and the exploitation of colonial labor and resources for profit remained vitally active, foreboding future conflict and war. There could be no hope for lasting peace and progress without a solution to this problem, but for the moment, alas, racist imperialism showed no sign of ending.[29]

Du Bois entered the 1950s apprehensive over what he saw as deepening declension at home and abroad, related to the powerful post-war resurgence of capitalist imperialism. Witnessing the triumph of reactionary pro-business political forces and rabid anti-Communist hysteria in post-war America, he feared that the United States was turning into a garrison state as it mobilized for international Cold War. White Americans were preparing to become the global guardians of Europe's imperialist tradition, which had made white people in the northern hemisphere affluent and colored people in the southern hemisphere poor.

Still willing to enter the thick of public battle as an octogenarian, Du Bois made international peace his great cause of the 1950s. The Korean War and the development of atomic weapons by the United States and the Soviet Union horrified him. Du Bois clamored for peaceful existence with the Soviets on two grounds. First, he taught, recent history showed "that war is not the path to the millennium," and the costs of nuclear war would outweigh any conceivable gain from it. Second, and equally important, was his belief that the threat of war came overwhelmingly from capitalist determination to use force to stem the world-wide tide toward socialist democracy. He pictured the United States as heading an aggressive imperialistic fight to keep control over colonial peoples and prevent the world's workers from asserting themselves and upsetting the international capitalist order. "Reluctantly the world is coming to believe that we actually want war," he said disheartenedly, "that we must have war . . . [to] keep our workers employed and maintain huge profits." He was sure "that the first step toward settling the world's problems was Peace on Earth" because American preparations for combatting Communism around the globe both threatened world peace and obstructed social progress nationally and internationally.

> I want progress; I want education; I want social medicine . . . a living wage and old-age security . . . employment for all and relief for the unemployed and sick; I want public works . . . services and . . . improvements . . . , [and] because . . . we cannot have these things, and at the same time fight, destroy and kill all around the world . . . I take my stand . . . and cry *Peace—No More War!*[30]

Fearlessly voicing such unpopular views, Du Bois became a pariah among white and black middle-class leaders. His Marxian critique of capitalism and strident opposition to the Cold War caused him to be harassed by the United States government as he organized on behalf of his views.[31] He found it increasingly difficult to get coverage of his views in the white press and newspapers, as well as in many black ones; his main public outlet in these years was in leftist journals such as *Masses and Mainstream*.

Du Bois had long since moved beyond the NAACP's program of seeking legal rights and now insisted that black Americans' problems could not be resolved apart from the anti-imperialist struggle of Third World peoples. By the 1950s Du Bois was considered an embarrassment by most black leaders. Even the NAACP broke relations with him and banned him from speaking to local chapters. Du Bois felt betrayed and recalled ruefully of these latter years in America, "The colored children ceased to hear my name."[32]

America's declension had grown so severe, he believed, that it had also overtaken blacks. In Du Bois's historical analysis, the recent upsurge in capitalism had, for the first time, created a sizable Afro-American middle class that identified its interests with white capitalist America. Educated Afro-Americans, that same "talented tenth" to whom he had once entrusted the race's mission, seemed to him as eager to chase private wealth and ignore social justice as whites. He could no longer envision black Americans leading the world's colored peoples, as he had dreamed in the 1920s and 1930s. Afro-Americans, like Anglo-Americans, had sold their souls and national birthright for the chance to grow rich on human exploitation. The promise of international democracy no longer seemed to reside in either American chosen people—black or white.

Between 1948 and 1963, Du Bois was at his furthest point of alienation from middle-class America. Harassed by the government and partially boycotted by the major media, he felt increasingly unable to get his message across or accomplish anything substantial in America. In 1961, the day before he left for the west African nation of Ghana to begin editing the *Encyclopedia Africana,* Du Bois joined the American Communist Party. In 1963, he became a citizen of Ghana, where he died later that year and was buried with national honors.

These facts have given rise to the widespread notion that Du Bois, by becoming a Communist expatriate, was expressing his final contempt for and rejection of America.[33] This popular myth is less than half-true. It is true that at the end of his life he was angered at his nation's conduct and treatment of dissenters like himself, although it is well to remember that he had always been bitter about whites' prejudicial treatment. And when he died, Du Bois was deeply discouraged about the amount of good that he or anyone else might accomplish anytime soon in the United States.

Nevertheless, Du Bois's actions were prompted more by his positive desire to edit a pan-African project in a newly independent black nation then by a wish to repudiate his spiritual bonds to the United States. For much of his career, he had dreamed of producing a comprehensive study of African society and history but had never found the time or money.

Thus, when Ghanaian President Nkrumah in 1960 renewed an invitation for Du Bois to come to Ghana to edit the *Encyclopedia Africana* and for the first time promised sufficient funds, the eighty-seven-year-old scholar determined to begin "the crowing undertaking of his life." Then in 1961, the United States Supreme Court upheld a part of an anti-subversive act that would strip suspected radicals of their passports and international travel rights. The upheld provision would become operational within ninety days.[34] Knowing he would probably be among those whose travel would be restricted once the ruling went into effect, Du Bois faced a drastic decision: either leave America immediately or risk never again seeing Africa and the wider world.

Du Bois officially joined the Communist Party of America while preparing to depart for Ghana. He decided to make a public announcement to set an example of nonintimidation and to protest the reigning political terrorism of McCarthyism.[35] Despite the major news media's having slighted him and his activities for years, it could not completely ignore Du Bois, and he figured correctly that he was too famous and his act too notorious to go unmentioned.

Du Bois's adoption of Ghanaian citizenship, on the other hand, far from being a premeditated political statement, was a spontaneous action. It would not have occurred at all had the new passport restriction not taken effect while Du Bois was in Ghana and had the official at the U.S. embassy not twice insultingly refused to renew the passports of Du Bois and his wife so that they might freely leave and re-enter Ghana. Seeing their dilemma, President Nkrumah graciously offered to grant Du Bois and his wife Ghanaian citizenship and passports. *At that moment,* according to Shirley Graham Du Bois, the couple decided to accept.[36] It was less a matter of Du Bois voluntarily forsaking his American rights and identity as having had them stripped from him; his adoption of Ghanaian citizenship did not initiate the loss of his status as an American so much as it acknowledged and formalized the loss.

## Du Bois's Unending
## American Jeremiad

The jeremiad's continued prominence in Du Bois's messages to Americans is the best indicator of his undying faith in the final redemption of his native country. Increasingly pessimistic about contemporary developments, which he interpreted as signalling a worsening and perhaps irreversible declension, Du Bois still professed faith in the promise of America's civil religion. In the early Cold War, Du Bois loudly bewailed America's "literal descent into hell in our day" and its slippage from its democratic past and mission. Most of his campaign speeches in 1950 when he ran as American Labor Party candidate for United States senator in New York were ringing jeremiads to the nation. These speeches had titles such as "Democracy Fails in America," "Civil Liberties," and "The American Way of Life."

In "Our American Heritage," Du Bois listed among the nation's great historic "gifts" to the world its former political and economic democratic practices. "We have helped the world forward," he declared, but in later times had "tried to undo what once we did well." In 1950 he warned that the "United States stands in grave danger of becoming a slave state" and "police tyranny," as evidenced by the current "loss of liberty" and attempts "to control thought" and curb free speech through government repression and McCarthyite intimidation of anyone who criticized Cold War militarism or domestic rule by big business. Whenever big business in America feels threatened, he declared, "their first impulse is to resort to the same tactics which the slave owner once used to stop abolitionists from discussing slavery."[37] He saw contemporary radicals like himself as playing a role analogous to the abolitionists in making possible American redemption—and they were receiving the same reward for their efforts.

Du Bois's latter-day tirades against the United States were genuinely prophetic in their juxtaposition of blistering attacks on social misdeeds and dogged assertions of faith in democracy's eventual triumph. "This America of ours, hope of our dreams, refuge to mankind," he indignantly thundered, *this* was the nation swiftly becoming "the greatest warmonger" in history. It was his duty to warn America that it faced "grave danger . . . unless soon it radically changes its present course." "We who have known a better America find the present scene almost unbelievable," he said, since a "great silence has fallen over the real soul of the nation." Nevertheless, he always summoned the faith to end optimistically. "The great silence on America's soul can be broken," he declared. "My words are not a counsel of despair," he roared, but "a call to new courage and determination" for Americans to overcome this crisis, as they had those of the past, with another outpouring of the democratic reform spirit. "What we have done, we can do again," he promised: "I still believe that someday this nation will become a democracy without a color line." He pledged to continue to "work for such an America."[38]

The most poignant proof of the amazing tenacity of Du Bois's remaining hopes for America is in his last autobiography, published in 1968. Never had Du Bois been so alienated from and angry with his homeland. His book was written at a low ebb of his expectations for democratic change forthcoming from America. His allegiance now was to international socialism as the only route to human progress, and much of the book describes his wide international travels and interests in the late 1950s. He is planning to leave for Africa to help it work out its post-colonial destiny and is about to become an American Communist.

Yet the autobiography still closes with a stirring American jeremiad. "I know the United States," he declares proudly. "It is my country and the land of my fathers. It is still a land of magnificent possibility. . . . But it is betraying its mighty destiny." Heatedly, he denounces its unconstitutional stifling of dissent, its military belligerence, and its selfish exploitation of most of the world's population. "This is what I call decadence!" he explodes. But faith in America's mythic past and future clearly prevails over present disillusionment in the book's final passage: "For this is still . . . a wonderful America, which the founding fathers dreamed until their sons drowned it in the blood of slavery . . . and greed. Our children must rebuild it. Let then the Dreams of the Dead rebuke the Blind who think that what is will be forever."[39]

Whatever else W. E. B. Du Bois was as he ended his life—an international socialist, an African nationalist—he died still a son and prophet of America.

# 6. Martin Luther King, Jr., and America's Promise in the Second Reconstruction, 1955–1965

W. E. B. Du Bois, by sheer will, maintained faith in eventual American and world progress, even though his analysis of post-war trends pictured white capitalist imperialism as a rising threat to international peace. Events led him to be deeply pessimistic about the chances of immediately alleviating white racism.

Yet even as this black jeremiah grew more disturbed about the vast scope of racial and social evil, ironically some of the very trends that he decried in his post-war jeremiads, such as U.S. international activism, were helping create conditions that would enable Afro-Americans to bring public opinion to bear against Southern racial discrimination in the greatest reform of American race relations since the Civil War. The Second World War, Cold War competition between the superpowers, decolonization in the developing non-white world, and revelations of Nazi genocide combined to discredit racism in the court of international opinion. In the United States a new Afro-American jeremiah, Martin Luther King, Jr., led a successful black revolt against racial segregation and mounted an effective assault on the white American conscience. As had the appeals of Frederick Douglass in the Civil War era, the moral persuasiveness of King's jeremiads momentarily merged with white Northern interests to form a national alliance between blacks and Northern whites and enforce a limited program of political equality upon an unwilling white South.

This second black-and-white, Northern-supported Reconstruction made it possible for King to avoid directly confronting *national* racism before 1965. The gathering white support for racial equality in public life that peaked between 1963 and 1965 encouraged King, like Douglass in his time, to focus on blacks' exodus from oppression in the South and on reconstructing the South as the key to democratizing America. Eventually, though, King's hopes for swift Southern and national reformation were dashed. After 1965, King, in a manner similar to Du Bois, grew more deeply distressed by the fierce tenacity of racism's hold on white America.

## Prologue to
## the Civil Rights Movement

From the turn of the century, when black subordination by law and custom was fully systematized, through the Second World War, caste was the American way in race relations.[1] The First World War raised hopes for fundamental change among many blacks, such as Du Bois, but these hopes were not fulfilled. The 1920s and 1930s saw a national revival of the Ku Klux Klan and extreme economic deprivation for most blacks. The first major stirrings of renewed black hope for national progress in race relations, as we saw in the previous chapter, originated in the New Deal and, even more dramatically, in the national war experience of the 1940s. Although progressive changes did occur, portending future black gains, realization of the potential for racial change suggested during the New Deal did not come about until after the Second World War, and not fully until the mid-1950s and 1960s.[2] Neither the president nor most public opinion, for example, questioned segregation in the armed forces when war came in 1941. In 1940, the national caste system seemed as entrenched and impervious to fundamental change as it had in 1860, but the Second World War, like the Civil War, was to open up unexpected possibilities of far-reaching change in national race relations.

The Second World War proved pivotal in fostering, internationally and domestically, a strong new moral consensus against racism. While battling the Axis powers militarily, the United States also engaged them in propaganda warfare. Japan centered its campaign for the loyalties of Asian populations on charges of white American racism, while Nazi Germany's strident commitment to Aryan purity and white racist democracy offered an inviting target for Allied counter-rhetoric.[3] Then, with the Allies' liberation of the Nazi concentration camps in 1945, the extent of racism's moral depravity shocked the world's conscience.

Racism's prominence as an international issue was heightened further in the era of Cold War and decolonization. The United States had emerged from the war as a globally active superpower greatly concerned about its image abroad. In its international competition with the Soviet Union for the allegiance of decolonizing, newly independent nations in Africa and Asia, the United States was disadvantaged by Jim Crow laws and Ku Klux Klan activities in the American South. These were heavily publicized and exploited in Soviet propaganda.

Afro-Americans first began receiving practical dividends from the new anti-racist moral climate in the form of victories in the federal courts. In 1944 the Supreme Court found the white-only Democratic Party primary elections held in Southern states to be unconstitutional. This case filed by the NAACP was the first victory in that civil rights organization's long-standing efforts to challenge and erode the legality of racial caste. The string of successive victories finally culminated in the historic 1954 decision in *Brown* v. *Topeka Board of Education,* in which the Supreme Court ruled segregation in public education to be unconstitutional. In so finding, the court overturned the "separate but equal" doctrine that had been the constitutional cornerstone for segregationary practices since 1896.[4]

The *Brown* decision provided the immediate spark for the domestic Civil Rights movement. Having made its bold decision, however, the Warren Court immediately backpedaled by not setting firm deadlines for state compliance with the desegregation order. Taking full advantage of this lenience, many white Southern political representatives vowed never to integrate Southern education and other public institutions.[5] White Citizens Councils organized "respectable" public resistance to desegregation across the South while less reputable organizations like the Ku Klux Klan and vigilante mobs responded with violence to attempts to implement school desegregation.[6]

White Southerners' violent resistance to the *Brown* decision created a division of national opinion over the South's treatment of blacks that resembled the sectional disputes of the Reconstruction era. The conscience of many Northern whites had been sensitized since 1945 to the anti-democratic situation in the Southern states where blacks were barred from political participation and Jim Crow laws sanctioned and enforced public racial separation. But it would first take intense political pressure created by a sustained wave of black activism and civil disobedience to mobilize the national conscience in a movement to dismantle legal racial discrimination. The *Brown* decision aroused great hopes for change among Afro-Americans. Blacks' heightened expectations and impatience with the slow pace of actual change gave rise to a new militancy in their demands for civil rights. The forceful weapon of mass direct action and civil disobedience was added to the NAACP's tactic of challenging racial discrimination in court. Black abolitionists' hope at the outset of the Civil War that slavery could be ended was paralleled by blacks' confidence after 1954 that Jim Crow was vulnerable and could be abolished. No individual made greater contributions to this dynamic movement for social change than Martin Luther King, Jr., who successfully pricked the conscience of white Americans for their shameful toleration of racism and betrayal of democratic principles.

Like many racial liberation leaders, King came from the privileged sector of the oppressed community and was thoroughly at home in the dominant Western Christian culture.[7] He was born and reared in the comfortable world of black middle-class Atlanta. His father, Martin Luther King, Sr. ("Daddy" King), who began work as an uneducated laborer, had risen to the position of pastor of a mostly professional middle-class black Baptist congregation. The Rev. Mr. King, Sr., had made himself a respected member of Atlanta's black bourgeoisie and raised his children to fear the Lord, work hard, and value money. M. L. King, Jr., grew up in a warmly supportive family and social environment and never lacked life's basic needs or comforts.

Not even a privileged black Southern youth, however, could escape the stinging barbs of racism. "As far back as I could remember, I had resented segregation," King wrote, and considered it "rationally inexplicable and morally unjustifiable." This tenet was taught him by his family. "Daddy" King had consistently spoken out against humiliating local racial practices and segregation. Angrily leaving a store with his son where the clerk would not wait on them until all the whites present had been served, his father declared, "I don't care how long I have to live with this thing, I'll never accept it. I'll fight it till I die."[8] King's early hatred of social injustice was honed by his extensive higher education. Gradually he adopted a theory of how best to resist and overcome social evil.

A precocious youth, King entered Morehouse College in Atlanta at age fifteen. Increasingly skeptical of the fundamentalist doctrines of the religious community in which he had been reared, he became a convert to liberal, or "modernist," Christianity. He came to endorse enthusiastically its synthesis of secular and scientific knowledge (such as biblical "higher criticism") with traditional religious faith and morality. He was also inspired by several of his professors who held it to be a Christian's duty to address social issues and oppose economic exploitation and racial oppression. Influenced by these socio-religious ideals, King formed his life-long conviction that any religion that is "concerned about the souls of men and is not concerned about the social and economic conditions that scar the soul, is a spiritually moribund religion." Thus seeing Christianity as a progressive social force, King developed at Morehouse College a strong "underlying urge to serve God and humanity through the ministry."[9]

After graduating from Morehouse in 1948, King attended Crozer Seminary in Pennsylvania, a prestigious white institution. There, and later studying for his Ph.D. in theology at Boston University, he continued "a serious intellectual quest for a method to eliminate social evil."[10] He borrowed widely as he constructed a philosophy that would offer moral yet effective means of fighting injustice. He was greatly influenced by the early twentieth-century Social Gospel theologian, Walter Rauschenbusch, who had protested the church's indifference to the living and working conditions of ordinary people in the industrial age. King was highly receptive to Rauschenbusch's criticism of *laissez faire* capitalism as he had been earlier to a Morehouse professor's belief that economic exploitation and racism were integrally related.[11]

King was attracted to examples of civil disobedience and non-violent resistance set by social activists and philosophers such as Henry David Thoreau and Mohandas Gandhi. As a student he was temporarily taken aback by Reinhold Niebuhr's trenchant critique of pacifism as passive *non*-resistance to evil, constituting, in effect, collusion with evil. King soon recovered, however, to defend Gandhian non-violence as an effective as well as moral way of achieving social progress. Agreeing that non-resistance to evil really would be morally and socially irresponsible, King called Niebuhr's characterization of pacifism a "serious distortion" of Gandhi's teaching of "non-violent resistance to evil." Gandhi had resisted evil vigorously and effectively, King argued. Precisely because "he resisted with love instead of hate," Gandhi's form of resistance possessed the greatest potential for effecting lasting social change. Violent resistance, according to King, "only multiplies the existence of violence and bitterness in the universe," whereas loving resistance to evil alone can "develop a sense of shame in the opponent and thereby bring about a transformation and change of heart."[12]

When King had finished his extensive education, he accepted a pastorship in Montgomery, Alabama. This was in 1954, the year when the Supreme Court rendered its decision against segregation in public education. He and Coretta Scott King, his wife and fellow social activist, went to the deep South from a strong sense of social duty. Although they preferred the less oppressive racial conditions in the North, they felt obligated, at least for a few years, to serve where blacks were in the most dire social and spiritual need.[13] Ironically, it was there that King would achieve international fame as the leader of the Montgomery bus boycott of 1955–1956.

By the mid-fifties, a mood of millennialistic hope for social change gripped the imagination of growing numbers of blacks, including Martin Luther King. The *zeitgeist,* or as King conceived it, God's will for freedom, was bringing forth a new social order in America and the world. And as events would shortly prove, divine providence had chosen American blacks, and even more mysteriously, Martin Luther King, as the vessels through which God would do his liberating work in this age.[14]

## In the Beginning at Montgomery

The particular event that initiated the grassroots movement to dismantle racial segregation and discrimination was the arrest of Rosa Parks, a respected black woman, for defying Montgomery city ordinances by refusing to yield her bus seat to a white person. Unexpectedly, Park's arrest roused the local black community to unprecedented protest. Montgomery blacks, used to quietly accepting unjust treatment by whites, united in spontaneous support of a boycott of the bus company until it agreed to change its racially discriminatory seating rules and hiring practices.[15]

King was a new, relatively uninfluential member of the black leadership group that met in his church on Friday afternoon to discuss how to respond to Mrs. Park's arrest. The leaders, mostly ministers, decided to stage a temporary, experimental boycott of the buses. They agreed to announce the plan in black churches on

Sunday and to ask their church members to support a boycott beginning on Monday. The leaders also founded an official organization, The Montgomery Improvement Association (MIA), and, to King's surprise, elected him president.[16]

King truly became the movement's leader in fact as well as title at a mass rally following the first day of the bus boycott. To the planners' delight, black compliance with the boycott unexpectedly had been nearly 100 percent. They decided late that afternoon, therefore, to extend the boycott and called a meeting at a black church that night to rally support and announce the boycott to the public. As MIA president, King was to give the evening's main speech. Acutely feeling his responsibility, King determined to make an appeal "militant enough to keep my people aroused to positive action" in seeking justice and yet "moderate enough" to keep their fervor "within controllable and Christian bounds," devoid of violence or hatred of whites. He also wished to defend the boycott before public opinion.[17]

King entered the pulpit that night as a virtual unknown, facing a sea of attentive black faces, reporters, and television cameras. First, he made plain that Montgomery blacks had gathered that evening from loyalty to the nation's lofty ideals, especially "because of our deep-seated belief that democracy . . . is the greatest form of government on earth." Then he methodically listed the indignities heaped upon blacks in the city buses leading up to Rosa Park's arrest and the boycott. Blacks had too long silently accepted such treatment, he contended. The crowd's murmurs of agreement ("Amen!" "Yes sir, tell it," "That's so") began rising, matching the growing fervor of King's voice, until he brought them to boil. "But there comes a time when people get tired," he cried in emotional rhythm: "We are here this evening to say to those who have mistreated us so long that we are *tired—tired* of being segregated and humiliated; *tired* of being kicked about by the brutal feet of oppression." Blacks would no longer be patient "with anything less than freedom and justice." The crowd leapt to its feet, enthusiastically urging the speaker on and answering his words with tumultuous cheers and applause.

King turned then to channel the people's aroused resolve into constructive, nonviolent protest. "Our actions must be guided by deepest principles of the Christian faith," he insisted, and "love must be our regulating ideal." He charged his followers to heed the words of Jesus: "Love your enemies . . . and pray for them." Pointedly, he contrasted the immoral activities of white supremacists who fomented "violence and lawlessness" with the protesters' peaceful acts that were "guided by the highest principles of law and order." In the crusade now beginning, he pledged, "there will be no cross-burnings, no white person will be taken from his home by a hooded Negro mob and brutally murdered."

He warned that if blacks failed to observe high ethical standards, their noble cause would degenerate into ignoble violence and "our protest will end up as a meaningless drama on the stage of history . . . shrouded with . . . shame." But, he promised, "if you will protest courageously, and yet with dignity and Christian love," then, "when the history books are written . . . [they] will . . . say, 'There lived a great people—a black people—who injected new meaning and dignity into the veins of civilization.' This is our challenge and our overwhelming responsibility."[18]

Pandemonium erupted as the people in the church wildly cheered, clapped, laughed, and cried. "This was the time that the people were brought face to face with the type of man that Martin Luther was," recalled one participant, "—not only the people who came . . . but those who nominated him, too. It was astonishing, the man spoke with such force."[19] That night a dynamic social movement and a charismatic leader met and magnified one another.

A year-long struggle culminated in the Montgomery bus boycott's final victory, but King was a major celebrity from the first mass meeting (there were many).[20] He became a hero to the local black community and, equally importantly, a fascinating figure to on-the-scene reporters and to those who observed him through the mass media. White media and national audiences were captivated by this black man who spoke with poetic eloquence and could, at one moment, exhort black congregations with revivalistic fervor and in the next discuss Gandhi and Aristotle for reporters. The media covered him extensively throughout the boycott, transmitting his words to a huge national and international audience.

Favorable media coverage, focused largely on King, proved invaluable in securing the ultimate victory. Projecting a local melodrama that pitted non-violent loyal American good against racist extremism and hateful violence to a large distant audience was a key to Montgomery and later civil rights successes. By their words and actions, the protesters contrasted their reasonable, legitimate goals and peaceful methods with white segregationists' irrational and vicious actions in a manner that won sympathy and support from neutral third parties.[21]

One such sympathy-garnering incident was when a bomb exploded on the front porch of King's home at a time when he was out but his wife and his infant daughter were inside. No one was hurt, but an angry crowd of blacks gathered. There was talk on the street of seeking revenge against whites, and weapons were brandished. King strode through the rubble of his porch and disarmed the crowd with his mesmerizing presence and rhetoric. "We must meet violence with nonviolence," he admonished. "Remember the words of Jesus. . . . We must love our white brothers. . . . We must meet hate with love." Everyone should go home, he said, for God was with them in this struggle and they must trust him, not force, to bring inevitable victory. Subdued, the crowd quietly dispersed. White policemen and reporters at the scene were amazed by King's performance.[22] Wire services immediately carried "the parable of the porch" around the world, which added to King's growing legend. For many onlookers, King had become a larger-than-life figure, a symbol of social morality and good will courageously confronting racist immorality.

In Montgomery as in later civil rights campaigns, national political intervention generated by the drama of well-staged local events proved critical in gaining final victory. Although the long bus boycott did not soften the hearts of local white segregationists, it did spark sympathetic responses around the nation, which could be translated into public pressure on blacks' behalf. A timely ruling by the U.S. Supreme Court that state and local Alabama laws requiring segregation on buses were unconstitutional, for example, finally helped break the resistance of Montgomery city officials to the MIA's demands.

The victorious Montgomery crusade raised King to national stature and international fame. He led many subsequent non-violent mass protests and civil disobedience campaigns against racist laws, as the excitement begun at Montgomery spread across the South. In a career that constantly risked violence, prison, and death, King led a swelling social movement to abolish racial caste and segregation in America.

## King's Moral Appeal
## and the American Jeremiad

The basic pattern was set in Montgomery and continued through King's later public crusades in which he performed as theorist, organizer, and symbol maker for the civil rights movement. First, his charisma and inspirational oratory helped create black unity and strengthen people's resolve to protest and struggle despite adversity. To do this, he would appeal to blacks' racial pride and sense of mission and destiny. Equally, if not more crucially, he was the chief public spokesman and interpreter of the civil rights movement to white America. King's remarkable talent for reaching the conscience of white Americans was vital in producing the conditions necessary for blacks to win their quest for equal rights.

His profound influence on American opinion, like that of Frederick Douglass before him, was primarily rooted in moral authority. King and Douglass each effectively marshalled the diverse but reinforcing cultural strands of evangelical Christianity, social reform, and civil religion in support of blacks' crusade for equality.[23]

King rhetorically clothed the civil rights movement in the sacred garb of the civil religion. Over and over, he proclaimed that the protesters were motivated by their deep love for America and a desire to make the nation all that it should be. The motto of the Southern Christian Leadership Conference (the civil rights organization of which he was president) was, he liked to remind audiences, "To Save the Soul of America." Speaking self-consciously as a Christian minister and American patriot, King portrayed blacks' present struggle as a new episode in America's greatest national spiritual traditions, religious and civil. "If we are wrong, the Constitution of the United States is wrong," he declared. "If we are wrong, God Almighty is wrong."[24] He always justified blacks' efforts to gain their rights as congruent with all Americans' highest values and most cherished self-image.

King masterfully aroused guilt in whites (especially those furthest removed from the immediate scene). He accused white Americans of violating their own democratic and Christian values when they denied rights and recognition to blacks as fellow citizens and human beings. In this vein, he spoke to whites in the sharply remonstrative tones of a jeremiah. But, having upbraided whites, he went on to assure them of blacks' basic attitude of forgiveness toward them.

After purposefully arousing guilt and anxiety in whites, he always forgave them their faults; he then tried to direct the psychic energy of their released guilt into constructive, redemptive acts that, he maintained, would lead America to its promised glory. In this disarming appeal to whites, King, like Booker Washington, Mary Bethune, and other black leaders before him, artfully raised and used popular stereotypes associating Afro-Americans with Christlike qualities of love, forgiveness, and nonviolence.[25]

The American jeremiad was a staple of King's rhetoric on behalf of black rights and equality, as it had been in the oratory of Frederick Douglass. King had a jeremiah's chiliastic understanding of the present. Throughout his career, he prophesied the dawn of a millennial social order that would bring freedom and democracy to blacks, America, and the world. "In a real sense we stand today between two worlds," he prophesied, "the dying old and the emerging [new]." An irresistible tide of human freedom was sweeping around the globe. "This is an era of offensive on the part of oppressed people" everywhere, he declared, as all "over the world men are in revolt against social and political domination" and lifting "the age old cry for freedom." To his mind, "Asia's successive revolts against European imperialism, Africa's present ferment for independence . . . and the determined drive of Negro Americans . . . are inextricably bound together."[26]

King characteristically presented the civil rights movement as part of the historic drama that had first secured democracy for white males and then for white women. He regretted that these earlier "American victories in the extension of Democracy" had not included blacks but simultaneously rejoiced that the climactic chapter in the national story of liberty's advance was now being written. He compared the struggles of civil rights workers with the heroic battles of the "men of 1776" and "the minutemen at Lexington and Concord." Contemporary blacks, by standing up to demand (however non-violently) their inalienable rights, were both following in the Founding Fathers' footsteps and moving the nation further toward its democratic destiny.[27]

Progress toward black freedom in America, he taught, had occurred in "three distinct periods in the history of race relations in this nation, each representing growth over a former period." First was "the era of slavery" in which a black was considered mere property, "a thing to be used rather than a person to be respected." Then followed "the period of restricted emancipation" and segregation, lasting from the Civil War to 1954, in which blacks escaped slavery but were still not fully free or equal. The final stage in fulfilling America's promise of freedom to Afro-Americans, "the period of constructive integration," opened with the 1954 *Brown* decision, which invalidated segregation. "As a result of this decision," King exulted, "we find ourselves standing on the threshold of the most creative period . . . of race relations in the history of our nation . . . now we stand on the border of the promised land of integration."[28]

As a jeremiah, King linked affirmation of America's past and future to sharp denunciations of the present generation's apostasy. Always proclaiming freedom's imminent dawn, he nevertheless persistently characterized the current social situation as one of crisis and national declension. "Midnight" was King's recurring metaphor for the discord of present society. It was "midnight in our world," he would often preach, "midnight within the social order." American race relations had reached a dangerous flashpoint between black determination and white Southern intransigence, which threatened a "reign of violence and terror." He found these tensions "indicative of the deep and terrible midnight that encompasses our national life."[29] "How we deal with this crucial situation," he warned, "will determine . . . our moral [and] . . . political health as a nation, and our prestige as leader of the free world." It would ultimately decide America's ability to serve "as a beacon of hope . . . for the world" and to become "truly, 'The land of the free and home of the brave.' "[30]

King's rhetoric also conformed to the American jeremiad in its drastic portrayal of two diametrically opposed American futures, doomsday or millennium. The national present was one of crisis portending disaster, King declared, but he stressed that "every crisis has both its dangers and opportunities" and "can either spell salvation or doom." There comes a time when " 'Every nation decideth which way, its soul shall go,' " he paraphrased the poet John Oxanham. Now was that time for America, and the issue over which the nation would either save or lose its soul was the burning question of civil rights. If Americans chose meanly, the cost would be high: "The price that America must pay for the continued oppression of the Negro is the price of its own destruction." "The hour is late; the clock of destiny is ticking out," King admonished whites, and so "we must act before it is too late" to grant blacks freedom and fulfill America's democratic mission.[31]

King's jeremiad always ended optimistically, prophesying American repentance and the dawn of a new democratic day. King corrected those who interpreted the nation's present deplorable state to mean "that we are retrogressing instead of progressing." "Far from representing retrogression and tragic meaninglessness," he said, social tensions "represent the usual pains that accompany the birth of anything new" and were in fact absolutely necessary to "start the move forward" into the new world that beckoned. If Americans would only now choose and act rightly, "we will emerge from the bleak and desolate midnight of corroding injustice into the bright and glittering daybreak of freedom and justice."[32]

The rhetorical fireworks with which King customarily concluded his orations underscored the millennialism that filled and sustained his social message. His speeches described in apocalyptic imagery the awe-inspiring fulfillment of God's will and the American dream. "In spite of the . . . frustrations of the moment I still have a dream," he declared, "that one day soon this nation will rise up and live out the true meaning of its creed . . ." and "the glory of the Lord shall be revealed."[33]

Although King directed most of his jeremiadic rhetoric toward whites, much of his function was to inspire and motivate blacks to social action. He therefore frequently appealed to Afro-American racial pride, duty, and messianic identity. Blacks in America, he taught, had a unique role that only they could play in accomplishing Providence's designs in history. If Afro-Americans did what God asked of them, to resist oppression firmly yet lovingly and nonviolently, King promised that "historians in future years will have to say there lived a great people—a black people," which by its courageous deeds "injected new meaning into the veins" of American and world civilization. King motivated his followers after he received the 1964 Nobel Peace Prize, for example, with a message praising the soldiers in "this mighty army of love." Because of their accomplishments, "the entire world now looks to the Negro in America for leadership in the whole task of building a [better] world."[34]

King's conception of black messianism reflected messianic imagery that traditionally portrayed blacks as Christlike. While King called everyone to be non-violent, loving, and forgiving toward those who wronged them, he felt that Afro-Americans were uniquely capable of it and thereby of serving millennial social ends. Blacks' historic experience of suffering was what gave them their special social role and redemptive potential. Urging Afro-Americans to stimulate America to fundamental change by their militant determination and willingness to sacrifice themselves, if need be, in nonviolent demonstrations, King said:

> Let us be those creative dissenters who will call our beloved nation to a higher destiny, to a new plateau of compassion, to a more noble expression of humaneness. . . . We are superbly equipped to do this. We have been seared in the flames of suffering. We have known the agony of being an underdog. We have learned from our have-not status. . . . We . . . have a passion for peace born out of our wretchedness and . . . misery.

Blacks were called by King willingly to suffer and sacrifice not just to improve their own conditions. Part of their mission was to heal whites of the moral illness of racism, thus transforming America and realizing its latent social potential. Because of their historic capacity to absorb and survive suffering, Afro-Americans, as no others, he believed, could "imbue our nation with the ideals of a higher and nobler order." "In dealing with out particular dilemma," he told blacks, "we will challenge the nation to deal with its larger dilemma."[35]

As the last sentence indicates, King was staunchly integrationist and critical of any form of black nationalism leading toward racial separatism and isolation.[36] He addressed the distinct but entwined missions of black and white Americans by adopting the black jeremiad's identification of Afro-Americans as a chosen people within a chosen people. King believed in the interconnectedness of humanity and held that black and white Americans would experience their mutual highest social good and fulfillment together.

In seeking fundamental change and progress on the national level, King experienced steep rises and dips in his hopes for current reform. Grounded in optimism about America and its future, he nevertheless keenly felt the impact of contemporary events and shifting social trends. From 1955 through 1959 his steadily rising hope was tempered by realization of the strength of social conservatism and political inertia in America. The period from 1960 to 1965 saw dramatic escalation of black reform activity and millennialistic expectations. These years also brought the greatest tangible signs of national racial progress and achievement. After 1966, however, King's expectations of swift and total American reformation were severely dashed. From then until his death in 1968, King increasingly felt frustrated and disappointed over white American resistance to thoroughgoing change. In surveying the bleak situation in 1967 and 1968, he had to struggle against total despair concerning white American reformability.

King's activities expanded rapidly after Montgomery. The MIA was supplanted by the Atlanta-based Southern Christian Leadership Conference (SCLC), which operated as a regional headquarters for planning and overseeing civil rights campaigns throughout the South. King traveled and spoke extensively around the country, drumming up support for the black cause and attracting large sums of money for the SCLC and other civil rights groups. He wrote many articles as well as a book between 1956 and 1960.[37] He also became a national political activist. He met with President Eisenhower and Vice-President Nixon, lobbied members of Congress, and led a 1957 Prayer Pilgrimage to Washington to pressure the federal government to enforce civil rights and energetically implement integration.

Although involved in many local civil rights campaigns, King gave highest priority to promoting social reform through national political action. He believed that vigorous federal action on behalf of civil rights was the most direct and effective way of achieving equality for Afro-Americans. King's objectives necessarily involved national politics, for, like Frederick Douglass, he sought to transform the federal government into an active agent of reform. The larger goal behind local civil rights demonstrations, therefore, was to elicit public sympathy and build support for prompt decisive governmental action. Given that he most sought action from the national government, it followed that he mainly addressed a predominantly white national audience with his jeremiads.

Although his jeremiads sought to melt the heart of all Americans, including Southern segregationists, some groups were singled out for special attention. Blacks, Northern liberals, labor unions, the white church, and white Southern moderates, according to King, all had a special covenantal duty to achieve American racial and social justice. These groups, in his mind, constituted the "saving remnant" within the American chosen people and were called to restore the nation to fidelity to its mission. Mobilizing these groups was critical for achieving the political pressure needed to move the government.

His jeremiad, therefore, most pointedly called upon these social groups to do their moral duty, to join the national progressive alliance through which he hoped blacks would achieve their freedom and America would find its salvation.

King's hopes for success quickened with the pace of events beginning around 1960. His efforts to influence the federal government had had little success during the Eisenhower administration, but the social and political climate then seemed to improve noticeably for civil rights forces in the early 1960s. The student sit-ins and freedom rides that dramatically contested segregation rocked the South between 1960 and 1962, giving powerful new impetus to the civil rights movement.[38] The increasingly violent confrontations between defiant nonviolent demonstrators and angry white mobs shocked the nation. Public opinion in the North began to grow impatient with white extremists' violent resistance to desegregation in the South. In 1961, the new liberal Democratic administration of John F. Kennedy also seemed to offer the movement fresh hope. Kennedy had fewer philosophical reservations about the energetic exercise of federal power than had Eisenhower.[39] Kennedy, moreover, had significantly benefited from black votes in his election (thanks to his well-publicized efforts during the campaign to secure King's release from a Georgia prison); he could be seen as owing blacks political consideration and favor.

King moved to capitalize on these changes and stepped up his public campaign to enlist the federal government in the civil rights crusade. The centerpiece of his propaganda campaign directed at the government was the call for a "Second Emancipation Proclamation" consisting of aggressive national executive action to guarantee blacks' civil rights. King wrote early in 1961 that the "new administration has the opportunity to be the first in 100 years of American history to adopt a radically new approach to the question of civil rights." But the administration had to start "with the firm conviction that the question is settled," just as the question of democracy versus monarchy was no longer debatable. The country, led by its president, King declared, "must decide" once and for all "that in a new era, there must be new thinking." The nation must realize, too, "that federal power is enormous and sufficient to guide us through the changes ahead." King blamed the "intolerably slow progress in civil rights" on "self-imposed limits in the use of bold, creative federal action" as much as on the recalcitrance of racist extremists. "History has thrust upon the present administration an indescribably important destiny—to complete a process of democratization which our nation has too long developed too slowly." "If we fail to make this positive decision," he feared, "an awakening world" would disregard America's pretense to world leadership and "conclude that we have become a fossil nation."[40]

In a subsequent magazine article evaluating the administration's performance in its first year ("Fumbling on the New Frontier"), King expressed sharp disappointment with the Kennedy administration and renewed his jeremiadic challenge to it. He used such disapproving adjectives as "cautious," "feeble," and "token" to describe the inadequate gestures offered by the president in place of the decisive leadership demanded by the national crisis. What was needed, King urged, was "massive social mobilization" of the nation and its resources to eradicate racism. The president's timidity was letting great opportunities pass. Frustrated by the administration's initial lack of desire to assume its rightful historic role, King compared Kennedy's hesitation to Lincoln's delay of the Emancipation Proclamation for fear of alienating slave-holding border states. Sooner or later, he predicted, President Kennedy would arrive "at an equally fateful decision." Meanwhile, the crisis worsened and "the clock of history is nearing the midnight hour." Yet the "opportunity is not yet lost," for the moment that the country and government recognized the urgency of national reforms to address the civil rights issue, he insisted, it "will lift the nation into a new era."[41]

Through 1962, King remained largely unsuccessful in getting federal support for the growing grass-roots movement to end racial segregation and discrimination. While the Kennedy administration privately expressed sympathy with the civil rights workers' goals and activities, it hoped to remain officially neutral in the divisive Southern struggle. The president's slim electoral margin and reliance on senior white Southern congressmen's support for his legislative priorities were major factors in Kennedy's early decision to stay clear of that explosive issue.[42]

Disappointed with the president and the creeping pace of change, King and the SCLC mounted a direct-action campaign against segregation in Birmingham, Alabama. It was intended to create a disturbance great enough to focus national attention and foment federal action on civil rights. The 1963 Birmingham campaign was planned and implemented mainly for its national impact. The SCLC code name for it was "Project C"—*c* for confrontation. Birmingham was the most segregated city in America, and King and his co-workers reasoned that if they could crack segregation there, they would reveal its vulnerability everywhere. The planners were also expecting help from Sheriff "Bull" Connor to stage a moral drama of good versus evil to the national audience. A blunt, outspoken despiser of "uppity niggers," Sheriff Connor was counted on to provide the violent displays necessary to command national media and public attention. As King said many times, he would never shy away from social tension and conflict, as these were often necessary to achieve lasting social progress.[43]

The 1963 campaign to desegregate Birmingham was the largest, most violent civil rights confrontation yet, and victory there proved to be the turning point in gaining national support for the movement. For over a month, thousands of black people marched in defiance of local authorities, and their determination was met by escalating official violence and repression directed by Sheriff "Bull" Connor. Night after night, national television carried riveting scenes of defenseless people being viciously attacked by policemen and dogs. A gale of national indignation broke, as Americans watched these horrifying images. The shocking acts of police brutality against peaceful men, women, and children were roundly denounced from public forums across America. Senator Wayne Morse declared that the scenes in Birmingham "would disgrace the Union of South Africa." Although reluctant to comment officially on the confrontation, President Kennedy, when besieged by reporters' questions at public appearances, admitted that what he saw in the papers about Birmingham made him "sick" but said that he could not intervene in a state affair.[44]

But the White House began to be deluged by demands that it do something to halt the brutality. At last—emboldened by the ground swell of national support for the activists, convinced that only basic national reform could avoid endless repetition of social chaos, and genuinely appalled by the events in Birmingham—President Kennedy changed his original position. He urged Birmingham officials to open negotiations with the SCLC. He also requested Birmingham businessmen, especially those of the United States Steel Company which did business with the federal government, to pressure city officials to meet King's conditions. In addition to the president's plea, city officials faced the unflagging zeal and determination of the civil rights forces, costly and unremitting violence and disorder, widespread condemnation in public opinion, and growing political and economic pressures. Finally, they acceded to most of the SCLC's conditions. The Battle of Birmingham was over. The stunning victory emboldened blacks around the nation, and in summer 1963 hundreds of new nonviolent direct action campaigns swept through the South.

Birmingham also broke the logjam of governmental activity in the field of civil rights. To King's delight, he dealt with a new John Kennedy now. Following Birmingham, the president dramatically appeared on national television to announce his support for sweeping federal civil rights legislation. He also became the first president to tell the American people that racial segregation and discrimination were morally wrong and intolerable. Indeed, Kennedy's message to the nation on civil rights echoed King's own language: "We are confronted primarily with a moral issue. It is as old as the Scriptures and as dear as the American Constitution."[45]

The SCLC organized the 1963 March on Washington for Jobs and Freedom to build national support for the administration's civil rights bill before it went to Congress. The march's larger significance, however, was that it symbolized a new national moral-political consensus against racism and for the banishment of racial discrimination from all areas of American life. Approximately a quarter-million sympathizers, nearly half of them white, gathered in the largest demonstration the national capital had ever seen to focus public attention on national civil rights reform. Those who came and those who heard the broadcasts and recordings were treated to some of King's finest oratory. Yet King said nothing on that day which he had not said repeatedly before. What was dramatically new was that the nation was now receptive to his message. When he cried "I have a dream" before the Lincoln Memorial, he employed powerful civil religious symbolism and rhetorically solidified the civil rights consensus. For this reason his speech has become a revered moment in the national memory.

For King and most of the nation, the March on Washington symbolized a new national beginning. By seriously commencing to purge itself of racism, the American nation was bringing itself into closer conformity with its ideals of freedom and democracy. The hopeful inauguration of this new America was an intoxicating experience for King and many others, which filled them with fresh courage and confidence.

The contagious warm feelings generated in Washington and throughout the country by the 1963 Washington March bears striking resemblance to the spirit of *communitas,* or common identity, that Catherine Albanese describes among early Americans during the exciting events of the Revolution. Albanese writes that a sense of having acted together in a momentous creative event inspired among the patriots an overwhelming feeling of fellowship. Usual social boundaries and divisions were momentarily eased and suspended during *communitas,* with its heady atmosphere of unity and good will and its proud sense of commonality as Americans acting heroically in the cause of freedom.[46]

In 1964 and 1965, the new moral consensus against racial discrimination that King's effective leadership and propaganda had done so much to produce was institutionalized as American policy. This period marked the zenith of racial reform and of King's heartfelt expectation of the rapid end of racist discrimination. After President Kennedy's assassination, Lyndon Johnson affirmed and expanded the federal government's newfound willingness to guarantee Afro-Americans' constitutional rights. Johnson guided the 1964 Civil Rights Act and the 1965 Voting Rights Act masterfully through Congress. Continuing progress, however, required continuing public pressure on the federal government, and this required further civil rights demonstrations. After signing the 1964 Civil Rights Act, for example, Johnson initially refused civil rights' activists request to seek additional legislation to secure black voting rights. It took a Birmingham-style success in Selma, Alabama, to dramatize the issue and prompt the president to submit such a bill to Congress.

The Selma civil disobedience campaign in 1965, like that in Birmingham in 1963, produced tremendous outpourings of public support that greatly influenced the national government.[47] Once President Johnson correctly assessed the public mood and political situation, he acted decisively. In March 1965 he went on national television to deliver a forceful speech asking a joint session of Congress to make national voting rights legislation its top legislative priority. Johnson's full-scale appropriation of King's jeremiadic vocabulary was striking. Blacks' fight for the right to vote was a challenge, he said, touching the core of "the values and purposes and meaning of our beloved nation." Johnson compared blacks' fight for the ballot to the patriotic revolutionary battles of Lexington and Concord. Furthermore, their acts "called upon us to make good the promise of America," and, should Americans prove "unequal to this issue," then "we will have failed as a people and a nation." But he knew Americans would meet this challenge. Taking a line from the civil rights movement anthem, he concluded emphatically, "And we *shall* overcome." Like Lincoln's Second Inaugural Address, President Johnson's 1965 "We Shall Overcome" speech echoed the public language and imagination used by the leading black jeremiah of the day. This use by the national leader of black rhetoric signified the national scope of Douglass's and King's victorious appeals to the nation.[48]

Congressional acts of 1964 and 1965 outlawing racial segregation and disenfranchisement were the most important legislative gains for blacks since Reconstruction, and their passage marked the peak of national racial reform in the 1960s. Not since the 1860s had Afro-Americans entertained higher, more millenniarian hopes for America. But in 1965 as in 1868, the window of opportunity for racial change showed that it could close as swiftly as it had opened. Moreover, in 1965 as in 1865, black expectations and demands continued to accelerate while white willingness to implement further reform faded. After 1965, King, like Douglass, was to learn that his ability to reach the conscience of Northern whites and win national support for racial reform was limited. White consciences had been successfully touched by Douglass to abolish slavery and by King to dismantle Jim Crow. But white consciences could not be quickly moved, however, to support economic reforms that, for blacks, were necessary to give substance to the legal forms of democracy. As of 1965, King's most challenging and disturbing encounter with racism in American culture still lay ahead.

# 7. King's Radical Jeremiad, 1965–1968: America as the "Sick Society"

The sun had shone brightly on the civil rights marchers who descended on Washington on August 28, 1963, to demand national political action against racism. It was a day full of contagious hope and optimism. Basking in the warm national response, many blacks could truly believe, as King suggested, that all was possible on that day signaling a new beginning toward genuine democracy in America. But, just before the march began, news of the death of W. E. B. Du Bois in Ghana circulated through the crowd, prompting, at least among blacks, removal of hats and lowering of heads. It was fitting that the shadow of Du Bois should dampen the otherwise unrestrained elation of the afternoon. For had he been there, he likely would have cautioned the jubilant crowd on how quickly to expect America to shed its racist habits and make the structural changes needed to accord blacks their full human rights and dignity.

In Du Bois's last pessimistic assessment of contemporary America, he glimpsed a flicker of hope in the nascent civil rights movement begun by the Montgomery bus boycott of 1955–1956 and then accelerated by the black student sit-ins against segregation. He had a brief respectful correspondence with King, whom he appraised as "honest" and "knowing the limits" of permissible protest. Commenting on the new movement, Du Bois found such activities "most encouraging" and wished King and the students well—*yet* he inevitably issued them a challenge. Gaining legal rights was all good and valuable, he agreed, but "still does not reach the center of the problem," which was securing "the chance for American Negroes to have money to spend because of employment by which they can make a decent wage." To move forward, blacks must "insist upon the legal rights which are already there and then . . . add to that an increasingly socialistic form of government." Establishing economic security, expanding social welfare, and otherwise changing "a government of wealth, for wealth, and by wealth" were needed to elevate blacks and all Americans to a level of true dignity. But Du Bois could not see America's ruling class accepting such reforms, which would cost it great treasure and power. "Does capitalism offer such a program?" he asked: "It does not, it offers war."[1]

Between 1963 and 1968, the national situation surveyed by Martin Luther King deteriorated with bewildering speed, and whereas his earlier focus had been on the racist sickness of the white South, after 1965 he increasingly addressed the social depravity of the whole nation. In late 1967, he recalled the radiant hope of the Washington March wistfully, as though it were already something from the distant past. "I must confess to you today," he told an audience, "that not long after talking about that dream I started seeing it turn into a nightmare" in the form of tragic riots, the war in Vietnam, and stony national indifference to the continuing challenge of social justice.[2] The disturbing developments of the later sixties challenged his earlier optimism about America's potential for swift, far-reaching reform. King's resulting disappointment approached despair in much the way as disheartening trends had once dimmed Du Bois's short-term expectations for America. These latter obstacles, furthermore, drove King to add to his initial civil rights agenda just those entwined issues of international peace and economic justice that Du Bois had stressed as the key to American social rejuvenation. But what had happened to alter King's mood and reading of the nation's direction so dramatically in so few years?

### King on the Liberal Mountaintop, 1963–1965

Between late 1963 and early 1965 King's optimism had soared. Reflecting the upswing of black militancy and confidence, the goals of King's jeremiad grew ever more bold and thoroughgoing. In a fall 1963 article, "In a Word—NOW," King demanded immediate passage of President Kennedy's pending civil rights bill, federal police action to halt Southern brutality, and legislation to enforce black voting rights and secure full employment. These items, he insisted, were *all* part of blacks' agenda for "NOW." A year later, King was elated over passage of the 1964 Civil Rights Act but displeased by

President Johnson's statement to the public that with it "the last vestiges of injustice" against blacks had been removed and private admonition to civil rights leaders that further protests were unnecessary, even "self-defeating."[3] But King had no intention of disbanding blacks' social crusade and declaring the promised land fully arrived. Pressing issues of black voting rights, poverty, and fair housing remained. Riding the still-rising tide of black protest, King planned to push harder and faster. "As I look forward toward 1964," he said, "one fact is unmistakably clear: the thrust of the Negro toward full emancipation will *increase* rather than *decrease*." If the American people and government procrastinated in adopting the urgently needed reforms, "the nation might well fasten its safety belt" for continuing social protest and unrest.[4]

King's ideas and hopeful expectations in this period were most systematically stated in his third book, *Why We Can't Wait,* published in early 1964. The book's main theme was that blacks demanded total unconditional freedom *now* and that no further delays or superficial steps were tolerable. *Now* was the time to unite American experience with American promise, he declared; otherwise, swirling clouds of revolt would continue to engulf the nation.

*Why We Can't Wait* significantly broadened the specific demands of King's jeremiad. Emphasis on the twin evils of racism and poverty ran throughout the book. Poverty's chains weighed as heavily on blacks as had segregation's bonds, King repeatedly insisted. Even as blacks were making rapid progress in securing legal rights, King began to stress the inadequacy of legal gains alone. Systematic "economic exploitation" also had to be addressed and uprooted. True equality "demanded a job that was secure and a pay check that lasted throughout the week." "The struggle for rights, is, at bottom, a struggle for opportunities" of every kind, he said, and blacks would never be free so long as they were subject to the crippling effects of "financial servitude."[5]

Accordingly, King championed a "gigantic Bill of Rights for the Disadvantaged" that would commit the federal government to mobilize national resources to abolish the scourge of economic deprivation. The massive governmental program that he envisioned "would immediately transform the conditions of Negro Life," as well as benefit millions of poor white Americans. Such an ambitious national undertaking "could mark the rise of a new era" of a just and democratic America.[6]

King anticipated that an American progressive alliance would come together to accomplish this national transformation. White America, he judged, was poised for extensive reform. The "surging power of the Negro revolt and *the genuineness of good will that has come from many white Americans* indicate," he felt, "that the time is ripe for broader thinking and action" (emphasis added). He advocated a grand interracial coalition, inspired by blacks' dynamic example, to forge a new America. Because of blacks' advancing political strength and momentum, the civil rights movement had matured to a new stage, he argued. Now it could unite politically with white progressives to promote an agenda embracing civil rights and national economic and social policy. The core of this dynamic alliance would consist of blacks, white labor, and middle-class liberals, and its instruments of change would be an aroused and committed federal government.[7]

Such was King's long-range social vision and hope until his death. But in 1964, unlike 1967–1968, he thought such a national political coalition eminently possible under the leadership of President Lyndon Johnson and the liberal Democratic Party. Johnson appeared to be a political miracle worker during his first eighteen months in office. Seizing the moment after Kennedy's assassination, LBJ pushed the historic 1964 Civil Rights Act through Congress as a tribute to the martyred president. He proved equally successful in breaking the legislative logjam against JFK's social welfare proposals such as Medicare. Johnson proceeded to score further impressive victories in moving his own social welfare legislation through Congress. Heading toward the 1964 presidential election, he described this program as a "War on Poverty" that would create "the Great Society" in America. Although Johnson did not provide as much federal protection to Southern civil rights workers as King wished, LBJ was clearly the closest thing yet to the activist president for whom King longed, and King showered praise on him in the book. He marveled at the "dimensions of Johnson's leadership" and lauded the president's "comprehensive grasp of contemporary problems" and statesman-like setting of "the twin goal of a battle against discrimination within the war on poverty."[8]

In retrospect, it is evident that even as the national civil rights consensus approached its climax between 1963 and 1965, the seeds of its destruction were present and growing. Just how fragile the national reform consensus was, how hard it would be to extend it beyond civil rights in the South, and how entrenched and pervasive were racially oppressive patterns within the nation as a whole would become clear to King only after 1965.

## Challenges to King's Dream and Leadership

One ominous development, starting in 1964 and worsening through 1968, was the outbreak of severe rioting by poor inner-city Northern blacks. The first surge of violent uprisings in big cities occurred in New York, Chicago, and Philadelphia in 1964. The spectacular victories of the Southern civil rights movement had captured national attention by then and the expectations of Afro-Americans everywhere had been dramatically raised. But a glaring gap arose between the visibly improving political circumstances of Southern blacks and the unchanged, even worsening socio-economic conditions of most Northern urban blacks. Despite dramatic gains in the South, the oppressive realities of Northern black ghetto life—slums, unemployment, inferior education, and *de facto,* not *de jure* segregation—remained untouched. The denied expectations of poor inner-city blacks began to explode in riots directed against white property in the racial ghettos of America's major cities.[9]

King responded to this alarming trend by seeking to halt black rioting as well as violent white repression and to mediate between the two sides. On the one hand, King unfailingly deplored outbreaks of lawlessness and argued that rioting held no positive solution to urban blacks' genuine social grievances. Riots and destruction of white property brought only temporary psychological satisfaction, he contended, while senseless violence hurt blacks' real interests by giving "the white majority an excuse . . . to look away from the cause of the riots—the poverty . . . deprivation and . . . degradation of the Negro" and to "talk instead of looting, and of the breakdown of law and order." At the same time, he cautioned whites against responding to the riots with counterviolence only and not also with constructive social reforms. He urged them to examine "the *reason* for violence," and he held "white leadership . . . as responsible as anyone for the riots, for not removing the conditions that cause them."[10]

But neither desperate, nihilistic black rioters nor outraged whites heeded King's call for mutual forbearance and dedication to finding nonviolent solutions to social problems. Touring the scene of a major riot in Harlem in 1964, King tried to calm black crowds and was booed and interrupted by angry ghetto-dwellers. He was also dismayed by seeing anti-Semitic and anti-white graffiti scrawled on building walls. Then in 1965, a round of even worse rioting opened, beginning with a terrific explosion in Watts, the black ghetto of Los Angeles. In every major city, it seemed, blacks were eager to destroy every symbol of white power and property within reach. Televised scenes of rampaging black rioters and looters became common. Blacks' most common media image now sharply contrasted with those earlier publicized scenes of *white* violence and black *nonviolence* on which the Southern civil rights movement had thrived. White public response was hostile, and white politicians called loudly for get-tough police measures and firmer enforcement of "law and order."

Meanwhile other blacks, including many student veterans of the Southern crusades and early followers of the non-violent creed, expressed anger at the violent white response to their efforts and mounting impatience with blacks' unilateral reliance on nonviolence. From the beginning, there had been a split of opinion in civil rights ranks between those, like King, who viewed nonviolence as an absolute moral commitment and pragmatists who wielded it as a weapon only as long as it secured positive results.[11] After the social efficacy of nonviolence seemed to wane after 1965, many increasingly militant black youths felt an urge to strike back at white foes rather than to continue to accept physical abuse passively.

The 1964 "Mississippi Freedom Summer" campaign was a key radicalizing experience for many young black activists, especially those in the main student civil rights organization, the Student Nonviolent Coordinating Committee (SNCC). The Freedom Summer was a plan to register black voters and politically organize them in the most regressive state of the deep South. The campaign was marred by many incidents of violence and even the murder of civil rights workers in the isolated rural Mississippi countryside. By summer's end, many students were carrying weapons for self-defense and vowing no longer to go as lambs to their slaughter.

Many individuals' turn from nonviolence during the Mississippi Freedom Summer was accompanied by their rising disillusionment with the movement's white allies. Latent racial tensions among the volunteers surfaced, as blacks accused white co-workers of holding condescending attitudes toward them and of merely "slumming" in a summer adventure among black Mississippians. Black students began arguing that continued reliance on whites represented admission of black inadequacy and inability to run their own movement. Many white student volunteers began feeling unwelcome and left the movement in 1964. Finally, the federal government's reluctance to protect workers in Mississippi and the fact that it took belated steps only after whites were killed led many blacks to conclude that the government was an unreliable and covertly racist ally. The Mississippi Freedom Summer left a bitter legacy among black activists of general distrust and suspicion toward whites. It exacerbated separatist trends and the inclination to contemplate and even romanticize the use of force to achieve racial liberation.

King became a prime target for the young radicals' discontent. He symbolized for many of them the unmanly passivity, lack of militance, and overwillingness to trust and cooperate with whites that they now rejected. Particularly damaging was King's role in the Mississippi Freedom Democratic Party (MFDP) episode at the 1964 Democratic National Convention. When the Mississippi state Democratic Party refused to permit black participation, volunteers organized the independent MFDP to challenge the regular white Mississippi delegations' credentials at the national convention.

King attempted to function as a mediator between the young radicals and national Democratic leadership. Originally he was the MFDP's leading advocate before party officials. But President Johnson adamantly ruled out seating the MFDP delegation and letting a racial confrontation mar his televised coronation as the Democratic presidential nominee. Johnson insisted that the MFDP accept a "compromise" that would seat that year's white Mississippi delegation while giving the MFDP a few nonvoting representatives and a promise to bar future delegations in whose selection nonwhites were not free to participate. Believing that Democratic liberalism was the blacks' best hope for national redress of their ills, King forsook immediate moral principle for long-term political considerations. He reluctantly accepted the party's decision and the onerous task of persuading the MFDP representatives to swallow the distasteful "compromise." Admitting the absolute justness of their cause, King advised them to accept this outcome and support Johnson's candidacy. MFDP and SNCC members refused, calling the seating of the all-white Mississippi delegation a predictable white liberal sell out. For his efforts, King lost enormously in respect and prestige among young militants and became permanently suspect as an apologist for white perfidy. Charges that he was an "Uncle Tom" prone to betray blacks' interests in dealings with whites became very common in black militant circles.

Events and experiences between 1964 and 1966 continued to aggravate disagreement and discord among black activists. Controversy over King's leadership and tactics rose again during the 1965 Selma campaign, when his decisions to draw black forces back from confrontation at crucial moments angered militant youths./Black Muslim leader Malcolm X, who was diametrically opposed to King's integrationist goals, nonviolent methods, and conciliatory stance toward whites, was invited to speak at SNCC meetings in 1964 and 1965./Deep disagreements continued to fester behind the public facade of black unity, until in 1966 student leaders like Stokely Carmichael openly broke with King and announced their own revolutionary program of "Black Power," a vague and emotionally charged slogan voicing determination to organize blacks separately and use all available means, including violence, to advance their interests.[12]

By late 1965, King lifted improvement of ghetto conditions to the top of his agenda. This move was precipitated by achievement of his main goal of 1964–1965, the national Voting Rights Act and by the disturbing trend toward black rage and militancy. In a November magazine article, "Next Stop: The North," King announced his intent to begin fixing attention on national (actually more Northern than Southern) socio-economic conditions. "The flames of Watts," he wrote, "cast light on the imperfections of the civil rights movement and the tragic shallowness of white racial policy." He confessed that the movement thus far had been "essentially regional, not national" and concerned with issues of legal and political discrimination primarily affecting Southern blacks. He had "long thought that the North would benefit derivatively from the southern struggle" and that "systematic changes" to better blacks' conditions would be voluntarily adopted by enlightened national leadership "without massive upheavals" as had occurred in the South. Now he admitted his earlier "miscalculation" and wrote that he had grown "disillusioned with the power structures" of the North and their lax, unimaginative response to pressing social problems. He now believed that dangerous urban conditions "would only be altered by a dynamic movement" generating enough public support and political heat to spur national leadership to action.[13] The pharaoh whose heart his words meant to melt and whose justice his actions sought to compel was now a white Northern urban pharaoh.

In 1966, the SCLC tried to put the new program into effect by launching a major direct-action campaign against city authorities in Chicago for several goals, most significantly massive spending increases for low-income public housing and an end of real estate companies' practices (tacitly supported by the city) to preserve residential racial segregation. The attempt to apply techniques learned in the Southern civil rights struggles to the vastly more complex socio-economic realities of the Northern metropolis was a bold, but to King, absolutely necessary gamble. Chicago represented his main attempt to show the oppressed that an intelligent non-violent campaign, unlike anarchistic rioting, could prompt the power structure to address their needs and make remedial changes. The 1966 Chicago campaign was King's key effort to save America's urban core from racial conflagration. He needed, he felt, a national victory on the scale of Birmingham or Selma in a campaign solely dedicated to urban issues. Overriding many SCLC staff members' pragmatic objections, King summarily decreed that his mission summoned him to Chicago.[14]

The Chicago campaign was a long and eventually violent confrontation between the SCLC-organized demonstrators led by King on one side and, on the other, Mayor Richard Daley's administration and angry mobs in white neighborhoods. Although the campaign began encouragingly with King leading 30,000 marchers to City Hall, major difficulties soon developed. King was frequently called away to civil rights demonstrations in the South and kept jetting in and out of Chicago. The movement often lost momentum in his frequent absences. It was during the Chicago crusade that the breach between King and Black Power enthusiasts became public knowledge during a Mississippi march, which helped undermine his influence everywhere.[15]

The confrontation between the SCLC and its local allies and Chicago's inflexible administration built for months. Then, late in the campaign, as King began leading marches against residential segregation into white ethnic working-class neighborhoods, the tension erupted in racist violence. Furious white mobs screamed "Kill the niggers!" and "We want Martin Luther Coon," and waved

Confederate flags and Nazi swastikas. They hurled bricks and bottles at the marchers over the heads of restraining policemen. One person threw a knife at King, another hit him with a brick in the ear. Shaken but safe at day's end, King exclaimed that in all his experiences in the deep South, never had he "seen anything so hostile and hateful" in whites "as I've seen here today."[16]

The campaign's climax had arrived. King pledged to keep leading marches into all-white Chicago suburbs, despite Mayor Daley's pleas and warnings that the police could not guarantee the marchers' safety. Embarrassed by the ugly racism exposed in his city and fearing an uncontrollable bloodbath, Daley finally agreed to open negotiations with the SCLC. Eventually a complex accord was hammered out between SCLC, the city, and Chicago real estate companies and banks to promote the goal of racially nondiscriminatory housing practices. King called off the SCLC campaign, claiming that these modest agreements signaled the city authorities' good faith and progress toward an open housing market in Chicago. No mention was made of alleviating slum conditions in the black West Side.

Chicago had not gone well and was, at best, a qualified success for King. Internal black divisions were pronounced throughout the campaign. King and SCLC were sharply challenged by young militants and Black Power advocates, including participants in demonstrations whose conduct King could not necessarily control. At the same time, there were many black ministers and politicians with ties to Daley's patronage machine who defended the mayor, attacked King, and undermined unified resistance in the black community.

King's forces were pitted against social problems more difficult to publicize effectively and a foe more subtle than they were used to handling. No single law or agent could be held accountable for ghetto poverty, but rather an interlocking web of social, economic, and political forces. Mayor Richard Daley was a far more powerful and wily foe than the stereotypical racist villains encountered in the movement's Southern heyday. Although not above resorting to repression to crush the movement, Daley relied mainly on political means. His Democratic machine's organization and patronage gave him influence deep within the black community, and he could manipulate public expenditures and welfare programs for his own ends. Daley's police and city government, moreover, were less guilty of overt brutality toward blacks than of sheer indifference toward ghetto crime and poverty.

With the exception of the final marches to white suburbs, the Chicago movement lacked dramatic scenes usefully contrasting hateful white violence with black nonviolence and morality. Mayor Daley was not the perfect foil that Bull Connor had been. Moreover, black violence was of far more concern to whites by 1966 than was white violence. A riot erupted in the West Side during King's presence in Chicago, for example, creating unfavorable publicity and prompting mutual recrimination and charges of blame between King and Daley. King also had difficulty getting pledges to observe nonviolence from many Chicago blacks, and his control over the actions of some demonstrators and marchers grew increasingly tenuous. The climate of opinion among blacks *and* whites amid widespread race riots was not propitious for King's direct action campaign.

SCLC's Chicago campaign was widely deemed a failure. Most black Chicagoans viewed its results skeptically; some openly derided it as a sellout. Daunted by the difficulties encountered in the campaign and disappointed by the public response, King seemed relieved to find a face-saving resolution. He lauded the agreements reached with the city, banks, and real estate interests, declared victory, and exited. The final accord proved difficult to enforce and fell short of the SCLC's original main goal of abolishing slum housing conditions. King's concrete demands had shrunk steadily through the campaign until they centered almost exclusively on the open housing issue, one of critical importance only to those blacks who could afford to leave the ghetto.

The lacklustre response to King's Chicago crusade was a sign of the times. In 1963, small changes, however incremental, had seemed breakthroughs pregnant with promise; by 1966, anything less than immediate total transformation of blacks' conditions seemed only to confirm the absence of real change. Moreover, Chicago had failed precisely where Birmingham and Selma had most dramatically succeeded, not so much in the details of the local resolution but in the all-important area of gaining national public support. By anyone's standards, including his own, Chicago was not a decisive vindication of nonviolence's promise for meeting America's urban racial crisis.

As black demands for change continued to accelerate during the later sixties and to center increasingly on national economic conditions rather than regional legal ones, white resistance to black demands and protests stiffened. By 1966, public opinion polls revealed that large white majorities opposed further concessions to blacks and favored tough "law-and-order" measures to repress social disturbances instigated by blacks. Televised scenes of black rioters and looters incensed many whites, helping to harden their growing sentiment that blacks had gotten enough and should be content with recent gains. When King took his nonviolent crusade northward, he received a hostile reception from the local politicians, even from many who, like Daley, had applauded his Southern campaigns.

By 1966, King's relations with the White House had grown strained. Among the factors militating against success in Chicago was the unwillingness of the federal government to intervene with outside pressure as it had in Birmingham and, most recently, at Selma. President Johnson had proved deaf to King's urgent requests for federal protection of civil rights workers in Mississippi. In place of the solicitous attention King's requests had been receiving from the White House since 1961, by 1966 he was getting curt, if any, replies.

The widening breach in King's relations with the White House stemmed from King's increasing vocal opposition to American military involvement in Vietnam. He had quietly watched the slow but steady buildup of American forces in Southeast Asia with rising apprehension since early 1965. When President Johnson took office there had been 23,000 U.S. advisors in Vietnam. Then, with little public fanfare or notice, the numbers of American military personnel in Vietnam rose rapidly. By June 1965 there were 75,000 U.S. troops, some in combat, and in August the president authorized sending 200,000 additional troops.[17]

King reacted with alarm to the sight of American money and matériel being poured into Vietnam. He saw no legitimate national interest being served and found the prospect of American soldiers battling Asian nationalists to prop up an unpopular dictatorship deeply disturbing. Opposed to all war, he was fiercely opposed to a war with racist imperialist overtones. He was most directly concerned by the war's diversion of governmental commitment and resources from desperately needed domestic wars on poverty and racial injustice. Having been awarded the international Nobel Peace Prize in 1964, King also took more seriously than ever his responsibility to speak to the needs of the whole world as well as America, especially in areas where the domestic and international causes of peace and justice intersected, as he believed they did in Vietnam.

Most of King's advisors opposed his risky course of speaking out against the war and U.S. foreign policy. In 1965, in the afterglow of Selma and before Chicago, King still enjoyed cordial relations with the president. King's aides warned him that to criticize Johnson's war policies would jeopardize federal support for the SCLC's upcoming campaign to abolish urban slums and poverty. Moreover, national public opinion was still very hawkish on the war. The head of SCLC's fund-raising activities thought that opposition to the war would alienate important contributors, including liberal labor unions. But as was often the case, King overrode his advisors' pragmatic counsel and declared that God and conscience called him to a certain stand. His followers, as a rule, then closed ranks behind their charismatic leader.[18]

In August, 1965, King first publicly voiced his growing doubts about American policy in Vietnam. In many forums he called for opening negotiations among the warring parties, including the United States and Viet Cong guerrillas, and offered personally to mediate to help end hostilities. For several weeks King repeated these ideas, as hostile public reaction came in from every quarter. The heads of the NAACP and National Urban League urged King to keep quiet, lest he endanger the Johnson-led consensus on civil rights and future government support.

President Johnson was furious, raging against King's ingratitude after all that he had supposedly done for him. The White House orchestrated a campaign to silence King, which included having pro-administration blacks pressure King to let foreign policy alone, encouraging press denunciations of King's pronouncements on Vietnam, and arranging intimidating briefings by administration figures to show King the errors of his thinking. Government officials, King recalled, "told me I wasn't an expert in foreign affairs and they were all experts. I knew only civil rights and should stick to that."[19]

When King stubbornly persisted and further suggested that the United States and United Nations should recognize the People's Republic of China, or Red China, and invite it to join peace negotiations, established leaders in and out of government, white and black, ferociously attacked him for his heresy. Liberal Democrats and labor union leaders protested as loudly as the White House—not to mention the apoplexy of Republicans and far right-wingers. King was suddenly in peril of losing his constituency among the federal government, white liberals, and the conservative wing of the black civil rights movement. Staggered by this barrage of criticism, King finally heeded his staff and backpedaled. He ceased making public statements about the war, as he and SCLC tackled the enormous challenge of the Chicago campaign. But the damage already done to King's relations with the White House was irreversible.

Lyndon Johnson, moreover, was not the only powerful member of the national government set on discrediting King by 1966. There had been a long-running public feud between King and J. Edgar Hoover, director of the Federal Bureau of Investigation (FBI). Civil rights workers had long complained that the FBI was indifferent to protecting the lives and rights of blacks in Southern civil rights demonstrations. King publicly questioned whether the FBI's heart was in civil rights law enforcement and criticized its policy of using Southern-born white agents to monitor civil rights demonstrations. King was startled and angered by Hoover's harsh public attacks against him in response to these remarks.[20]

Hoover was an arch-conservative who had disliked King and the disruptive civil rights movement from the start. Moreover, by 1962, Hoover was convinced that King was either an active Communist or Communist dupe, and in either case, a grave danger to the Republic. King was then unaware that he had been under heavy FBI surveillance since an informant told the bureau in 1961 that Stanley Levison, one of King's assistants, was a former Communist Party member, a charge which appears to have been true. Levison, a New York lawyer with a long-standing interest in civil rights, joined King's forces during the Montgomery bus boycott. Earlier in 1955 he had resigned from the Communist Party and had no further contact with it. Discovering this past, the FBI jumped to the conclusion that Levison remained an active Communist whose resignation was just a cover for his assignment of making the civil rights movement an agent of Communist designs. In 1962 the bureau launched a full-scale investigation of King including extensive electronic surveillance and wiretapping of his home and SCLC offices.[21]

Director Hoover compiled charges of Communist infiltration against King and presented them as proven fact to the Kennedy White House. Skeptical of Hoover's objectivity, the president and Attorney General Robert Kennedy nevertheless warned King that he had Communists on his staff whom he must purge. Robert Kennedy also authorized continued FBI surveillance of King, probably to protect the administration from Hoover.

King was perplexed by these charges. He said that he did not care what people had done before they joined him and that he took Levison and Jack O'Dell, another figure fingered by the FBI, at their word that they were no longer involved with the Communists. Although he temporarily broke relations with these men, King eventually disregarded the Kennedys' advice, taking the position that if anyone had proof of these charges, they should bring it forth, but, lacking that, he trusted the word of a proven friend more than he did the FBI.[22]

King's decision to resume ties with Levison confirmed his alliance with Communism in J. Edgar Hoover's mind. As long as President Kennedy remained in office, Hoover's campaign to expose and ruin King was somewhat restrained. By 1966, however, Hoover had found a soulmate in LBJ, who enthusiastically joined the vendetta and authorized a secret government campaign to undermine King's reputation and public authority.[23]

## King's Radical Jeremiad, 1966–1968

The traumatic trends of the later sixties—racial polarization, burning cities, bloodshed abroad and division at home over Vietnam, and a national lack of will for reform and reconciliation—disturbed and depressed King. American society seemed to be reaching the breaking point. Campus demonstrations erupted, as America's youth spilled out of classrooms and onto the streets to protest the Vietnam conflict and the draft. Some of the students, many of whom had begun their social activism in the civil rights movement, became New Left revolutionaries espousing radical critiques of American society and foreign policy. Apolitical hippies opted out of conventional society and chose lifestyles and dress that flamboyantly rejected its values. The terms "Generation gap" and "counter culture" became widespread, describing a massive disillusionment among American youth with established society. At the same time, hard-line "law-and-order" politicians such as California Governor Ronald Reagan became conservative folk heroes by vowing to get tough with campus radicals. And conservative American workers, or "hard hats," beat up, "un-American" hippies and demonstrators.

Amid the gathering crisis, King grew convinced that America verged on self-destruction and felt more strongly than ever a prophetic duty to warn America against its folly. A sense of desperate urgency drove King between 1966 and 1968: *someone* had to warn the people, reach and rally them back from sinful madness to repentance and revival. King sought to forge a new national consensus extending beyond enforcement of civil rights to a firm commitment to erase poverty from national life. It was an unsuccessful crusade. Unlike the consensus against racial discrimination in public life that he had helped create by 1963, Americans did not listen with open ears or willing hearts to the social prophecy he preached after 1965.

King's social genius had been his unique ability to combine militance with moderation. He had consistently been radical enough to push America toward major change while staying near enough to middle-class opinion and institutions to affect and direct them. Although the white South had never willingly accepted the changes that he advocated, between 1963 and 1965 he had been successful in winning over much white Northern opinion and the federal government to his point of view. As he extended his social crusade and issued a jeremiad decrying *de facto* discrimination caused by Northern socio-economic practices, however, his national influence with whites waned, and he lost the government's favor. When he began finally to demand economic redistribution at home and to denounce American policy abroad, he became a virtual pariah among most whites. Moreover, not only could he no longer unite whites and blacks, he could no longer even unite blacks behind his charismatic leadership, as he was increasingly caught in the cross fire between young black militants who called him a compromising Uncle Tom and established black leaders who echoed white charges that he was radical and unpatriotic. What was a molder of social consensus and builder of coalitions to do in a society that, by the late sixties, had no stabilizing center?

Quixotic as this quest seemed by 1967, King committed his remaining energies to achieving a reform consensus. Realistically, King could see no basis for rallying his splintering social allies and mobilizing them into a national political force. He would nevertheless *try* to articulate the vision, frame the issues, and inspire those actions that he believed necessary for national redemption. The burden of leadership weighed heavily on him in these years, as he felt that he did not measure up to his awesome responsibility. His wife recalls that the terrible race riots of 1967 left King more distressed than she had ever seen him. "He felt that people were looking to him for a creative solution" to the crisis and that "he had not been able to propose one. He said, 'People expect me to have answers, and I don't have any answers.'"[24] So King struck out more desperately and boldly to find the solutions America needed.

King had been edging beyond the civil rights reform consensus even before it peaked in 1965; with that concensus's collapse, his conception of the socio-economic changes required to realize Afro-American freedom and fulfill America's mission was dramatically widened and radicalized. The radical thrust of King's final public message and jeremiad is best documented in his last book, *Where Do We Go from Here: Chaos or Community?*, published in early 1967.

The book opened with a nostalgic re-enactment of President Johnson's signing of the 1965 Voting Rights Act, back, King recalled, when optimism seemed "easy." Within a year, however, came the hate-filled violence of Watts and Chicago, the defiant voice of Black Power, the mounting white backlash, and deep national division over America's misadventure in Vietnam. There had been an enormous "change of mood" in the country. With the Voting Rights Act, King asserted, "one phase of development in the civil rights revolution came to an end" and "a new phase opened"—one whose implications Americans were not yet ready to accept. Although a majority of white Americans had come to agree that blacks "should be spared the lash of brutality," it was now clear that they "had never been truly committed to helping him out of his poverty." When "the freerunning expectations of the Negro crashed into the walls of white resistance," the "result was havoc."[25]

Dramatic loss of white support for the changes needed by blacks prompted hard re-thinking by King. "Why is equality so assiduously avoided?" he asked rhetorically, and why did "white America delude itself" about "the evil it retains?" The answer lay in economic self-interest. "The practical cost of change for the nation up to this point has been cheap," he said, and national reforms "obtained at bargain rates." It cost very little and required no redistribution of wealth to desegregate Southern restrooms and lunch counters. "The real cost lies ahead," he declared, in adopting those economic reforms needed to create genuine equal opportunity in America. King attributed white Americans' hardening opposition to their "dawning awareness that Negro demands will necessitate structural changes" and "impinge upon the basic system of social and economic control" that nationally favored whites and exploited blacks.[26]

King's current analysis led him to revise his view of the national past. The white backlash, he belatedly realized, might have been anticipated. He now perceived a historic pattern in which every instance of democratic progress had been followed and compromised by fresh bursts of white racism. "Ever since the birth of our nation, white America has had a schizophrenic personality on the question of race," King wrote, and "has been torn between selves— a self in which she proudly professed the great principles of democracy" and a self in which America practiced racism, "the antithesis of democracy." King blamed the current halt in American racial progress on this continuing "tragic duality" in white American culture. "There has never been a solid, unified and determined thrust to make justice a reality for Afro-Americans," he declared, and the nation's current retrogression was "an expression of the same vacillations" and "lack of commitment" that had always characterized the white American approach to racial justice.[27]

Every significant step toward interracial freedom had been diluted by the continuing racism in Anglo-American culture. King saw this tragic ambivalence symbolized by the attitudes of the Founding Fathers and other great white national heroes. Great as they were, "not one of these men had a strong, unequivocal belief in the equality of the black man." In the lives of Washington and Jefferson, King found "the developing dilemma of white America, the haunting ambivalence, the intellectual and moral recognition that slavery is wrong, but the emotional tie to the system [that was] so deep and pervasive" in society that they were unwilling to root it out. The same compromising duality was reflected in Abraham Lincoln's agonizingly slow movement toward the Emancipation Proclamation despite his moral recognition of the barbarism of slavery. "A civil war raged within Lincoln's own soul," King wrote, "between the Dr. Jekyll of freedom and the Mr. Hyde of slavery" which immobilized him for most of the war.[28]

King dwelt on the parallel between the present and the Civil War era in first dramatically arousing, then dashing black hopes for justice. He wrote that when emancipation came, it carried "the beautiful promise" of democracy for Frederick Douglass. Yet eventually, Douglass concluded that emancipation had conveyed a largely illusory freedom to blacks who were soon abandoned by the white public and national government to lives of racial subordination, social degradation, and economic deprivation. Without land and economic wherewithal, blacks had languished in inequality down to the present day. Recently, the great legal gains of the civil rights movement and modest beginnings of a war on poverty had, like Reconstruction, "seemed to herald a new day" for blacks. But now, as after Reconstruction, this promise was being betrayed by white indifference, economic selfishness, and ingrained racism. A tragic historical cycle was being repeated.[29]

King called American racism a "congenital deformity" that had "crippled the nation from its inception" and struck deep and powerful roots in American society. It was among the earliest, most formative influences on American culture, he noted, "not just an occasional departure from the norm, on the part of a few bigoted extremists." Racism as a national way of life began with "extermination of the American Indians" and the "ghastly blood traffic" of the African slave trade. Indeed, of the two warring strains in the American psyche, "the positive one, our democratic heritage," he noted, "was the later development on the American continent" and its development had always been conditioned and inhibited by a powerful racism.[30]

Stressing that racism's primary motive was economic, King held that it also had "a profound impact in shaping the social-political-legal structure of the nation," which still bore its imprint.[31] In the face of racism's pervasive historic influence, it was the height of irresponsibility for the nation to bestow abstract legal rights on blacks without also altering the social-economic structures that had been built on and around the exploitation and inferior status of the subjugated group. And yet this was just what white America, in 1967 as in 1868, proposed to do.

Despite his new emphasis on the centrality of racism in America, King did not counsel despair for its future. "The racism of today is real, but the democratic spirit" that opposed it was equally real and would, he predicted, eventually prevail in the nation's inner struggle to find its true self. "America has strayed to the far country of racism," he warned, away from its moorings in Judeo-Christian ideals and democracy. "*But it is not too late to return home,*" he cried. If America swiftly returned to its better self, the democratic creed would be restored at home and go on to recapture the imagination of the people of the world; if America failed this test, however, it would betray its mission and commit "national suicide." Deciding which way the country would go, he concluded, "is white America's most urgent challenge today."[32]

"The future of the deep structural changes we seek," King told blacks, "lies in new alliances" with other minorities and with labor, liberals, and progressive elements in the church and middle-class. Coalition building, not separatism, was the route blacks needed to follow, he argued, since blacks' position could be transformed only within the larger transformation of America's political and economic structures. Economic, not explicitly racial issues, moreover, had to be the centerpiece of this movement's agenda, for only by altering America's economic structures could the exploitation of blacks and poor whites truly be ended. King therefore reiterated his proposal for a national "Bill of Rights for the Disadvantaged" to devote at least a trillion dollars to uprooting and abolishing poverty.[33]

This national political coalition would be only the surface expression of a deeper "revolution of values" in American life. Ending "the evils of racism, poverty and militarism," he preached, meant that "a new set of values must be born." Only a total reformation of American society and its values could reverse the nation's downward spiral toward disaster. "For its very survival's sake," King urged, "America must re-examine old presuppositions and release itself" from reflexive habits of racism and defense of property over human need.[34]

In his final chapter, "The World House," King gazed beyond America, descrying a worldwide march toward freedom and a necessary role for America in this historical process. The world was "at a turning point," he proclaimed, as the flow of history, which for several centuries had favored Europe, began a reversal from "the era of colonialism" now "at an end." As "a freedom explosion" spread through the oppressed colored world, King prophesied, the "earth is being redistributed," and "we 'are shifting our basic outlooks.'" Revolutionary times demanded "new attitudes" and "mental outlooks," for today "our very survival depends on our ability to stay awake, to adjust to new ideas . . . and to face the challenge of change." To get in tune with the day's new trend, nations should cooperate in peacefully removing the last vestiges of racism and imperialism on which the passing order was based. It was time for "an all-out war against poverty," he exclaimed. "The wealthy nations . . . must promptly initiate a massive, sustained Marshall Plan for Asia, Africa and South America."[35]

The United States, the world's richest and most powerful nation, had a special obligation to bring about this transformation. King, the jeremiah, scored America for its "continued alliance . . . with racism and exploitation throughout the world." "If we are not diligent" in rooting out every lingering trace of "racism in our dealings with the world," he feared that "we may soon see the sins of our fathers visited upon ours and succeeding generations." Sadly, America was not now fulfilling its duty to lead the world toward justice but rather was waging a war to thwart national independence in Vietnam. When he saw "our country . . . intervening in . . . a civil war, mutilating hundreds of thousands of Vietnamese children with napalm," and refusing to open negotiations to stop the slaughter, he wrote darkly, "I tremble for our world." Vietnam was a microcosm of the "nightmare" of "today's possible nuclear destructiveness and tomorrow's even more calamitous prospects" of worldwide descent into uncontrollable violence. "Before it is too late," he cried, America must wake from habits of racism and war "and read the warnings on history's signposts."[36]

"Our only hope today lies in our ability to recapture the revolutionary spirit" of the American heritage, King wrote, "and go out into . . . [the] world declaring eternal opposition to poverty, racism and militarism." "America," he proclaimed, "can well lead the way in this revolution in values" and in creating a just international order. America had to start at home with a Marshall Plan for its own poor and then organize one for the whole world. All was possible, he promised, if America would only show the will to change course, stop resisting the world trend, and instead join it and lead humanity "to the new world which is now possible," the City of God.[37]

King's main activity in 1967 was assuming national leadership in the mushrooming anti-war movement. Silent on Vietnam in 1966 as the price of trying to keep the support of white liberals and the government, King decisively ended his self-censorship. The war and not civil rights, he grasped, had become the central source of division in the country, and his analysis could no longer separate America's internal sickness from its follies abroad.

King's public coming out into the peace movement was his speech at New York City's Riverside Church in April 1967, a media event affording King a forum from which to address the nation on Vietnam. King declared that he was criticizing his beloved country reluctantly and only after long agonizing thought and out of loyalty to its truest self and ideals. He reminded his audience that the SCLC's motto was "To Save the Soul of America."

King felt compelled to denounce the Vietnam War for several reasons, especially his commitment to America's poor. "A few years ago," he lamented, there had seemed "a real promise of hope for the poor," as the nation took its first tentative steps in a war on poverty. Then came the Vietnam buildup,

> and I watched the [anti-poverty] program broken . . . as . . . some idle political plaything of a nation gone mad on war, and I knew that America would never invest the necessary funds . . . in rehabilitation of its poor so long as adventures like Vietnam continued to draw men and skills and money like some demonic destructive suction tube.

He felt that "I could never again raise my voice against the violence of the oppressed in the ghettos without having first spoken clearly to the greatest purveyor of violence in the world today—my own government." He also felt obliged to protest the war as a recipient of an international peace prize and as a minister of Jesus Christ, "a calling that takes me beyond national allegiances." "I speak as a citizen of the world," he declared, against American actions in Vietnam.

King ended the speech with the same revolutionary international jeremiad with which he concluded *Where Do We Go from Here?* "The war in Vietnam," he contended, "is but a symptom of a far deeper malady within the American spirit," an inner moral sickness outwardly expressed in America's futile attempt to arrest world change. The irresistible world freedom movement required a fundamental "revolution of values," but America was failing this test. Until the United States woke up to change and began working with conviction to end domestic and international poverty, it was rapidly "approaching spiritual death." He delivered a jeremiadic challenge to America to decide immediately whether it would change imminent salvation or eternal damnation. And he predicted that, by returning to its own revolutionary roots, America could "lead the way" to the new world.[38]

King was blasted by the American establishment for the "traitorous" Riverside address. President Johnson was beside himself with anger, and a White House aide exclaimed, "My God, King has given a speech on Vietnam that goes right down the commie line!" *Life* magazine denounced it as "a demagogic slander" sounding "like a script for Radio Hanoi." More deeply disturbing to King was the only slightly less vitriolic editorial denunciations of the speech by respected liberal newspapers like the *New York Times* and *Washington Post*. King sat down and wept when he read national press reactions to the speech.[39]

The president and FBI now regarded King as "the most dangerous man in America." Hoover credited the speech to the sinister hand of Communism by way of Stanley Levison. A flow of FBI reports on King's growing involvement in anti-war protests based on extensive surveillance of King streamed to the president. Johnson was obsessed by King's potential for providing charismatic leadership to the budding peace movement and feared that King was preparing to run for president in 1968 on an anti-Johnson peace ticket, a fear assiduously fanned by the FBI. Hoover's attempt to smear King by tying him to Communism never achieved credibility beyond the extreme right-wing fringe, and so his efforts to bring down the black leader now centered on offering FBI tapes of King's sex life to newspapers. To Hoover's disbelief and consternation, no news agencies would publish his carefully gathered dirt. Frustrated, the FBI resorted to sending prostitutes to King's hotels in an attempt to entrap him, and a composite "highlight" tape was mailed to King's home with an attached note recommending suicide as the only way to escape exposure as a moral degenerate.[40] King was distressed to learn the depth of the government's enmity toward him and lengths to which it would go to break him, but he did not let it overwhelm him. By 1967 he steeled himself to face federal hostility as yet another disheartening social fact which he was bravely, almost fatalistically, determined to press on against.

King's major theme in 1967 and 1968, next to Vietnam, was the need for deep structural economic changes in the United States and the world, as part of a fundamental "revolution of values." Institutionalizing this value revolution would entail, minimally, nationalization of certain industries, massive renovation of slums, a guaranteed national income, and a complete overhauling of American foreign policy and overseas investments. A national annual income increasingly appealed to King as the most direct and efficient way of immediately remedying poverty.[41]

All the while, King groped for a political vehicle to use in accomplishing these goals. Somehow a progressive alliance had to be formed around a dynamic movement for nonviolent social change. King valiantly tried to create such an instrument. As autumn approached in 1967, he told Coretta King, "We must have a program centered around jobs and economic activities. We have to think in terms of some creative non-violent action in these areas." She writes that he was "searching for a way."[42] Out of this sense of social crisis and imminent catastrophe came King's last urgent attempt to save America and resurrect the promise of peaceful social change: the National Poor People's campaign.

In August 1967, King broached an idea to close advisors that he would form a massive civil disobedience campaign to dramatize the plight of the poor and demand remedial government action. A nonviolent poor people's army would be recruited from around the nation and march on the national capital where it would hold sit-ins in Congress and government offices, immobilizing Washington and its operations. The Poor People's March was to be a popular interracial movement focused on economic and class issues. Its immediate goal would be to shake the center of national power out of its slumber of neglect.

King's aides were aghast at the breathtaking dimensions of his plan and tried to talk him out of it. He was proposing that the SCLC gather several thousand poor people representing a cross section of the nation—inner-city blacks, Appalachian whites, native Americans and Chicanos from the West, drill them for three months in non-violent techniques, then march them to Washington, D.C., to stage demonstrations to disrupt the federal government. They questioned whether the SCLC had organizational and financial resources (contributions to SCLC had dropped precipitously) to pull off such an ambitious enterprise. They warned of likely public hostility and forceful government repression. But King was not to be dissuaded. The stakes were too high, he insisted, and the current crisis too severe to hold back from bold action. As he talked on fervently to his advisors about this, his "last and greatest dream," one aide realized with a jolt that "we are going for broke this time."[43] King was indeed going for broke, for the Poor People's Campaign was, in his mind, nothing less than America's last chance for survival.

From December 1967 to his death in April 1968, the Poor People's Crusade was King's dominant concern. He threw himself into its preparation with desperate energy. He was indefatigable in drumming up public support for the proposed march. He crisscrossed the country, publicizing the campaign and seeking for it recruits and contributions. He spent most of February and March lining up volunteers among poor people in the deep South. Touring rural Mississippi, he was moved to tears by the shocking malnutrition and lack of adequate clothing and shelter that he saw in poor tenant farmers' shacks. He vowed to bring them all and many other poor people to Washington for the whole nation to see and acknowledge—*then* maybe America would do something about them. As was his custom, even in the midst of work on a national campaign, he also supported local movements seeking his aid and presence, shuttling back and forth between projects.

Preparations for the Washington March did not go well. Money and volunteers were not sufficiently forthcoming, and SCLC workers persisted in asking King to cancel it. The country's mood seemed unreceptive, and prominent public officials were denouncing the plan. As aides had feared, it had further contributed to King's plummeting popularity among whites. Whereas King had once appeared to many whites as a patriotic dissenter in whom they could take pride, after 1965 they considered him mainly a radical rabble-rouser or, worse, traitor. King was very discouraged and privately battled despair. "We're in terrible shape with the poor people's campaign," he confessed to one SCLC worker. "It just isn't working. People aren't responding."[44]

The federal government's reaction to the announced plan verged on hysteria. President Johnson publicly called on King not to hold the march, stating that lawlessness would not be tolerated and troops would be mobilized to deal with any mobs, adding emphatically, "Dr. King better believe that." The FBI was even more panicky about the revolutionary overtones of the planned Poor People's Campaign, regarding it as a Marxist plot to foment class hatred and insurrection that the Bureau had a patriotic duty to crush.[45]

By 1968 America's elite regarded King as a dangerous threat, although, considering his diminishing effectiveness, his opponents doubtlessly were overestimating him. But it was a threat they themselves had done much to create. In promoting King's program and leadership style to the center of national attention as a safe and responsible way of affecting unavoidable and acceptable change, they had stamped King with public legitimacy and approval that, once given, was not easy to retract. No matter what less acceptable changes he came to advocate, King retained ready access to the media and a residue of social and political influence. The Johnson administration, corporate America, and the right wing of organized labor, all of whom had earlier supported King, recognized the growing danger to their interests represented by King's leftward drift after 1965. Black Panthers and student revolutionaries were one thing, for the authorities clearly had the means to crush them. But when Martin Luther King began to provide charismatic leadership to a populistic crusade to challenge national power centers, elite fears of social revolution grew intense.

As King's jeremiad shifted from its earlier focus on political equality to structural economic change, it increasingly resembled the late socialist jeremiad of W. E. B. Du Bois. Domestically and internationally, the central problem facing America had become, for King as it had been for Du Bois, the gap between the rich and poor. Although King was not a Communist, his growing stress on class issues and peace as America's main challenges mirrored the substance of Du Bois's radical jeremiads from the later 1940s through 1963.[46] As King's civil religious prophecy grew to resemble that of Du Bois, King's treatment by the American establishment came to parallel that accorded Du Bois—with one major difference. King, who was still respectable and legitimate in many Americans' eyes, represented a far graver threat to the *status quo* than had the aging, isolated Du Bois.

No wonder, then, that by 1968, King could relate to Du Bois better than ever before. Amid feverish shuttling between the rural South, Washington, D.C., and a black garbagemen's strike in Memphis, King paused to deliver an address honoring the centennial of Du Bois's birth. King praised Du Bois for his indomitable courage in fighting inequality in an age when "there was far more justification for frustration and hopelessness" than now, "and yet his faith never wavered." King declared, "He confronted the establishment as a model of militant manhood and integrity," and he paid a high price. "He defied them and, though they heaped venom and scorn on him, his powerful voice was never stilled." He also noted that Du Bois "was a radical all his life." King sought "to remind white America of its debt to Dr. Du Bois" for "a gift of truth for which they should eternally be indebted to him." Instead, white Americans had persecuted and rejected him. Although Du Bois was internationally honored, King observed, "he was an exile . . . to the land of his birth," as was so often the prophet's fate. But "history cannot ignore W. E. B. Du Bois," King declared, for his spirit and legacy had not died: "He will be with us when we go to Washington in April when we demand our right to life, liberty and the pursuit of happiness."[47]

Events in 1967 and 1968 so deeply discouraged King that close friends worried about his state of mind.[48] His national influence was in steep decline, and his dream of creating a national moral and political consensus uniting blacks, labor, and white liberals seemed to have turned to ashes. President Johnson, whom in 1964–1965 King had imagined as leading this progressive coalition, had turned into a monster, railing against war protesters and black rioters and spending vast sums on destruction in Vietnam while America burned. And at the same time that King had lost much white support for challenging national economic patterns and foreign policy, he was spurned by many blacks for his presumed lack of courage and overwillingness to compromise with white authorities. He was caught and rendered ineffective in the raging riptide of national polarization.

## Faith and Despair in King's Final Jeremiad

Such facts haunted King and mocked his efforts to bring the nation to peaceful resolution of its terrible multiple crises. A dearth of positive response to the planned Poor People's March worried him, since he regarded this as a last-ditch effort to reach the country's conscience and save its soul. Despite his brave front, his deep private pessimism began seeping into his public statements.

As King saw diminishing evidence of redemptive action forthcoming from the nation, the jeremiadic threat of divine vengeance came out ever more forcefully in his rhetoric. "I seriously question the will and moral power of this nation to save itself," he confided to his wife. He called America more and more a desperately "sick society" whose disease was so advanced that it might prove fatal. "Truly America is much, much sicker than I realized when I began in 1955," he told a confidante.[49]

On March 31, 1968, at the Washington National Cathedral, the Rev. Dr. Martin Luther King, Jr., preached his last Sunday sermon. His text was from the book of Revelation concerning the end days: "Behold I make all things new, former things are passed away." A great revolution was sweeping through the world, he once again declared, and America, for its very soul and survival, had to stay awake and responsive to it. As ever, millennialist faith ultimately prevailed in King's rhetoric. He would "maintain hope" that America would respond favorably to this revolution and to the upcoming Poor People's Campaign and so "make America the truly great America that it is called to be." Finding confirmation in "the sacred heritage of our nation and the eternal will of God," he yet predicted America's redemption and the dawn of "a new day of justice and brotherhood."

In the longer middle sections of his sermon, however, King dwelt vividly on the very real possibility of America's eternal damnation. He told the parable of the rich man "who went to hell because he didn't see the poor" and proclaimed that "this can happen to America," too, if it did not act soon to "help bridge the gulf between the haves and the have-nots." America had the wealth and power to do so; "The real question is whether we have the will." He and many others would soon go to Washington, he announced, "to see if the will is still alive." "The judgment of God is upon us today . . . and something must be done quickly," he cried. "I pray God that America will hear this before it is too late."[50]

So he prayed, but what did he expect? Like Frederick Douglass after Reconstruction and Du Bois after the First World War, King no longer found temporal evidence pointing to America's imminent reformation. On the level of day-to-day experience, he no longer expected immediate progress; in the realm of prophecy, however, he kept faith in America's promise, and he continued to act in accordance with that faith.

Later that week, King was drawn into appearing in Memphis again to aid the sanitation workers' strike. There he gave his last mass address to the social movement he had led since 1955. He again dwelt at length on the rampant social immorality and sickness of the times. With visible emotion he struggled to deny the final reality of these trends. Only the coming day, he insisted, which God had allowed him to glimpse from the mountain top ("I've seen the promised land") was truly real, even though, he mused, it may not come soon and he might not be present when it did. The sermon that he was to deliver the following Sunday was entitled, "Why America May Go to Hell."[51]

King did not live to give that sermon nor to lead the Poor People's

March scheduled for the next week. Between speeches and marches at Memphis, King was shot and killed while on his hotel room balcony. King's last crusade to save America and promote social justice did not succeed, and his attempt to lead a civil religious revival and forge an enlarged consensus for reform died with him. Perhaps history was kind to allow him this exit. One of King's associates, Andrew Young, said, "Martin had done about all that he could. . . . He was being abused. . . . The burdens of this nation were weighing so heavily on him, God decided Martin had had enough."[52] One does not need Young's faith to conclude that King's attempt to lead America down the path he envisioned for it was on the verge of defeat, whether he had lived or not.[53] Sad experience had recently sobered him, giving him a chastened appreciation of the power of racism to delay social progress. Like Douglass and Du Bois before him, King ended his life as a disappointed, yet ultimately faithful, jeremiah, still pursuing and prophesying the final fulfillment of America's democratic promise.

# Conclusion: The Black Jeremiad and the Jackson Phenomenon

The Afro-American jeremiad has been a leading feature of black protest rhetoric and thought from before the Civil War though the modern civil rights era, but its success in achieving major reforms has not been constant. The Civil War and civil rights eras represent the twin peaks when issues of vital concern to Afro-Americans commanded national attention and redress. Voiced by Frederick Douglass between 1863 and 1872 and Martin Luther King, Jr., between 1956 and 1965, compelling moral appeals to Americans were instrumental in creating a favorable climate of opinion necessary for realizing substantial social, legal, and political reform. Douglass and King used the powerful ritual of the jeremiad to legitimate the goals which they sought, raise guilt among white Americans, and prod for social change.

Unique contemporary conditions significantly contributed to the temporary positive responses received by Douglass's and King's jeremiads. The Civil War and Second World War gave unprecedented impetus to anti-racist trends in the North, and perceptions of white Northern self-interest in both periods encouraged the use of national political power to force change in Southern racial practices.

Even these two great leaps forward, fostered by unusually propitious national and international conditions, had important limits. At its height, reform went only as far as guarantees of civil and legal equality and mainly affected the unique Southern caste system. When black jeremiahs expanded their agendas to include structural economic changes that would reconstruct the North, too, a reform consensus among blacks and white Northerners failed to materialize. Most whites, including many who had lent crucial support to the struggle against slavery and for blacks' legal rights, balked at subsequent proposals for economic change. Whereas black leaders like

Douglass, Du Bois, and King considered economic reforms necessary to give substance to the forms of democracy, most whites regarded such proposals as illegitimate invasions of personal property rights. Not only did impetus for reform halt at the wall of economic redistribution but, as changing conditions altered Northern whites' perception of their interests in relation to black aspirations, even previous gains in the civil and political sphere became vulnerable to encroachment or reversal. Frederick Douglass, W. E. B. Du Bois, and Martin Luther King, Jr., were all most successful stressing the need for civil rights and least effective in advocating basic economic change.

This record suggests that the Afro-American jeremiad is, paradoxically, both radical and conservative. In affirming normative American social beliefs, the jeremiad helps sustain the current order. Sacvan Bercovitch's thesis that the American jeremiad's primary function is to maintain social control points to its predominant conservatism. For Bercovitch, the American jeremiad offers a symbolic, formulaic analysis of contemporary society that precludes more radical analyses, and it defuses potentially disruptive social discontent by transferring it to the soothing realm of rhetorical ritual.[1] To the extent that major black intellectual and political figures have employed a rhetoric anchored in social consensus, they have had to keep their goals within its non-revolutionary bounds.

On the other hand, the jeremiad typically voiced by national black leaders seems consistently to have been more searching in its examination of American social faults and bolder in prescribing reform than its white counterparts. For example abolitionism, the first great American social cause championed by black jeremiahs such as Douglass, was initially considered a suspect radical cause violating norms of respectable behavior and opinion. Furthermore, after Douglass had helped forge a public consensus to end slavery, he pushed on in his jeremiads to demand sweeping racial political and legal equality and—when this seemed forthcoming—for opportunities for economic equality.

A similar pattern emerges in the careers of W. E. B. Du Bois and Martin Luther King, who labored to transform once radical causes such as racial desegregation into eminently respectable, moderate goals in the minds of most Americans. Yet at moments when the parameters of tolerable reform shift somewhat, prominent black jeremiahs have typically re-positioned themselves to champion new, more radical issues on the outer edge of the prevailing social-political consensus. Although black jeremiahs like Douglass, Du Bois, Bethune, and King made great contributions to American society in their times, it is significant that these leaders all eventually came to be considered too radical even by many whites who had formerly supported them.[2]

The tradition of the black jeremiad offers another telling example of how a non-dominant group's acceptance of the cultural norms and values of a dominant group is a double-edged phenomenon. Recently scholars have noted the internalization of the ideology of domesticity by most nineteenth-century American women and of slaveholders' paternalistic ideology by black slaves. The assumption by blacks' and women of cultural ideals and conventions promulgated by the powerful on the one hand placed important limits on these groups' militant resistance and efforts at autonomy; but on the other hand, these cultural norms provided an ideological shield behind which women and slaves steadily advanced their rights and freedom.[3] The black jeremiad may well reflect the influence of hegemonic ideology upon subordinate groups' public ideas and programs, but it also illustrates the shrewd and artful tendency of an oppressed group to refashion values taught by privileged classes—even as it accepts them—into ideological tools for its own ends. This probably accounts for the black jeremiad's most distinct and paradoxical trait. The black jeremiad always strives to speak to and within a changing American consensus and yet it is usually at the forward edge of that consensus, prodding it toward ever more thorough and inclusive social change.

Some scholars perceive a historic turn in this century among Afro-Americans away from loyal faith in America's mission toward a concentration on separate racial issues and identity. Leonard Sweet argues that, since the 1920s, more and more blacks have considered their black and American identities inimical and have decisively chosen exclusive racial over interracial social concerns and loyalties. Sweet sees Du Bois's post-war disillusionment with America's promise for blacks as generally symptomatic of twentieth-century black thinkers' growing alienation from the vision of America shared with whites. He contends that sharpening awareness among blacks of America's "hopeless contradictions between professions and practice" and between "myths and realities" has bred rising cynicism—not just about the nation's present state but about its very potential for improvement. Sweet does not, however, account for the upsurge of black hopes for America that was unleashed by the Second World War and brought to a peak in the civil rights movement. Wilson Moses' study of black messianism also notes the fading of Afro-American belief in America's mission, but he sees this diminution as a post-1960s phenomenon.[4]

Moses is correct in saying that widespread black disaffection from white America and its institutions followed in the wake of the early civil rights crusade. By the late 1960s, King was fighting a rising tide of black cynicism regarding the chances for progress through cooperation with whites, and the end of the sixties saw another popular resurgence of black nationalism and racial separatism. But Moses' thesis, like that of Sweet, is contradicted by evidence of a strong subsequent revival of black millennial hopes for America.

## Jackson: National Black Jeremiah of the Seventies and Eighties

If black faith in America can be measured by the vitality of the black jeremiad tradition, the rhetoric and public activities of the Rev. Jesse Jackson in the 1970s and 1980s seem to indicate that such faith is still flourishing.

Jesse Louis Jackson joined the civil rights movement as a student in 1963 when he arrived at Greensboro, North Carolina, to take part in the sit-ins. He quickly became a local leader in the Congress of Racial Equality, one of the main direct action groups. Next, he attended Chicago Theological Seminary while deepening his ties to civil rights organizations. When King's SCLC launched its Chicago crusade in 1966, Jackson became an important local staff member. In 1967, he was appointed head of Operation Breadbasket, the economic arm of SCLC's Chicago program. Through strategic use of boycotts, publicity, and negotiation, Operation Breadbasket aimed to gain more jobs and economic opportunities for blacks and more equitable relations between blacks and the business community. After King's assassination, Jackson, adroit in self-promotion, converted Breadbasket into his own organizational base, People United to Serve Humanity (PUSH). In the early 1970s, PUSH organized black consumers and negotiated "covenants" with dairy, beverage, food, and other corporations. The purpose of these covenants was to create more economic opportunities for blacks, including jobs, management positions, shelf space for black products, and use of black banks. PUSH grew into a multi-faceted national organization active in a wide range of civil rights and social issues. After the mid-1970s, Jackson gained much publicity by crusading in American schools for study, discipline, and achievement and against promiscuity, drug use, and failure. Jackson's interests, while remaining broad, turned increasingly political in the 1980s. PUSH organized major voter registration drives and, most dramatically, Jackson mounted in the 1984 and 1988 races for the Democratic presidential nomination the first credible presidential campaign by a nonwhite in American history.[5]

In his ambitious efforts over the last two decades to lead social-political reform and attract mass followings among blacks and whites, Jackson has repeatedly used still-vibrant themes of American messianism and millennialism in formulating his own national jeremiad. Jackson, as reformer-jeremiah, unceasingly criticizes present social immorality and declension, urges repentance and reform, and promises that victory and salvation will follow as the result of Americans' right actions.

A staple of Jackson's public statements since the sixties has been an expression of keen displeasure over the nation's "present state of spiritual decadence and despair." In 1980, for example, he deplored "the conclusion of a decade of moral decadence." In 1985, he said, "Today we have a crisis in America. We are a nation adrift. Our spiritual power and the power of our people are in jeopardy." "America is on a collision course" with disaster, and a national shift in direction is imperative.[6]

Jackson believes that during the 1970s America began to drift away from the social progress and gains in justice of the civil rights movement. For him, this downward turn in America's democratic destiny was accelerated by Ronald Reagan's election to the presidency in 1980. In his 1984 presidential bid, Jackson crisscrossed the country proclaiming that there was "agony" and "darkness across the land" because of Reaganomics. America's worst sin in the eighties was its waning commitment to civil rights and equality. The "Regan Revolution" opposed and tried to roll back every major advance made by disadvantaged groups in the last two decades; its policies, Jackson declared, "must be seen as a reversal of all past White House and congressional actions."[7]

Economically, federal policies in the early eighties lopsidedly benefited powerful corporations and the rich at the expense of lower- and middle-class Americans, Jackson contended. He accused Reagan of "taking from the poor and giving to the rich" in a "reverse Robin Hood process," swelling the numbers of impoverished Americans. He castigated the Reagan administration as "pro-rich, pro-aristocratic, pro-agribusiness, pro-military, and pro-big business" and, conversely, as anti-poor, anti-minorities, anti-women, anti-consumer, and anti-environment. Greedy, irresponsible corporations committed economic violence against American workers in the 1980s. Internationally, the government had adopted a course of "manifest destiny, military adventurism, gun-boat and big-stick diplomacy." In South Africa, Central America, and elsewhere, the United States was aligning with forces of tyranny and oppression against popular democratic movements. America's conduct in the early eighties, he warned, would lead to a dangerous world of greater tensions, conflict, and war.[8]

Americans, argued Jackson, must therefore reexamine "every aspect of United States foreign and domestic policy that has favored . . . the few over the many." "As a nation, we must change direction," since "our very lives are at stake."[9]

Gravely concerned by society's current condition, Jackson is nevertheless optimistic as America approaches "a crossroad" between "danger and opportunity." "If we make certain decisions, we will face a decade of greater danger. If we choose other options, the 1980s can be a decade of greater opportunities," Jackson declared. "I still believe the country can be saved" *if* it seeks "new values and new vision."[10]

Jackson's grand political goal is to bring together an interracial "Rainbow Coalition" composed, foremost, of those he habitually calls by names such as "the disinherited," "the rejected," and "the despised." This populist movement should include minorities, lower-income groups, women, gays, workers, farmers, and all those suffering from social discrimination and economic dislocation. Next, his strategy requires that these groups unite with all Americans seeking progressive social and political change and, finally, with the middle class. The poor and the middle class, while often antagonistic, really have more common interests than not, and the national interest, he proclaims, would be served by building a coalition from "the bottom up," extending into the middle class.[11]

Beyond advocating its constituents' interests, this alliance is called to save the nation, redeem the national mission, and build a new and better America. His movement, says Jackson, heeds "the call of this nation's highest and noblest principles that we might fulfill our mission . . . and be the source of hope for people yearning to be free everywhere." America has a mission, Jackson believes, and he works assiduously to define it for the nation and to stir people to action. Addressing the 1984 Democratic National Convention, he stated that, although Americans were not perfect, they were "called to a perfect mission: to feed the hungry, to clothe the naked, to house the homeless, to teach the illiterate, to provide jobs for the jobless, and to choose the human race over the nuclear race." The task of the Rainbow Coalition, he declares, is to "inspire our party and the nation to fulfill this mission" and enable America to "fulfill the promise of democracy."[12]

Although Jackson addresses missionary language to the nation at large, his core constituency is among Afro-Americans and he aims much nationalistic messianic rhetoric directly at them. He constantly invokes racial pride and mission to bolster black self-esteem and to encourage self-help, reform, and resistance to injustice. "We're not slaves brought here to serve white folks," he reminds black audiences, "We're God's children sent here to save the human race." "Hold your heads high" and never "give up," he exhorts them, for "God didn't bring us this far to leave us." "God has a purpose for us!" He sometimes states that Afro-Americans' distinct place in society makes them a "nation within a nation."[13]

Jackson's racial nationalism, though, always complements and never contravenes his American nationalism. He posits an entwined millennial destiny for white and black America. Blacks cannot proceed alone, socially or politically, he preaches, "for until white America is what it ought to be, black America cannot be what it ought to be." In championing a black agenda, he asserts that "what is good for black Americans is good for *all* Americans." Blacks, because they are "in the front and bearing the brunt of social and economic deterioration and in the rear of social and economic development," are "a weathervane for this society," signaling the direction of the whole nation. Racial justice, moreover, is a vital precondition for every kind of social justice. "Race is still the number-one unfinished task of this democracy," he declares, since it connects so many social problems and hinders all progressive change. Overcom-

ing racism is the key to unlocking America's mission: "The resolution of the race question in this country would liberate us to liberate
others around the world."[14]

Including more than blacks, Jackson's proclaimed constituency
embraces the poor, the rejected, and disinherited of whatever race.
He finds social messianic potential in this group, moreover, precisely
because of its history of unmerited suffering and unjust social treatment. The disadvantaged have a special role to play in remaking
society. He holds "that the vision to save the nation will not come
from the palace" but from "the stable" and that "the rejected stones
will form the cornerstone" of a more democratic public policy. It is
instructive that he customarily uses biblical metaphors to describe
the redemptive traits of blacks and the poor. It is a Jackson article of
faith that "unearned suffering is redemptive," as quintessentially
revealed in the humble circumstances and suffering of the messiah.
"Jesus was rejected . . . and born in the slum," Jackson notes, like
himself and the core of his followers.[15]

The final end of a progressive alliance of rejected people spear-
heading a crusade for social change, according to Jackson, is to
deliver America from its dangerous current shortcomings and to
build, first, a more democratic America, and eventually, a better
world. He and his supporters are taking on "the burdens and re-
sponsibilities of helping to create a new national and world order."
"Ultimately," Jackson declares, "our struggle is a struggle to change
the character of our nation and thus to enable us to be leaders and
servants in the world."[16]

Jackson clearly delivers a jeremiad, at once critical of and faithful
to America. The specific jeremiad that he delivers bears a close
resemblance to that of Martin Luther King, Jr., especially in King's
final radical days. Jackson himself has repeatedly (and controver-
sially) portrayed himself as the sole, direct inheritor of King's charismatic leadership and mission. In much substance, Jackson's crusade
does in fact pick up approximately where King's agenda ended.
While still trying to expand minority rights and diminish white
racism, for example, Jackson resolutely insists, as did King, on tying
the black cause to interracial political reform, based on shared
economic interests with poorer Americans. He holds that the main
arena for social action has moved beyond civil rights to economic
rights, to what he calls "silver" rather than civil rights.[17] Transcending the need for specific policy changes is America's need to find new

values, to undergo what King called a "revolution of values." Only through such an inner moral transformation would the nation become firmly committed and dedicated to eradicating poverty and distributing material benefits more equitably at home and abroad.

The Rainbow Coalition must be more than just political; it must be prophetic and a national moral and spiritual crusade. King, the prophet, initiated this movement, Jackson states, and left America with "a charge" and "a promise." King charged Americans to care for the weak, to fight discrimination and deprivation, and "to shake the foundations and reshape the priorities" of the nation. His promise to those who accepted this task was, "you'll get there one day"; that "if you hold on and hold out, joy is coming"; and that there is "a new city whose builder and maker is God." King, according to Jackson, reminded Americans of God's promise that "if my people, who are called by my name, will . . . pray and seek my face, then . . . I'll give back your land."[18]

## Present and Future
## for the Black Jeremiad

During the great upswing of millennialist hope among black Americans between 1954 and 1965, there were major breakthroughs to fuel the black faith in America. But Jackson's jeremiad and reform program seem more related to King's unsuccessful crusade after 1966 than to his spectacularly productive earlier career. The events of the later sixties deeply discouraged King and other blacks despite the recent significant gains made partly by moral appeal to whites. How much more quickly may blacks' faith in white commitment to democracy wane when black jeremiahs cannot produce tangible results to justify continued participation in the American civic faith?[19]

If, as many cultural historians fear, blacks no longer believe their fellow Americans to be responsive to forms of moral suasion such as the American jeremiad, this loss of faith marks a major historic change in black cultural traditions with ominous implications for American race relations. In this regard, it seems significant that Douglass, Du Bois, Bethune, and King were most optimistic about their country when white Americans showed concern over the quality of their political democracy. Washington, on the other hand, seems to have reacted to a situation in which white society showed more concern for private interests in the marketplace than for a virtuous democracy. It may be that today's white public is as absorbed with private economic gain and hostile to non-white demands for public justice as in Washington's day. Whites' antagonistic response to King's final crusade and, arguably, to Jackson's calls for political reform may signal to blacks the selfish indifference of whites to the plight of the nation's burgeoning non-white population and the colored global majority. Robert Bellah, a leading scholar of American civil religion, believes that the tradition of a democratic public interest has been gradually weakening while the tradition glorifying private self-interest has been gaining strength.[20] If this trend continues, it may be more difficult for future black leaders to believe that they can appeal to the conscience of white America.

It is always tempting to view the national present as unhealthy and to despair for the future, given Americans' cultural tendency to see the present as a declension from a more heroic past. As the subjects of this book indicate, however, there is nothing new about America's failure to deal forthrightly with the challenges of racism and social justice or about the betrayal of frequently soaring Afro-American patriotic expectations. High hope is a necessary condition for grievous disappointment. Afro-American hope for America has often run low but eventually has welled up to burst forth again. Scholars have erred in interpreting the phenomenon of black disappointment in America as a one-time event of the 1920s, late 1960s, or whenever; it seems more accurate to regard the ebb and flow of black hopes for America as a recurrent historical pattern—at least, until now. If the past is the best guide to the future and the Jackson phenomenon indicative at all of contemporary black attitudes, then it is premature to forecast the demise of the black American jeremiad and of the resilient hope on which it rests.

# Notes

## Introduction

1. Martin Luther King, Jr., address to the March on Washington, 1963, *Southern Christian Leadership Conference Newsletter* 1 (Sept. 1963): 5–8.

2. The conventional name for Americans of African descent historically has been subject to change. Most recent is the trend toward adopting "African-American," although it is unclear whether a firm consensus for it has emerged. In this study, I have used mainly two identifications, "Afro-American" and "black," since Afro-American is but a shortened form of African-American and black is still the most common colloquial term.

3. America's symbolic meaning to early modern Europeans is well discussed in Charles L. Sanford, *The Quest for Paradise: Europe and the American Moral Imagination* (Urbana: Univ. of Illinois Press, 1961).

4. John Winthrop, "A Modell of Christian Charity," in *Puritan Political Ideas, 1558–1794*, ed. Edmund S. Morgan (Indianapolis: Bobbs-Merrill, 1965), 90–91; Thomas Paine, "Common Sense," in *The Writings of Thomas Paine*, ed. Moncure Conway (New York: Burt Franklin, 1902; reprint 1969), 1:118–19; Thomas Jefferson, first inaugural address, in *God's New Israel: Religious Interpretations of American Destiny*, ed. Conrad Cherry (Englewood Cliffs, N.J.: Prentice-Hall, 1971), 107.

5. Ronald Reagan, 1980 presidential debate with John Anderson, New York *Times*, 22 Sept. 1980, B7; Reagan's speech accepting the Republican nomination, New York *Times*, 18 July 1980, A8; State of the Union address, 26 January 1982, *Public Papers of the President of the United States, Ronald Reagan, 1982* (Washington, D.C.: Office of the Federal Register, National Archives and Records, General Services Administration, 1982), 72. These speeches contain many samples of the civil religious imagery recurrent in Reagan's rhetoric.

6. The term "civil religion" became common scholarly coin with publication of Robert Bellah's seminal article, "Civil Religion in America," *Daedalus* 96 (Winter 1967): 1–21. The best collection of interdisciplinary essays on the topic is *American Civil Religion*, ed. E. Richey and Donald G. Jones (New York: Harper & Row, 1974).

7. Ernest L. Tuveson's *Redeemer Nation: The Idea of America's Mil-*

*lennial Role* (Chicago: Univ. of Chicago Press, 1968) is among the better studies tracing the development of American millennial identity.

8. Perry Miller, *The New England Mind: The Seventeenth Century* (New York: Macmillan, 1939), first drew serious attention to the phenomenon of the American jeremiad. Recent notable scholarship which continues to examine the importance of the jeremiad tradition in the national culture includes Sacvan Bercovitch, *The American Jeremiad* (Madison: Univ. of Wisconsin Press, 1978); David W. Noble, *The End of American History: Democracy, Capitalism and the Metaphor of Two Worlds in Anglo-American Historical Writing, 1880–1980* (Minneapolis: Univ. of Minnesota Press, 1985); and James Moorhead, *American Apocalypse: Yankee Protestants and the Civil War, 1860–1869* (New Haven: Yale Univ. Press, 1978).

9. John Winthrop, "A Modell of Christian Charity," in Morgan, *Puritan Political Ideas*, 90–91. Bercovitch points out that the jeremiad tradition was begun by Winthrop even before the colonists had disembarked from their ships at Plymouth Bay; see *American Jeremiad*, 3–6.

10. Bercovitch, *American Jeremiad*, 6–7.

11. Bercovitch notes "the persistence of the Puritan jeremiad throughout the eighteenth and nineteenth centuries, in all forms of the literature, including the literature of westward expansion," *American Jeremiad*, 10–11. He also suggests its influence over American novelists in the nineteenth and twentieth centuries, ch. 6.

12. Martin Marty, Foreword, in Catherine Albanese, *Sons of the Fathers: The Civil Religion of the American Revolution* (Philadelphia: Temple Univ. Press, 1976), ix–x.

13. See note 12, above.

14. The classic work on the influence of radical English "Real Whig" political ideology on Revolutionary political thought is Bernard Bailyn, *The Ideological Origins of the American Revolution* (Cambridge: Harvard Univ. Press, 1967).

15. American colonists' use—and transformation—during the Revolution of a sacred past derived from England is the theme of Albanese's book. Late colonial Anglo-American identification with the myth of a free Anglo-Saxon past is also well treated in Reginald Horsman, *Race and Manifest Destiny: The Origins of American Racial Anglo-Saxonism* (Cambridge: Harvard Univ. Press, 1981); see especially ch. 2, "Liberty and the Anglo-Saxons."

16. I follow Catherine Albanese in using the patriarchal terminology and symbolism that characterized colonial and early national public language.

17. Albanese, *Sons of the Fathers*, 6, 9.

18. George B. Forgie contends that Lincoln and his political contemporaries felt dwarfed by the Founding Fathers, were jealous of their predecessors' opportunities for achieving immortality, and discouraged over their own poor prospects for greatness in *Patricide in the House Divided: A Psychological Interpretation of Lincoln and His Age* (New York: Norton, 1979), especially ch. 1, "The Founding Heroes and the Post-Heroic Generation."

19. Albanese, *Sons of the Fathers*, 15. Leonard I. Sweet has written on Afro-Americans' positive view of the mythology of America and their own role in it in *Black Images of America, 1784–1870* (New York: Norton, 1976). Sweet's excellent study, unfortunately, treats only the nineteenth century.

20. Leading studies of abolitionism include: Merton Dillon, *Crusade Against Slavery: Friends, Foes, and Reforms, 1820–1860* (Algonac, Mich.: Reference Publications, 1986); Louis Filler, *The Crusade against Slavery* (New York: Harper, 1960); and Betty Fladeland, *Men and Brothers: Anglo-American Antislavery Cooperation* (Urbana: Univ. of Illinois Press, 1972). Herbert Aptheker, *Abolitionism: A Revolutionary Movement* (Boston: Twayne Publishers, 1989), will likely have an impact on the field. The pioneering work on widespread slave resistance and rebellion was Aptheker, *American Negro Slave Revolts* (New York: Columbia Univ. Press, 1943; reprint, New York: International Publishers, 1969). For investigations of the complex forms and degrees of resistance, see John Blassingame, *The Slave Community* (New York: Oxford Univ. Press, 1972); Eugene Genovese, *Roll, Jordan, Roll* (New York: Pantheon, 1974); and Gerald Mullin, *Flight and Rebellion* (New York: Oxford Univ. Press, 1972).

21. Wilson Jeremiah Moses, *Black Messiahs and Uncle Toms: Social and Literary Manipulations of a Religious Myth* (University Park: Pennsylvania State Univ. Press, 1982), 30–31.

22. The Exodus metaphor is well described along with other key motifs of Afro-American slave Christianity in Lawrence Levine, *Black Culture and Black Consciousness: Afro-American Folk Thought from Slavery to Freedom* (New York: Oxford Univ. Press, 1977), and Albert J. Rabiteau, *The "Invisible Institution" in the Antebellum South* (New York: Oxford Univ. Press, 1978). The concept of black messianism is capably introduced by Moses in *Black Messiahs and Uncle Toms*, ch. 1. Moses suggests the significance of historic suffering and oppression in black millennialist traditions especially in relation to the biblical "suffering servant" theme associated with the messiah in Isaiah. Leonard Sweet writes on Afro-Americans' understanding of slavery as part of God's providential redemptive design in *Black Images of America*, ch. 5.

23. Thomas Jefferson, *Notes on the State of Virginia* (New York:

Harper & Row, 1964; reprinted from *The Writings of Thomas Jefferson,*
ed. H. A. Washington (New York: 1861), 8:156.

24. David Walker and Henry Garnet, *Walker's Appeal and Garnet's
Address to the Slaves of the United States* (New York: Arno Press, 1969;
first published, New York: J. H. Tobit, 1848), 1, 19. My discussion of
Walker here is indebted to Wilson Moses' discussion of the jeremiadic
quality of Walker's rhetoric. Charles V. Willie has argued that most great
racial liberation leaders were from the most privileged sectors of the oppressed society and were among those members of their race most thoroughly educated and acculturated in the norms of the dominant culture. See
"A Theory of Liberation Leadership," *Journal of Negro History* 68 (Winter
1983); 1–7.

25. W. E. B. Du Bois, *The Souls of Black Folk* (A. C. McClurg, 1903),
17.

26. For useful introductions to Garvey and Garveyism, see Robert A.
Hill, *Marcus Garvey* (Berkeley: Univ. of California Press, 1987), and Tony
Martin, *Race First: The Ideological and Organizational Struggles of Marcus
Garvey and the U.N.I.A.* (Westport, Conn.: Greenwood Press, 1976). For
an excellent analysis of Garveyism as a civil religion and of Garvey's consid-
erable theological creativity, see Randal Burkett, *Garveyism as a Religious
Movement: The Institutionalization of a Black Civil Religion* (Metuchen,
N.J.: Scarecrow Press and American Theological Library Association,
1978), and Roderick McLean, *The Theology of Marcus Garvey* (Washington, D.C.: Univ. Press of America, 1982).

27. A good although hostile study of the Black Muslim cult is C. Eric
Lincoln, *The Black Muslims in America* (Boston: Beacon Press, 1963). An
excellent, more sympathetic scholarly treatment is E. U. Essien-Udom,
*Black Nationalism: A Search for Identity in America* (Chicago: Univ. of
Chicago Press, 1962).

28. *The Autobiography of Malcolm X,* with Alex Haley (New York:
Grove Press, 1964), is indispensable for understanding Malcolm's ideas and
activities. Published editions of his speeches and public statements include
Malcolm (Little) X, *By Any Means Necessary,* ed. George Breitman (New
York: Pathfinder Press, 1970), and *The End of White World Supremacy,* ed.
Benjamin Goodman (New York: Merlin House, 1971).

29. An excellent example of Malcolm's nearly-but-not-quite jeremiadic
rhetoric toward white Americans is the speech "God's Judgment of White
America" printed in *The End of White World Supremacy,* 121–48.

30. While highly respecting his work on black messianism, I sharply
disagree with Wilson Moses' characterization of the period in which the
black jeremiad flourished. Moses considers the black jeremiad "mainly a
pre–Civil War phenomenon" exclusively associated with abolitionism
(*Black Messiahs and Uncle Toms,* 31). This view slights the continued

presence of the tradition into the twentieth century as a key tool for protesting all forms of American racial injustice.

## Chapter 1

1. Benjamin Quarles, *Frederick Douglass* (Washington, D.C.: Associated Publishers, 1948), remains the best scholarly biography of Douglass. A more recent intellectual biography is Waldo E. Martin, *The Mind of Frederick Douglass* (Chapel Hill: Univ. of North Carolina Press, 1984). Dickson J. Preston, *Young Frederick Douglass: The Maryland Years* (Baltimore: Johns Hopkins Univ. Press, 1980), offers valuable insights into Douglass's formative years. There is uncertainty about the date of Douglass's birth, although sometime in 1817 seems most probable.

2. Frederick Douglass, *Life and Times of Frederick Douglass: Written by Himself* (New York: n.p., 1892; reprint, n.p., 1962), 78–79.

3. Gerald Mullin, *Flight and Rebellion: Slave Resistance in the Eighteenth Century* (New York: Oxford Univ. Press, 1972).

4. Douglass, *Life and Times*, 213–14.

5. Douglass, *Narrative of the Life of Frederick Douglass, an American Slave: Written by Himself* (Boston: Anti-Slavery Office, 1845).

6. Douglass, "The War with Mexico," *The North Star*, 21 Jan. 1848.

7. Douglass, "The Dred Scott Decision," quoted in *The Life and Writings of Frederick Douglass*, ed. Philip S. Foner, 4 vols. (New York: International Publishers, 1950–1954) 2:407–12. For many years Foner's has been the standard published edition of Douglass's speeches and papers. This set is currently being supplanted, however, by *The Frederick Douglass Papers*, ed. John W. Blassingame (New Haven: Yale Univ. Press, 1979). As few volumes in the Blassingame edition are yet out, I will usually quote from Foner, except when the material appears only in Blassingame.

8. The introduction to Series One in *The Frederick Douglass Papers*, ed. Blassingame (hereafter cited as *FD Papers*) contains a valuable description and discussion of Douglass's oratorical style and method, especially 1:xxii–lv.

9. Douglass, *Frederick Douglass' Paper*, 30 July 1852, in *FD Papers* 1:xlv.

10. Douglass, "Self-Elevation—Rev. S. R. Ward," *Frederick Douglass' Paper*, 13 April 1855, in Foner, ed., *Life and Writings* 2:360. While Douglass's rhetoric definitely had nationalistic aspects, his black nationalism was not invidious toward nonblacks and never vitiated his broad universal concern for human liberty and progress. He considered ending his people's own acute oppression complementary and, indeed, prerequisite to establishing general social justice. On Douglass's fundamental adherence to middle-class values and social ideals, see Martin, *Mind of Frederick Douglass*, 81–82.

11. Douglass, "Colored People Demand Respect," Rochester, New York, 13 March 1845, in *FD Papers* 2:113; "Work and Self-Elevation," *Frederick Douglass' Paper,* 5 May 1854.

12. Douglass, "West India Emancipation Speech," 1 Aug. 1880, quoted in Martin, *Mind of Frederick Douglass,* 134; "The Future of the Colored Race," in Foner, ed., *Life and Writings* 4:195.

13. Douglass, "Self-Help: An Address Delivered in New York, New York, 7 May 1849, as reported by the New York *Herald,* 8 May 1849," in *FD Papers* 2:168–70.

14. Douglass, "A Letter to the American Slaves from those who have fled from American Slavery," *North Star,* 5 Sept. 1850.

15. Douglass, "A Nation in the Midst of a Nation," address delivered in New York, New York, 11 May 1853, in *FD Papers* 2:424–27.

16. Douglass, "Prejudice and Opportunity," *Frederick Douglass' Paper,* 12 Aug. 1853; in *FD Papers* 2:449. See note 10 above on the basic compatibility of his goals of racial liberation and social justice for all.

17. Douglass, "The Nation's Problem," 16 April 1889, in *Negro Social and Political Thought, 1850–1920,* ed. Howard Brotz (New York: Basic Books, 1966), 318–19.

18. Douglass defended historical African civilization and culture in combating racist theories of white superiority and black inferiority. See below and Waldo Martin's discussion of Douglass's views on Africa in *Mind of Frederick Douglass,* 202–13.

19. Douglass, "Why Is the Negro Lynched?" in Foner, ed., *Life and Writings* 4:513; "A Nation in the Midst of a Nation," in *FD Papers* 2:438. "The Destiny of Colored Americans," *North Star,* 16 Nov. 1849, is another valuable text on this subject.

20. Reginald Horsman, *Race and Manifest Destiny: The Origins of Racial Anglo-Saxonism* (Cambridge: Harvard Univ. Press, 1981).

21. George Fredrickson, *The Black Image in the White Mind: The Debate on Afro-American Character and Destiny, 1817–1914* (New York: Harper & Row, 1971; Torchbook ed., 1972), 98.

22. Samuel George Morton, *Crania Americana; or, A Comparative View of the Skulls of Various Aboriginal Nations of North and South America to Which Is Prefixed an Essay on the Varieties of the Human Species* (Philadelphia, 1839). Fredrickson, *Black Image in the White Mind,* ch. 3, gives a useful explication of Morton's views and of the American school of ethnology. A more recent treatment of the subject is found in Horsman, *Race and Manifest Destiny,* ch. 7.

23. Frederick Douglass, "The Proclamation and a Negro Army," *Douglass' Monthly* (hereafter *DM*), March 1863. Like most of Douglass's important statements, this one was originally delivered as a speech and subsequently printed in his newspaper.

24. Douglass, "The Color Line," 1881, in Foner, ed., *Life and Writings* 4:342–43, 350.

25. Douglass, "The Claims of the Negro Ethnologically Considered," in Foner, ed., *Life and Writings* 2:308, 291, 295–96.

26. Douglass, "The Future of the Colored Race," in Foner, ed., *Life and Writings* 4:195.

27. Douglass, "We Ask Only for Our Rights," an address delivered in Troy, N.Y., 4 Sept. 1855, quoted in *FD Papers* 3:94–95.

28. Martin, *Mind of Frederick Douglass*, 199.

29. See, for example, Douglass, "Condition of the Country," *DM*, Feb. 1863.

30. Douglass, "Colored Men's Rights," an address delivered in New York City, 14 May 1857, in *FD Papers* 3:146; "The Color Line," 1881, in Foner, ed., *Life and Writings* 4:343; "Citizenship and the Spirit of Caste," *Frederick Douglass' Paper*, 21 May 1858; "Colored Men's Rights," in *FD Papers* 3:146.

31. Douglass, "Claims of the Negro Ethnologically Considered," in Foner, ed., *Life and Writings* 2:306; "The Prospect in the Future," *DM*, Aug. 1860.

32. Douglass, "The Color Line," 1881, in Foner, ed., *Life and Writings* 4:351–52. Waldo Martin notes with chagrin Douglass's "blindness . . . to European antiblack prejudice," calling it "shortsighted and wrongheaded" in *Mind of Frederick Douglass*, 115. In an article blasting Northern white Free Soilism for its attitude of contempt toward blacks, Douglass could still point to England as an example of total freedom from racial prejudice. See Douglass, "The Unholy Alliance of Negro Hate and Anti-Slavery," *Frederick Douglass' Paper*, 5 April 1856, and "The Color Line," 1881, in Foner, ed., *Life and Writings* 4:346–47.

33. A good example among many of Douglass's jeremiads declaring Northern guilt for the national crime of slavery is his "The Blood of the Slave on the Skirts of the Northern People," *North Star*, 17 Nov. 1848, in Foner, ed., *Life and Writings* 1:343–47.

34. On conditions of blacks in the antebellum North, see Leon Litwack, *North of Slavery: The Negro in the Free States, 1790–1860* (Chicago: Univ. of Chicago Press, 1961), and August Meier and Elliott Rudwick, *From Plantation to Ghetto*, 3d ed. (New York: Hill & Wang, 1976), ch. 3.

## Chapter 2

1. David W. Blight has written about the spiritual meaning that Douglass saw in the war in "Frederick Douglass and the American Apocalypse," *Civil War History* 31 (no. 4, 1985): 309–28, and in *Frederick Douglass'*

*Civil War: Keeping Faith in Jubilee* (Baton Rouge: Louisiana State Univ. Press, 1989).

2. This is William W. Freehling's conclusion, e.g., in "The Founding Fathers and Slavery," *The American Historical Review* 77 (Feb. 1972), reprinted in *American Negro Slavery: A Modern Reader,* ed. Allen Weinstein et al. (New York: Oxford Univ. Press, 1979), 3–19, especially 9, 14.

3. The Constitution, David B. Davis concludes, was "open-ended" regarding slavery because it embodied a national compromise in which "both sections had agreed to defer the question to the future"; both slavery's critics and supporters seemed to think that time was on their side. See Davis, "The Constitution and the Slave Trade," in *The Problem of Slavery in the Age of Revolution* (Ithaca, N.Y.: Cornell Univ. Press, 1975), reprinted in *American Negro Slavery,* 28–29.

4. Garrison, quoted in James B. Stewart, *Holy Warriors: The Abolitionists and American Slavery* (New York: Hill & Wang, 1976), 98–99; Garrison, "No Union with Slaveholders," *The Liberator,* 31 May 1844.

5. George Fredrickson borrowed the concept from the sociologist Pierre L. van den Berghe, *Race and Racism: A Comparative Perspective* (New York: John Wiley & Sons, 1967), 17–18, and applied it very effectively to his study of white antebellum racial thought in *The Black Image in the White Mind: The Debate on Afro-American Character and Destiny, 1817–1914* (New York: Harper & Row, 1971), 61–70.

6. J. C. Calhoun, quoted in Richard Hofstadter, *The American Political Tradition and the Men Who Made It* (New York: Knopf, 1948; reprint New York: Vintage Books/Random House, n.d.), 80. Hofstadter's provocative essay, asserting the social-political sophistication of pro-slavery thought, shares important themes with Fredrickson's analysis of Southern "Herrenvolk" democracy and egalitarianism.

7. Increased contacts through such forums as the National Negro Convention movement with black leaders, many of whom advocated black political struggle and some of whom, like Henry Garnet, asserted the just necessity of slave rebellion, led Douglass to alter his exclusive reliance on moral suasion. See Martin, *Mind of Frederick Douglass,* 56–58.

8. Douglass, *North Star,* 16 June 1848.

9. See David B. Davis, *The Slave Power Conspiracy and the Paranoid Style* (Baton Rouge: Louisiana State Univ. Press, 1969), on this belief held by many antebellum Northerners. On the antebellum Republican Party's beliefs see Eric C. Foner, *Free Soil, Free Labor, Free Men: The Ideology of the Republican Party before the Civil War* (New York: Oxford Univ. Press, 1970). Antebellum white Northern prejudice and caste practices toward blacks are well documented in Leon Litwack, *North of Slavery: The Negro in the Free States, 1790–1860* (Chicago: Univ. of Chicago Press, 1961).

10. See discussion of Douglass's evolving interpretation of the Constitu-

tion's pro- or anti-slavery leanings in Waldo Martin, *Mind of Frederick Douglass*, 36–38, and in *Life and Writings of Frederick Douglass*, ed. Philip Foner, 2:51–54.

11. So far did Lincoln avoid threatening slavery early on that he directed that all slaves fleeing to Union armies be returned to their masters. When two field generals balked at returning valuable laborers that the enemy could use against Union forces and declared all slaves reaching their lines free, Lincoln publicly countermanded their declarations. See August Meier and Elliott Rudwick, *From Plantation to Ghetto*, 3d. ed. (New York: Hill & Wang, 1976), for details.

12. Douglass, "How to End the War," *DM*, May 1861.

13. Douglass to Samuel May, 30 Aug. 1861, in Foner, ed., *Life and Writings* 3:159; "Signs of the Times," editorial column in response to letter from S. Dutton, 14 Oct. 1861, *DM*, Nov. 1861. See also Blight's discussion in "Frederick Douglass and the American Apocalypse," 315–18.

14. Douglass, "The Union and How to Save It," *DM*, Feb. 1861.

15. Bercovitch, *American Jeremiad*, 198.

16. Douglass, "The Reasons for Our Troubles," *DM*, Feb. 1862; "The Decision of the Hour," July 1861; "The Union and How to Save It," Feb. 1861; "The Slaveholders' Rebellion," Aug. 1862.

17. For a useful overview of practical considerations affecting the decision for emancipation, see David H. Donald, *Liberty and Union* (Lexington, Mass.: D. C. Heath, 1978), 144–53.

18. A marked upswing in newspaper editorials and visiting delegations to the White House urging emancipation as well as Congressional action to legalize military confiscation of slave "contrabands" working in Southern war efforts were evidence of a significant shift in Northern sentiment in favor of conditional abolition and military enlistment of blacks. See, e.g., discussion in Meier and Rudwick, *From Plantation to Ghetto*, 157–58.

19. Douglass, "January First, 1863," *DM*, Jan. 1863; "The Proclamation and a Negro Army," March 1863.

20. Douglass, "The Proclamation and a Negro Army." It is revealing that Douglass so excitedly compared the Emancipation event to the nation's revolutionary founding. His attitude toward the former parallels Catherine Albanese's description of the thrilling, religious feeling experienced by the patriots in her *Sons of the Fathers*. Each generation believed it had entered a creative time outside of ordinary history, felt connected to the past heroic acts of their fathers, and believed their own present creative acts both faithfully reflected and imitated their inherited tradition of liberty as well as broke new ground in advancing freedom. See the explication of this American cultural phenomenon in Chapter 1, above.

21. Douglass, *North Star*, 3 Dec. 1847.

22. I hope to counter the misleading view of Wilson Moses regarding the

longevity of the black jeremiad expressed in *Black Messiahs and Uncle Toms,* 31. See Introduction, note 30.

23. Douglass, Speech at the 32nd Annual Convention of the American Anti-Slavery Society, *The Liberator,* 26 May 1865; "The Mission of the War," New York *Tribune,* 14 Jan. 1864.

24. Douglass, "The Mission of the War," New York *Tribune,* 14 Jan. 1864; "Reconstruction," *Atlantic Monthly,* Dec. 1866, 761–65, in Foner, ed., *Life and Writings* 4:199, 203.

25. Douglass, *Anti-Slavery Standard,* 29 May 1869; "Plan to Buy Land to Be Sold to Freedmen," quoted in Foner, ed., *Life and Writings* 4:31–32.

26. Douglass, "Condition of the Country," *DM,* Feb. 1863; "The Present and Future of the Colored Race in America," *DM,* June 1863. In the latter, Douglass blamed the baneful, contaminating influence of Southern slavery for past discriminatory laws in Northern states.

27. Douglass, "Salutory of the Corresponding Editor," *The New National Era,* 27 Jan. 1870.

28. Douglass, "The Proclamation and a Negro Army," *DM,* March 1863; "Emancipation, Racism, and the Work Before Us," an address delivered in Philadelphia, 4 Dec. 1863, in *FD Papers,* 3:608–9.

29. Woodward reaches these conclusions about Reconstruction, e.g., in the essays, "Political Legacy of Reconstruction," *The Journal of Negro Education* 26 (1959): 231–40, reprinted in *The Burden of Southern History* (New York: Random House, 1961), 89–107; and "Seeds of Failure in the Radical Race Policy," *American Counterpoint: Slavery and Racism in the North-South Dialogue* (New York: Little, Brown & Co., 1964), reprinted in *Reconstruction in the South,* 2d ed., ed. Edwin C. Rozenc (Lexington, Mass.: D. C. Heath & Co., 1972), 245–63.

30. See C. Vann Woodward's *Reunion and Reaction: The Compromise of 1877 and the End of Reconstruction,* 2d ed. (Garden City, N.Y.: Doubleday, 1956), and relevant portions of his *Origins of the New South, 1877–1913* (Baton Rouge: Louisiana State Univ. Press, 1951), for the political dynamics behind the end of Reconstruction. W. E. B. Du Bois, *Black Reconstruction in America, 1860–1880* (New York: Harcourt, Brace & Co., 1935) has had a revolutionary impact on the historiography of Reconstruction generally and is still one of the best studies of the subject.

31. Douglass, "The Civil Rights Case," speech at the Civil Rights Mass-Meeting, Lincoln Hall, 22 Oct. 1883, in Foner, ed., *Life and Writings* 4:393–94, 403.

32. Douglass, "Why Is the Negro Lynched?" in Foner, ed., *Life and Writings* 4:511, 491, 515, 523.

33. Although increasingly dissatisfied with Republican policies toward blacks, Douglass remained an active party member and held several federal appointments, including Marshall of the District of Columbia and U.S.

Ambassador to Haiti. At the same time, he continued to be outspoken in protesting wrongs where and as he saw them.

## Chapter 3

1. Booker T. Washington, "An Account of a Speech before the National Negro Business League," Atlanta, Ga., 30 Aug. 1906, in *The Booker T. Washington Papers,* ed. Louis R. Harlan et al., 13 vols. (Urbana: Univ. of Illinois Press, 1972–85), 9:63 (hereafter, *BTW Papers*).

2. These and other of Washington's childhood experiences are told in Louis R. Harlan, *Booker T. Washington,* 2 vols. (New York: Oxford Univ. Press, 1972, 1983), 1:16–17. Harlan's study is the best scholarly biography of Washington. My account of Washington's life and activities draws mainly on Washington's own recollections plus Harlan.

3. His conviction about the wisdom of blacks looking to paternalistic white elites for aid was reinforced by an incident in which General Ruffner tried to intervene in a local dispute to save blacks from Ku Klux Klan violence. See Washington, *Up from Slavery* (New York, 1901; Dell Publishing, 1965), 63–64.

4. General Armstrong's letter is quoted in Harlan, *Booker T. Washington,* 1:110. See also Harlan's description of young Washington's hero-worship of the general, ch. 3.

5. There was, for example, the black migration to Kansas by the so-called "Exodusters" and renewed interest in African colonization after Reconstruction as voiced by leaders such as Bishop Henry M. Turner. See, for example, Nell Irvin Painter, *Exodusters: Black Migration to Kansas after Reconstruction* (New York: Alfred A. Knopf, 1977).

6. Washington, "The Atlanta Exposition Address," reprinted in *Up from Slavery,* 154–59.

7. The best analysis of national press reaction to the Atlanta address is in Rayford W. Logan, *The Betrayal of the Negro: From Rutherford B. Hayes to Woodrow Wilson,* revised edition of *The Negro in American Life and Thought: The Nadir, 1877–1901* (New York: Collier Books, 1965), ch. 14. President Cleveland's congratulatory message is reprinted in Washington, *Up from Slavery,* 160–61.

8. An excellent analysis of Washington's thought and its close fit with his day's dominant social-intellectual trends appears in C. Vann Woodward, *Origins of the New South, 1877–1913* (Baton Rouge: Louisiana State Univ. Press, 1951; reprinted, 1971), 356–60.

9. On conservative trends in Anglo-American social thought during the Gilded Age, see, e.g., Richard Hofstadter, *Social Darwinism in American Thought,* revised ed. (New York: Braziller, 1967).

10. See note 7.

11. Harlan, *Booker T. Washington,* vol. 1, ch. 8, describes Washington's use of espionage to undermine rival educators in the 1880s. In vol. 2, chs. 2 and 4, Harlan details Washington's covert acts against black opponents after the turn of the century. See also August Meier, "Booker T. Washington and the Negro Press," *Journal of Negro History* 38 (Jan. 1953): 67–90, for analysis of Washington's control over black newspapers.

12. See Wilson Moses, *Black Messiahs and Uncle Toms,* ch. 6, for another analysis of Washington's civil-religious symbolism.

13. Washington, "Address at the Dexter Avenue Baptist Church," Montgomery, Ala., 19 May 1901, in *BTW Papers* 6:113; *Selected Speeches of Booker T. Washington,* ed. E. David Washington (Garden City, N.Y.: Doubleday, Doran, and Co., 1932), 81.

14. Washington, *Up from Slavery,* 97–98, 109–10.

15. Washington, "Democracy and Education," 30 Sept. 1896, in *Negro Social and Political Thought, 1850–1920: Representative Texts,* ed. Howard Brotz (New York: Basic Books, 1966), 364; "An Address in Atlanta," 25 Sept. 1899, in *BTW Papers* 5:218.

16. George Fredrickson, *The Black Image in the White Mind: The Debate on Afro-American Character and Destiny, 1817–1914* (New York: Harper & Row, 1971); S. P. Fullinwider, *The Mind and Mood of Black America* (Homewood, Ill.: Dorsey Press, 1969); and Wilson Jeremiah Moses, *Black Messiahs and Uncle Toms: Social and Literary Manipulations of a Religious Myth* (University Park: Pennsylvania State Univ. Press, 1982)—all incisively treat the cultural tradition of blacks as Christlike.

17. Washington, *Up from Slavery,* 157; quoted in Minneapolis *Journal,* 2 Feb. 1896, in *Booker T. Washington,* ed. Emma Lou Thornbrough (Englewood Cliffs, N.J.: Prentice Hall, 1969), 72.

18. Washington, *Up from Slavery,* 157.

19. Washington, "A Fragment of an Address at the Metropolitan A.M.E. Church," Washington, D.C., 18 Mar. 1904, *BTW Papers* 7:469; "An Address on the Twenty-Fifth Anniversary of Tuskegee Institute," Tuskegee, Ala., 4 Apr. 1906, *BTW Papers* 8:568; "An Address before the Christian Endeavor Society," Nashville, Tenn., 7 July 1898, *BTW Papers* 4:439; *Up from Slavery,* 159; *The Future of the American Negro* (New York: Negro Univ. Press, 1899; reprint, 1969), 24–25.

20. On Washington's involvement in Africa, see Louis Harlan, "Booker T. Washington and the White Man's Burden," *American Historical Review* 71 (Jan. 1966): 441–67. Washington, "Industrial Education in Africa," *Independent* 60 (13 Mar. 1906): 616–19. Herbert Aptheker links Washington's cooperation with colonialism to his support of monopoly capitalism generally and of its whole program, including imperialism. This also holds, in his view, for Washington's hatred of unions, program of industrial education, and bowing to the establishment of Jim Crow racism. On these

central and connected contemporary issues, Aptheker stresses that the views of Washington and W. E. B. Du Bois fundamentally diverged. See, for examples, chs. 6 and 7, "American Imperialism and White Chauvinism" and "The Niagara Movement," in Aptheker, *Afro-American History: The Modern Era* (New York: Citadel Press, 1971).

21. Washington, *Up from Slavery*, 24–25.

22. Washington, *Future of the American Negro, BTW Papers* 5:360–61; "Lawbreaking Negroes Worst Enemy to Race," Atlanta, Ga., 30 Aug. 1906, *BTW Papers* 9:62–63.

23. Robert Bellah labels the myth of the self-made individual the doctrine of "Salvation and Success in America" in *The Broken Covenant* (New York: Seabury Press, 1975), 70.

24. Washington, *Up from Slavery*, 118, 205.

25. Bercovitch, *American Jeremiad*, 154–57.

26. Washington, *The Future of the American Negro*, 209, 178, 95–96, ix; *Character Building: Being Addresses Delivered on Sunday Evenings to the Students of Tuskegee Institute by Booker T. Washington* (New York: Doubleday, 1902), 119–31; *Black Belt Diamonds: Gems from the Speeches, Addresses, and Talks to Students of Booker T. Washington* (New York: Fortune and Scott, 1898; reprint, Miami: Mnemosyne Publishing, 1969), 56.

27. Washington, *Future of the American Negro*, 231–32, 198; *Up from Slavery*, 223; *Future of the Negro*, 85; *Selected Speeches*, 81.

28. Washington, "What Is It That The Negro Needs Most?" Tuskegee Institute, 23 Nov. 1907, *BTW Papers* 9:407; *Future of the American Negro*, 104–5, 179.

29. Washington, *Selected Speeches*, 81; *Up from Slavery*, 40; *Selected Speeches*, 76–77.

30. Washington, *Black Belt Diamonds*, 115; *Future of the American Negro*, 151.

31. Washington, "An Address in Atlanta," 25 Sept. 1899, *BTW Papers* 5:217–18; "Address at the Metropolitan A.M.E. Church," 22 May 1900, *BTW Papers* 5:528.

32. Washington, *Black Belt Diamonds*, 72; *Selected Speeches*, 94.

33. Martin Marty distinguishes between "priestly" and "prophetic" genres of civil religion in his essay, "Two Kinds of Two Kinds of Civil Religion," in *American Civil Religion*, ed. Russell Richey and Donald Jones (New York: Harper & Row, 1974), 139–57.

34. The best source of information on Wells and her career is her own *Crusade for Justice: The Autobiography of Ida B. Wells*, ed. Alfreda M. Duster (Chicago: Univ. of Chicago Press, 1970). Best known as Ida B. Wells, she usually used the last name of Wells-Barnett after her marriage to Ferdinand Barnett in 1895.

35. Ibid., 49.

36. Ibid., 52. In the editorial, Wells urged Memphis blacks—outnumbered, outarmed, without legal protection—to take the only recourse open: leave town. Many did, and in two month's time, six thousand people had left. Most of these moved to the Oklahoma territory in the Black Exoduster movement that was enthusiastically endorsed in the *Free Speech*. Some others moved North.

37. Wells, *Crusade for Justice*, 64.

38. Ibid., 65–66.

39. Wells, like Frederick Douglass before her, took her propaganda crusade to the British Isles as a way of embarrassing Americans before the world and gaining greater domestic attention.

40. Wells, *Crusade for Justice*, 65. A useful description of the social function and mythology of lynchings appears in Donald L. Grant, *The Anti-Lynching Movement: 1883–1931* (San Francisco: R. & E. Research Associates, 1975), ch. 1.

41. Taking information from established newspapers also had the practical advantage of relieving Wells from the time and expense of collecting all her own material from scratch. She also selectively supplemented previously published information with her own on-the-scene interviewing and investigative reporting.

42. Ida Wells-Barnett, *A Red Record: Tabulated Statistics and Alleged Causes of Lynchings in the United States, 1892–1893–1894* (Chicago: Donohue & Heneberry, 1895), reprinted in Wells-Barnett, *On Lynching: Southern Horrors, A Red Record, Mob Rule in New Orleans* (Salem, N.H.: Ayer Co., 1987), 43–45. (Note: all following citations of these three pamphlets refer to their reprinting in the *On Lynching* edition). Ida B. Wells-Barnett, "Lynching and the Excuse for It," *The Independent* 53 (16 May 1901): 1133–36, reprinted in *Lynching and Rape: An Exchange of Views*, ed. Bettina Aptheker (San Jose, Cal.: American Institute for Marxist Studies, 1977), 33.

43. Wells, *Southern Horrors: Lynch Law in All Its Phases* (New York: New York Age Print, 1892); in *On Lynching*, 6.

44. Wells, *Crusade for Justice*, 70; *Southern Horrors*, 11.

45. Wells, *Southern Horrors*, 11; *Crusade for Justice*, 70; *Southern Horrors*, 13.

46. Wells, *Southern Horrors*, 13–15.

47. Ibid., 14–15.

48. Wells, "Preface," *Southern Horrors; Crusade for Justice*, 219.

49. Wells, *Southern Horrors*, 23–24.

50. Wells, *Crusade for Justice*, 72. Frederick Douglass denounced lynching, e.g., in "Why Is the Negro Lynched?" 1894, in Philip Foner, ed., *The Life and Writings of Frederick Douglass*, 4 vols. (New York: International

Publishers, 1950–54), 4:491–523. Douglass and Wells prominently contributed to Wells, ed., *The Reason Why the Colored American Is Not in the World's Columbian Exposition* (Chicago: published by the author, 1893).

51. Washington's correspondence is peppered with derogatory comments about Wells and Barnett. He once wrote to his personal secretary, "Miss Wells is fast making herself so ridiculous that everybody is getting tired of her"; Washington to Emmet Jay Scott, 21 July 1900, *BTW Papers* 5:589. For similar expressions of enmity toward the Wells-Barnetts, see Washington to Charles William Anderson, 16 June 1904, *BTW Papers* 7:533, Timothy Thomas Fortune to Washington, 27 Sept. 1899, *BTW Papers* 5:220–21, and Charles William Anderson to Washington, 31 May 1909, *BTW Papers* 10:127.

52. BTW, "Account of a Speech before the National Negro Business League," Atlanta, Ga., 30 Aug. 1906, *BTW Papers* 8:63.

53. Washington, "Speech before National Negro Business League," *BTW Papers* 9:62; interview with Washington in Indianapolis *Freeman*, 28 Aug. 1897, 4.

54. For an indication of Wells's pronounced distaste for Washington's habit of telling degrading "darky" stories to whites, see *Crusade for Justice*, 331.

55. Washington, "A Protest Against Lynching," Tuskegee, Ala., 22 Feb. 1904, *BTW Papers* 7:447–48.

56. See, for example, Washington, "Lynch Law and Anarchy," *The Sunday School Times*, 2 Nov. 1901, *BTW Papers* 13:500–4.

57. Washington to Oswald Garrison Villard, 16 Nov. 1904, cited in Grant, *The Anti-Lynching Movement*, 14.

58. Wells, *Red Record*, 98–99.

59. Wells, *Crusade for Justice*, 169.

60. Wells, *Red Record*, 7, emphasis added; "Introduction," *Mob Rule in New Orleans* (Chicago: n.p., 1900).

61. Wells, *Red Record*, 98–99.

62. Wells, "Lynching and the Excuse for It," in Bettina Aptheker, *Lynching and Rape*, 34; Wells, *Red Record*, 97; Wells, "Introduction," *Mob Rule in New Orleans*.

63. Frederick Douglass's letter to Ida B. Wells, 25 Oct. 1892, reprinted as introduction to Wells, *Southern Horrors*.

64. See Barbara Welters, "The Cult of True Womanhood: 1820–1860," *American Quarterly*, Summer 1966, 151–74; and Nancy F. Cott, *The Bonds of Womanhood: "Woman's Sphere" in New England, 1780–1835* (New Haven: Yale Univ. Press, 1978) for descriptions of the nineteenth-century "cult of true womanhood" and emergent "ideology of domesticity." Cott's work is particularly instructive on how this socially conservative,

constrictive ideology could be used to justify considerable expansion of women's social role and activities.

65. See Barbara Welter, "The Feminization of American Religion," in *Clio's Consciousness Raised: New Perspectives on the History of Women,* ed. Mary Hartman and Lois Banner (New York: Harper & Row, 1974), 137–57; and Ann Douglass, *The Feminization of American Culture* (New York: Knopf, 1977).

66. Examples of Wells's own frequent references to the race's threatened "manhood" appear, e.g., in *Crusade for Justice,* 280–81, and in *Red Record,* 11.

67. Wells, *Crusade for Justice,* 248–52. See all of ch. 30, "A Divided Duty."

## Chapter 4

1. W. E. B. Du Bois, *Dusk of Dawn: An Essay toward an Autobiography of a Race Concept* (New York: Harcourt, Brace and World, 1950; reprint ed., 1968), 18. The best-known book biographies of Du Bois are Elliott Rudwick, *W. E. B. Du Bois: Propagandist of the Negro Revolt,* 2d ed. (1962; reprinted, New York: Antheneum Press, 1972), and Francis L. Broderick, *W. E. B. Du Bois: Negro Leader in Time of Crisis* (Stanford, Calif.: Stanford Univ. Press, 1959). Unfortunately, both works reflect their authors' pronounced Cold War era biases and are often highly negative, especially of Du Bois's latter career. Manning Marable, *W. E. B. Du Bois: Black Radical Democrat* (Boston: Twayne Publishers, 1986), is a valuable interpretive survey of Du Bois's thought; another useful intellectual overview and attempt at categorization is Joseph DeMarco, *The Social Thought of W. E. B. Du Bois* (Lanham, Md.: University Press of America, 1983). Analyses of Du Bois's literary works include Arnold Rampersad, *The Art and Imagination of W. E. B. Du Bois* (Cambridge: Harvard Univ. Press, 1976), and Herbert Aptheker, *The Literary Legacy of W. E. B. Du Bois* (White Plains, N.Y.: Kraus-Thomson, 1989), a collection of Aptheker's introductory essays to various editions of Du Bois's literary works.

One cannot do research on Du Bois for long without coming across the substantial work, editorial and otherwise, of Herbert Aptheker. Many of the sources cited herein are most accessible to readers in his and others' editions of Du Bois's writings. Of particular value as a research tool is *The Complete Published Works of W. E. B. Du Bois,* comp. and ed. Herbert Aptheker, 37 vols. (Millwood, N.Y.: Kraus-Thomson, 1973–1986). This series includes *Annotated Bibliography of the Published Works of W. E. B. Du Bois* (1973), *Selections from the Crisis* (1983), *Newspaper Columns* (1986), *Creative Writings* (1985), *Writings in Periodical Literature* (1982), *Pamphlets and Leaflets* (1986), and new editions of all Du Bois's books.

Other compilations by Aptheker, not part of the Kraus-Thomson series, include *The Correspondence of W. E. B. Du Bois*, 3 vols. (Amherst: Univ. of Massachusetts Press, 1973–1979), and *Against Racism: Unpublished Essays, Papers, Addresses, 1887–1961* (Amherst: Univ. of Massachusetts Press, 1985). Dr. Aptheker was also the original holder and editor of Du Bois's papers, now in the Papers of W. E. B. Du Bois archival collection at the University of Massachusetts, Amherst, cited hereafter as Du Bois papers.

2. Rampersad, *Art and Imagination of W. E. B. Du Bois*, 22. Rampersad provides an excellent discussion of Puritanism's lasting imprint on Du Bois's social values.

3. Du Bois, *Dusk of Dawn*, 10–11; Du Bois, *The Autobiography of W. E. B. Du Bois: A Soliloquy on Viewing My Life from the Last Decades of Its First Century*, ed. Herbert Aptheker (New York: International Publishers, 1968), 75.

4. Du Bois, "Reminiscences of William Edward Burghardt Du Bois," interviews by William T. Ingersoll, 1963, Columbia Oral History Collection, Columbia University, 8; Du Bois, *Dusk of Dawn*, 14; Du Bois, *Autobiography*, 94.

5. Du Bois, *Dusk of Dawn*, 20.

6. Du Bois, *Autobiography*, 107; Du Bois, "My Evolving Program for Negro Freedom," in *What the Negro Wants*, ed. Rayford W. Logan (Chapel Hill: Univ. of North Carolina Press, 1944), 36.

7. Du Bois, "My Evolving Program," in *What the Negro Wants*, 37.

8. Du Bois, "W. E. B. Du Bois," interview by Moses Asch, 1961, Folkways Recording, Schomburg Center for Research in Black Culture, New York Public Library, Oral History Tape Collection; Du Bois, *Dusk of Dawn*, 101.

At age fifteen, Du Bois began writing columns for the New York *Globe* on the activities of the black community of Great Barrington, and these articles show his keen interest in blacks' collective actions and welfare. The young man frequently gave advice and exhortations to local blacks. See for examples, his columns of 14 April, 5 May, and 29 Sept. 1883, and of 17 May 1884, in *Newspaper Columns by W. E. B. Du Bois*, ed. Herbert Aptheker, 2 vols. (White Plains, N.Y.: Kraus-Thomson, 1986), 1:1, 2, 7, 14. While Du Bois's racial pride was quite strong, it must be said that he was never chauvinistic and that the reach of his social concern was invariably catholic. All his life, for example, he was a stout supporter of equal rights for women. Noting Du Bois's urgent concern first for his own people, Herbert Aptheker writes that Du Bois "never thought of this in any exclusionary sense or with any invidious content." Rather, he regarded ending "the specially onerous oppression and exploitation" of blacks as "part of the necessary effort to eliminate inequality and injustice" against any oppressed group. Aptheker, "W. E. B. Du Bois and Africa," in *Racism, Imperialism, and Peace*, ed. Marvin Berlowitz and Carol Martin (Minneapolis: MEP Publications, 1987), 178. These points hold equally true for Frederick Douglass; see note 10, Chapter 1, above. A recent treatment of Du Bois's racial nationalism is Sterling Stuckey, *Slave Culture: Nationalist Theory and the Foundations of Black America* (New York: Oxford Univ. Press, 1987), ch. 5, "W. E. B. Du Bois: Black Cultural Reality and the Meaning of Freedom."

9. Du Bois, "My Evolving Program," 37–38.

10. Du Bois did occasionally try to enter general student social life at Harvard University, as when he tried out for and was rejected by the glee club. See Du Bois, *Dusk of Dawn*, 35, on his racially isolated social experience at Harvard.

11. Du Bois, "My Evolving Program," 37.

12. Du Bois, *Autobiography*, 157.

13. Ibid., 206; Du Bois, *Dusk of Dawn*, 51.

14. Rampersad, *Art and Imagination of W. E. B. Du Bois*, 36–39. For all its force and undeniable brilliance, Du Bois's writing style conformed more to the ideals of the nineteenth than the twentieth century. Du Bois's writing reflected the gentility and refinement admired by the Victorians, and his language was poetic but also slightly quaint and anachronistic.

15. As previously noted, Du Bois's penchant for middle-class criticism of black social behavior went back as far as high school. See note 8 above.

16. Du Bois, *Autobiography*, 194.

17. Du Bois, *The Philadelphia Negro* (Philadelphia, 1896; reprinted in *The Seventh Son: The Thought and Writings of W. E. B. Du Bois*, 2 vols., ed. Julius Lester (New York: Random House, 1971), 1:223.

18. Ibid., 223–24.

19. Ibid., 221, 226–28.

20. Du Bois, letter to Booker T. Washington, 24 Sept. 1895, Du Bois papers, microfilm reel 3.

21. Du Bois recalled the Hose lynching incident in several memoirs. Quotations here are from Du Bois, "A Pageant in Seven Decades, 1868–1938," 70th Birthday Address, 23 Feb. 1938, Atlanta University, papers of W. E. B. Du Bois, reel 86, reprinted in *W. E. B. Du Bois Speaks: Speeches and Addresses*, ed. Philip S. Foner, 2 vols. (New York: Pathfinder Press, 1970), 1:39. *Dusk of Dawn*, 67; *Autobiography*, 222.

22. Du Bois, "A Pageant in Seven Decades," in *W. E. B. Du Bois Speaks*, 1:48.

23. Du Bois, *The Souls of Black Folk* (Chicago, 1903; reprint, New York: New American Library, 1969), 87–89.

24. Ibid., 91–95.

25. Du Bois, "Niagara Address to the Nation," 16 Aug. 1906, Harpers Ferry, W. Va., reprinted in Foner, ed., *W. E. B. Du Bois Speaks*, 1:170–73.

26. See, for example, Du Bois, "Black Social Equals," 1908, unpublished manuscript rejected by *McClure's* magazine, Du Bois papers, reel 82; and "Marrying of Black Folk," *Independent*, no. 69, 13 Oct. 1910, 1812–13.

27. The most thorough treatment of Washington's efforts to undo the Niagara Movement is in Louis R. Harlan, *Booker T. Washington*, vol. 2, ch. 2, "Damning Niagara." In addition to external hostility, Niagara suffered from internal weaknesses, too, such as depending on a tiny membership base of educated black professionals. See Herbert Aptheker, "The Niagara Movement," in *Afro-American History: The Modern Era* (New York: Citadel Press, 1971), 127–28. He especially notes Niagara activists' success in gradually prying away from the Tuskegee camp important white former Washington supporters such as Oswald Villard and Moorfield Storey and bringing them over to the radicals' viewpoint.

28. On the archetypal place of abolitionism in Du Bois's social imagination, see Howard-Pitney, "Afro-American Jeremiahs," doctoral thesis, University of Minnesota, 1984, 172–73, 243–46, 335. Du Bois's 1909 biography, *John Brown* (n.p.: George Jacobs, 1909), reveals the author's emotional identification with the great abolitionist martyr and his tendency to link abolitionism to Progressive reform. In the 1950s, Du Bois, then extremely radical, compared abolitionism to the contemporary Communist movement. See, for example, "Abolitionism and Communism," unpublished article, 1952, Du Bois papers, reel 83.

29. Du Bois usually addressed both blacks and whites, although his messianic rhetoric was directed at different times more to one than the other. Most major causes such as black economic and cultural nationalism, pan-Africanism, liberal reform, and socialism found some expression in this thought throughout his life. What is most significant are marked shifts in the predominance of some concerns over others across time. It is a matter of measuring the frequency with which he made certain proposals and the relative balance between his various ideological commitments that best describe the trajectory of his evolving thought.

30. Du Bois, "The Crisis," *The Crisis*, 10 Nov. 1910.

31. Du Bois, "Don't Be Bitter," *Crisis*, May 1914.

32. Du Bois, "Optimist and Pessimist," *Crisis*, March 1912.

33. Du Bois, "Easter," *Crisis*, April 1912; "Emancipation," *Crisis*, Jan. 1913.

34. Du Bois, "The Present," *Crisis*, Aug. 1917; "The Black Soldier," *Crisis*, June 1918.

35. Du Bois, "Awake, America," *Crisis*, Sept. 1917.

36. Du Bois, "Returning Soldiers," *Crisis*, May 1919; "Forward," *Crisis*, Sept. 1920.

37. Du Bois, "My Mission," *Crisis*, April 1919; "Africa," *Crisis*, April

1924. Herbert Aptheker, "W. E. B. Du Bois and Africa," in *Racism, Imperialism, and Peace,* 178–96, offers an incisive analysis of Du Bois's writings and views on Africa.

38. Du Bois, "Criteria for Negro Art," *Crisis,* Oct. 1926.

39. Du Bois, "Co-operation," *Crisis,* Nov. 1918.

40. Du Bois, "My Evolving Program," 61–62. See also *Dusk of Dawn,* 295–96. For Du Bois's repeated arguments for his plan in *The Crisis* see, for example, "Segregation," Jan. 1934; "Segregation in the North," April 1934; and "The Anti-Segregation Campaign," June 1934. One of the most comprehensive statements of his position during the 1930s was "The Negro and Social Reconstruction," 22 May 1936, in *Against Racism,* 103–58.

41. Du Bois, *Dusk of Dawn,* 296.

42. Du Bois, "Co-operation," *Crisis,* Nov. 1918; "Thrift Calls," *Crisis,* Jan. 1921.

43. Du Bois, *Dusk of Dawn,* 217, 220.

44. Du Bois, "Black and White Workers," *Crisis,* March 1928; Du Bois, *Dusk of Dawn,* 205; "Marxism and the Negro Problem," *Crisis,* May 1933. He railed angrily at white workers for "voting navies to keep China, India, Mexico and Central America in subjection" and for being content to be "paid high wages . . . while 'niggers' and 'dagoes' and 'chinks' starve, slave, and die." Du Bois, "Black and White Workers," *Crisis,* March 1928.

45. Du Bois, "The Class Struggle," *Crisis,* Aug. 1921; Du Bois, "Marxism and the Negro Problem," *Crisis,* May 1933.

46. Du Bois, *Dusk of Dawn,* 326, 5–6, 282.

47. Ibid., 6–7.

## Chapter 5

1. The best book-length study of Bethune is Rackham Holt, *Mary McLeod Bethune: A Biography* (Garden City, N.Y.: Doubleday, 1964). For brief useful discussions of her significance in the New Deal period, see relevant portions of Harvard Sitkoff, *A New Deal for Blacks: The Emergence of Civil Rights as a National Issue* (New York: Oxford Univ. Press, 1978), and John Kirby, *Black Americans in the Roosevelt Era: Liberalism and Race* (Knoxville: Univ. of Tennessee Press, 1980). A highly critical opinion of her political effectiveness in the National Youth Administration is expressed by B. Joyce Ross, "Mary McLeod Bethune and the National Youth Administration: A Case Study of Power Relationships in the Black Cabinet of Franklin D. Roosevelt," *Journal of Negro History* 60 (Jan. 1975): 1–28.

2. Mary McLeod Bethune, " 'I'll Never Turn Back No More!' " *Opportunity* 16 (16 Nov. 1938): 324–26.

3. Bethune, "Clarifying Our Vision with the Facts," Proceedings of the

22d Annual Meeting of the Association of the Study of Negro Life and History in Washington, D.C., 3 Oct. 1937, *Journal of Negro History* 1 (Jan. 1938): 11.

4. Bethune, "The High Cost of Keeping the Negro Inferior," n.d., Mary McLeod Bethune Papers, 1923–1942, Armistad Research Center, New Orleans, La., microtext, box 2, folder 14; "Certain Unalienable Rights," in *What the Negro Wants*, ed. Rayford W. Logan (Chapel Hill: Univ. of North Carolina Press, 1944): 253.

5. Bethune, "Certain Unalienable Rights," in *What the Negro Wants*, 248–58; " 'I'll Never Turn Back No More!' " 326.

6. Bethune, "President's Address to the 15th Biennial Convention of the National Association of Colored Women," Civic Auditorium, Oakland, Calif., 2 Aug. 1926, 9, Bethune papers, box 2, folder 16; "Closed Doors," n.d., 9, Bethune Papers, box 2, folder 18.

7. Bethune, " 'I'll Never Turn Back No More!' " 326, 324; "What Are We Fighting For?" Address for Panel I, Industrial Production, 1942, 12–13, Bethune papers, box 2, folder 13.

8. Bethune, "Certain Unalienable Rights," 256.

9. Bethune, "Certain Unalienable Rights," 257.

10. Bethune, " 'I'll Never Turn Back No More!' " 326.

11. Bethune, "Certain Unalienable Rights," 256; "What Are We Fighting For?" 12–13, Bethune papers, box 2, folder 13.

12. Bethune, "Closed Doors," 7; "President's Address to 15th Biennial Convention of the National Association of Colored Women," 9–10.

13. Bethune, "What Are We Fighting For?" 12–13.

14. Albertus Bethune eventually disappeared from her life after ten years of marriage; the two never saw each other again. See Holt, *Mary McLeod Bethune*, 124–26, on her marriage.

15. Mary Bethune, quoted in Edwin R. Embree, *Thirteen Against the Odds* (Port Washington, N.Y.: Viking Press, 1944; reissue, Kennikat Press, 1968), 15.

16. Holt, *Mary McLeod Bethune*, 110.

17. Bethune, "The Negro Woman in American Life," n.d., 1–5, Bethune Papers, box 2, folder 7.

18. Holt, *Mary McLeod Bethune*, 115; Bethune, "My Secret Talks with FDR," *Ebony*, April 1949, 42–51; reprinted in *The Negro in Depression and War*, ed. Bernard Sternsher (Chicago: Quadrangle Books, 1969), 55.

19. Ross, "Mary McLeod Bethune and the National Youth Administration," 4–5.

20. Ibid., 5.

21. Bethune, Minutes of the Association of Southern Women for the Prevention of Lynching (ASWPL) Annual Meeting, 11 Jan. 1935, ASWPL Papers; Bethune to Jessie Daniel Ames, 24 Mar. 1938, ASWPL Papers. Both

statements appear as quoted in Jacqueline Dowd Hall, *Revolt Against Chivalry: Jessie Daniel Ames and the Women's Campaign Against Lynching* (New York: Columbia Univ. Press, 1979), 244, 247–48.

22. Ross, "Mary McLeod Bethune and the NYA," 7–8.

23. It is an interesting question whether Bethune consciously used a feminine speaking manner as her most effective technique in a sexist society or whether she actually had internalized those social roles and values. Did she try other rhetorical styles and find her audiences unreceptive to them? Unfortunately, I have no evidence that would help answer this question.

24. Executive Order 8802 which established a Fair Employment Practices Committee was promulgated in response to labor leader A. Philip Randolph's plans for a massive black march on Washington to protest racial discrimination in national war production.

25. Sitkoff, *A New Deal for Blacks,* 335. See Kirby, *Black Americans in the Roosevelt Era,* especially ch. 9, for another assessment of the ambiguous but, on balance, positive and emboldening legacy of the New Deal for black Americans.

26. See Kirby, *Black Americans in the Roosevelt Era,* especially ch. 8, "Race, Class, and Reform: The Intellectual Struggle," on the trend among black liberal thinkers toward emphasizing class and downplaying racial factors in analyzing the "Negro Problem" during the 1930s and 40s. This incisive chapter treats thinkers such as Ralph Bunche, Charles Johnson, and W. E. B. Du Bois. Du Bois's sharpening convictions on the centrality of race and racism to black and white Americans were not well received during this era.

27. Du Bois, *In Battle for Peace: The Story of My Eighty-Third Birthday* (New York: Masses and Mainstream, 1952), 180.

28. Du Bois, *Color and Democracy: Colonies and Peace* (New York: Harcourt, Brace, 1945).

29. Du Bois, "Prospects of a World without Race Conflict," *American Journal of Sociology* 49 (March 1944): 450–56.

30. Du Bois, "I Take My Stand," *Arena* (London), June-July 1951, 50–54; Du Bois, *In Battle for Peace,* 24.

31. Du Bois's peace activism made him suspect in the eyes of the United States government. In 1949, for example, he organized an international peace conference in New York City which publicly endorsed peaceful relations with the Soviet Union, and he attended peace congresses in Paris and Moscow. To coordinate such activities between conferences, he helped found the New York Peace Information Center in 1951. He was subsequently indicted by a federal grand jury for failing to register the center as a "foreign agency" of the Soviet Union. He stood trial but was acquitted.

32. Du Bois, *Autobiography,* 395.

33. This popular legend is asserted, for example, by Stephen B. Oates in

his discussion of Du Bois in *Let the Trumpet Sound: The Life of Martin Luther King, Jr.* (New York: New American Library, 1982), 263–64.

34. Du Bois considered the *Encyclopedia Africana* project to be his last crowning scholarly achievement. See Shirley Graham Du Bois, *His Day Is Marching On: A Memoir of W. E. B. Du Bois* (Philadelphia: J. B. Lippincott, 1971), 323. The Supreme Court decision in question, *Communist Party v. S.A.C.B.*, upheld section 6, restricting travel of suspected radicals, of the McCarran Internal Security Act of 1950. Section 6 was later struck down by the court in *Aptheker v. Secretary of State* (1964).

35. This is according to Herbert Aptheker, Du Bois's close friend and colleague during these years. Aptheker identified the motives behind Du Bois's decisions to go to Ghana, join the Communist Party, and become a Ghanaian citizen. Aptheker, interview with writer, San Jose, Calif., 1 Aug. 1989.

36. This is confirmed by Aptheker as well as by Shirley Graham Du Bois, who was with Dr. Du Bois at the U.S. embassy in Ghana when they were denied American passports. Mrs. Du Bois said that their acceptance of Ghanaian citizenship implied no statement about the United States. Instead, she stressed the positive basis of Dr. Du Bois's decision—his gratitude to and pride in his African host country. See *His Day Is Marching On*, 352–53.

37. W. E. B. Du Bois, "Our American Heritage," 4 July 1954, Camp Unity, New York; and "Civil Rights," WMCA radio broadcast, New York, 19 Oct. 1950, both in Du Bois papers, reel 81, 13–15; reel 80, 1–3.

38. Du Bois, *In Battle for Peace*, 163–64; Du Bois, "The United States," May 1961, Du Bois papers, reel 83: 2; "Peace Is Dangerous," pamphlet, portions delivered as speech in Town Hall, New York, 28 Sept. 1951, Du Bois papers, reel 86: 14–15.

39. Du Bois, *Autobiography*, 419–23.

## Chapter 6

1. A useful overview of twentieth-century racial trends and realities before the civil rights movement is provided in Harvard Sitkoff, *The Struggle for Black Equality, 1954–1980* (New York: Hill & Wang, 1981), ch. 1.

2. The potential national impact of the growing black vote, for example, first became clear to political observers in the 1948 presidential election, in which the black vote was widely regarded as a pivotal factor in Harry Truman's re-election.

3. Wartime Japan also was overtly racist, as has been recently demonstrated by John Dower in *War without Mercy: Race and Power in the Pacific War* (New York: Pantheon Books, 1986).

4. The "separate but equal" doctrine, overturned by *Brown*, had been established by the Supreme Court in 1896 in *Plessy v. Ferguson*. For an

extensive narrative account of the legal campaign leading to the 1954
*Brown* decision, see Richard Kluger, *Simple Justice: The History of* Brown
*v.* Board of Education *and Black Americans' Struggle for Equality* (New
York: Knopf, 1975).

5. Resistance to the Supreme Court's desegregation order was offered
by the white Southern social-political order from top to bottom. "The
Southern Manifesto," a statement that announced defiance of the order and
invoked states' rights against federal intrusion, was signed by nineteen
Southern senators and seventy-seven members of the House of Representatives.

6. The best-known instance of early violent white resistance to desegregation of public education occurred in Little Rock, Arkansas, in 1957. See
Sitkoff, *The Struggle for Black Equality,* 29–33, for a description of events
in Little Rock.

7. For a theory of race liberation leaders' social origins, see Introduc-
tion, n. 24 above. General biographies of King include David L. Lewis,
*King: A Critical Biography* (Baltimore: Pelican Books, 1970), and Stephen
B. Oates, *Let the Trumpet Sound: The Life of Martin Luther King, Jr.* (New
York: New American Library, 1982). A literate and readable book is Taylor
Branch, *Parting the Waters: America in the King Years, 1954–63* (New
York: Simon & Schuster, 1988). Notable recent scholarly studies of King's
activities include David J. Garrow, *Bearing the Cross: Martin Luther King,
Jr., and the Southern Christian Leadership Conference* (New York: William
Morrow, 1986), and Adam Fairclough, *To Redeem the Soul of America:
The Southern Christian Leadership Conference and Martin Luther King, Jr.*
(Athens: Univ. of Georgia Press, 1987). I will customarily refer the reader to
Garrow for more information about King's public campaigns and activities.

8. Among the several sources for these boyhood stories is Coretta Scott
King, *My Life with Martin Luther King, Jr.* (New York: Holt, Rinehart &
Winston, 1969), 82–83. King's family had an established history of social
activism and service. His maternal grandfather, A. D. Williams, was the first
president of the Atlanta chapter of the National Association for the Advancement of Colored People.

9. King, *Stride toward Freedom: The Montgomery Story* (New York:
Harper & Row, 1958), 91; typescript carbon of why King felt called to the
ministry, Martin Luther King, Jr., Collection, Special Collections Depart-
ment, Mugar Library, Boston University (hereafter cited as BU Collection),
drawer 3.

10. King, *Stride toward Freedom,* 91.

11. Walter Rauschenbusch's *Christianity and the Social Crisis* (1917)
had a major formative impact on King's ideas and attitudes about social
justice. Walter Chivers, King's sociology teacher and advisor at Morehouse,
stressed the causal connection between capitalist exploitation and racism in

his courses. John J. Ansbro, *Martin Luther King, Jr: The Making of a Mind* (Maryknoll, N.Y.: Orbis Books, 1982), provides an excellent introduction to the influential sources of King's ideas. See Ansbro, ch. 4, on King's conception of the social mission of the church.

12. King, student lecture notes, systematic theology, BU Collection, drawer 14; *Stride toward Freedom*, 98–99. See Ansbro, *The Making of a Mind*, ch. 4, on issues concerning nonviolence and the moral imperative of resisting collective evil.

13. See King's recollection about his decision to accept a pastoral position in Montgomery in *Stride toward Freedom*, 18–19.

14. On King's self-identity as a chosen instrument of divine will, see, e.g., ibid., 63, 69–70, and Coretta Scott King, *My Life with Martin Luther King*, 82–83.

15. For a well-researched account of the Montgomery bus boycott and King's role in leading it, see David Garrow, *Bearing the Cross*, ch. 1. Fairclough, *To Redeem the Soul of America*, ch. 1, "The Preachers and the People," contains perceptive sociological analysis of the vital leadership provided by King and other black ministers in the Montgomery bus boycott and civil rights movement generally.

16. The black leaders who chose King calculated that the MIA president, who would be the focus of local white hostility, should be a young man who could move on and continue his career elsewhere.

17. King, *Stride toward Freedom*, 59–60.

18. Quotations come from transcriptions of a tape recording of King's mass address of 5 Dec. 1955 at the Holt Street Baptist Church in Donald H. Smith, "Martin Luther King, Jr.: In the Beginning at Montgomery," *Southern Speech Journal* 34 (Fall 1968): 12–16.

19. Observers' remarks quoted in Oates, *Let the Trumpet Sound*, 72.

20. For King's account of the Montgomery boycott campaign, see King, *Stride toward Freedom*.

21. A number of students of political conflict have commented on King's skillful use of highly charged symbols to win public support. David Garrow's *Protest at Selma: Martin Luther King, Jr., and the Voting Rights Act of 1965* (New Haven: Yale Univ. Press, 1978) ably analyzes the strategies used and social dynamics manipulated by King in the Selma demonstrations to gain national voting rights legislation. Two political scientists, Roger Cobb and Charles Elder, use King and the civil rights movement to illustrate how the intelligent use of symbols by one side in a social-political conflict may help it prevail. See *Participation in American Politics: The Dynamic of Agenda-Building* (Baltimore: Johns Hopkins Univ. Press, 1972), especially chs. 8 and 9.

22. King, *Stride toward Freedom*, 137–38; C. Scott King, *My Life with Martin Luther King*, 130.

23. Andrew Michael Manis, *Southern Civil Religions in Conflict: Black and White Baptists and Civil Rights, 1947–1957* (Athens: Univ. of Georgia Press, 1987), offers a useful consideration of King and other black Southern Christians' uses and understanding of American civil religion.

24. King, address at Holt Street Baptist Church, Montgomery, Ala., 5 Dec. 1955, in David H. Smith, "Martin Luther King," *Southern Speech Journal* 34 (Fall 1968): 12–16.

25. August Meier has written perceptively about how King's rhetoric, by both arousing guilt in whites and offering forgiveness, provided a powerful emotional catharsis for many white listeners; see "On the Role of Martin Luther King, Jr.," *New Politics* 4 (Winter 1965): 52–59.

26. King, "Crisis and the Church," *Council Quarterly* (n.d.), 1, clipping in BU Collection, drawer 13; King, statement to the press at the beginning of the Youth Leadership Conference, 15 April 1960, Raleigh, N.C., BU Collection, drawer 4.

27. King, part of a speech at a meeting launching the Crusade for Citizenship in Miami, Fla., 12 Feb. 1958, BU Collection, drawer 1.

28. King, "The Future of Integration," 1–2, speech delivered at the State University of Iowa, Iowa City, 11 Nov. 1959, BU Collection, drawer 1.

29. King, "A Knock at Midnight," sermon printed in *Strength to Love* (New York: Harper & Row, 1958), 42.

30. King, "The Future of Integration," 1–2. King clearly continued the black patriotic dissenting tactic of presenting the nation's response to blacks' demands for justice as the supreme test of its democratic mission. See Leonard Sweet on this "testing" theme in black American protest, in *Black Images of America* (New York: W. W. Norton, 1976).

31. King, "The Crisis in Human Relations," 11–12, BU Collection, drawer 10.

32. King, address accepting the Social Justice Award of the Religion and Labor Foundation, 1, BU Collection; "The Crisis in Human Relations," 12, BU, drawer 10.

33. King, "Address to the March on Washington, 1963," *Southern Christian Leadership Conference Newsletter* 1 (Sept. 1963): 5, 8.

34. King, *Where Do We Go from Here: Chaos or Community?* (New York: Harper & Row, 1967; Bantam ed., 1968), 158. This is almost the exact phrasing of King's challenge at the close of his original mass address at Holt Street Baptist Church in Montgomery on 5 Dec. 1955. "A Mighty Army of Love," *SCLC Newsletter* 2 (Oct.–Nov. 1964): 7.

35. King, *Where Do We Go from Here?* 157–58. See S. P. Fullinwider, *The Mind and Mood of Black America: Twentieth-Century Thought* (Homewood, Ill.: Dorsey Press, 1969), especially ch. 8, "The Moral Equivalent of Blackness," on King's portrayal of Afro-Americans as a uniquely

Christlike people with a special historical mission and destiny. These are similar to the themes explored in Wilson Moses, *Black Messiahs and Uncle Toms* (University Park: Pennsylvania State Univ. Press, 1982).

36. See, for example, King, "Letter from a Birmingham Jail," in King, *Why We Can't Wait* (New York: Signet, 1964), 87, and King, *Where Do We Go from Here*, 55–56 and 62. For a systematic treatment of King's intellectual response to separatist black nationalism, see Ansbro, *Making of a Mind*, 204–24.

37. The book was *Stride toward Freedom: The Montgomery Story*.

38. For more about the student sit-ins and freedom rides, see Sitkoff, *The Struggle for Black Equality*, chs. 3 and 4; on King and the SCLC's relation to these student protests, see Garrow, *Bearing the Cross*, ch. 3.

39. Eisenhower's cautious conservatism and gradualistic approach to social change frustrated King, leading him to write that the president could not be

> committed to anything which involved a structural change in . . . American society. His conservativism was fixed and rigid, and any evil defacing the nation had to be extracted bit by bit with a tweezer because the surgeon's knife was an instrument too radical to touch this best of all possible societies.

Untitled, undated manuscript during Eisenhower administration, BU Collection, drawer 10, no. 25.

40. King, manuscript of untitled article written for *The Nation* magazine, BU, drawer 1.

41. King, "Fumbling on the New Frontier," *Nation*, 3 March 1962, 190–93.

42. Early in his administration, President Kennedy, in deference to white Southern Democrats, appointed many segregationists to Southern federal benches. Passing a national tax-cut bill, moreover, was the president's highest domestic goal through 1962 and he needed Southern votes.

43. SCLC's Birmingham campaign is detailed in Garrow, *Bearing the Cross*, ch. 5.

44. President Kennedy quoted in Oates, *Let the Trumpet Sound*, 235.

45. Ibid., 245.

46. Albanese, *Sons of the Fathers*, 48–53.

47. The most sophisticated analysis of the strategy behind the successful 1965 Selma campaign is Garrow, *Protest at Selma*. See also n. 21 above.

48. Lyndon Johnson quoted in Sitkoff, *The Struggle for Black Equality*, 193–95. The Kings were jubilant over the president's message. Hearing the speech at home on television, Coretta Scott King told herself, "Thank goodness, they've finally got the message of what my husband has been saying for years." C. Scott King, *My Life with Martin Luther King*, 264.

Chapter 7

1. Du Bois's comments about King, quoted in Stephen B. Oates, *Let the Trumpet Sound: The Life of Martin Luther King, Jr.* (New York: New American Library, 1982), 263; Du Bois, "Socialism and the American Negro," speech to Wisconsin Socialist Club, University of Wisconsin, Madison, 9 April 1960, recorded by Lee Baxandall, Schomburg Center for Research in Black Culture, New York Public Library, Oral History Tape Collection (hereafter Schomburg Center); Du Bois's comments on student sit-ins in "W. E. B. Du Bois"; interview by Moses Asch, 1961, Folkways Recording, Tape Collection, Schomburg Center.

2. Martin Luther King, Jr., "Conscience and the Vietnam War," in *The Trumpet of Conscience* (New York: Harper & Row, 1967), 75–77. The essays in this book were first delivered as the Massey lectures over the Canadian Broadcasting Corporation in November and December 1967.

3. King, "In a Word–NOW," *The New York Times Magazine*, 29 Sept. 1963, 91–92; Johnson quoted in Oates, *Let the Trumpet Sound*, 274.

4. King, "The Negro Revolution in 1964," editorial in *SCLC Newsletter*, Jan. 1964, reprinted in *Negro History Bulletin* 31 (May 1968): 18–19.

5. King, *Why We Can't Wait* (New York: Signet Books, 1964; rev. ed., New York: New American Library, 1968), 24, 136.

6. Ibid., 136.

7. Ibid., 135, 141–42. In 1964, after Birmingham, King and SCLC figures such as Bayard Rustin were charting a grand strategy for the movement which called for shifting from protest to politics. Much of the SCLC leadership felt that the future of the movement and its goals lay in forming a national political alliance to alter American economic institutions and move the country leftward. See David J. Garrow's account of these discussions and ideas in *Bearing the Cross: Martin Luther King, Jr., and the Southern Christian Leadership Conference* (New York: William Morrow, 1986), 287–88, 352–54.

8. King, *Why We Can't Wait*, 146.

9. See August Meier and Elliot Rudwick, *From Plantation to Ghetto*, 3d ed. (New York: Hill & Wang, 1976), 301–3, for a brief description of the 1960s urban race riots.

10. King, "Playboy Interview: Martin Luther King, Jr.," *Playboy*, Jan. 1965, 78.

11. King followed Gandhi in distinguishing between *satyagraha*, commitment to nonviolence as a total way of life and inviolable moral principle, and *duragraha*, the pragmatic use of nonviolence simply as an effective social tool. David J. Garrow ably discusses King and SCLC's strategic use of nonviolence *and* of the violence that so often met it in *Protest at Selma*. See

also James Colaiaco, *Martin Luther King, Jr.: Apostle of Militant Nonviolence* (New York: St. Martin's Press, 1988), ch. 8.

12. Harvard Sitkoff summarizes the disillusioning and radicalizing impact of the 1964 Mississippi Freedom Summer and 1965 Selma March on young black activists in *The Struggle for Black Equality, 1954–1980* (New York: Hill & Wang, 1981), ch. 6.

13. King, "Next Stop: The North," *Saturday Review*, 13 Nov. 1965, 33.

14. Garrow describes King's Chicago campaign in *Bearing the Cross*, chs. 8, 9.

15. See Sitkoff, *Struggle for Black Equality*, 209–10 and 212–17, on the birth of "Black Power" during the 1966 Mississippi March.

16. King quoted in "Dr. King Felled by Rock," *Chicago Tribune*, 6 Aug. 1966, 1.

17. American troop totals in Vietnam cited in Oates, *Let the Trumpet Sound*, 375.

18. For some indication of many SCLC leaders' misgivings about King's public dissent from U.S. policies in Vietnam, see Garrow, *Bearing the Cross*, 552. King's most decisive response to other civil rights activists' objections to his anti-war stance appeared in "Quote and Unquote," *SCLC Newsletter*, June–July 1965, 4.

19. King quoted by David Halberstam, "The Second Coming of Martin Luther King," *Harper's* Magazine, Aug. 1967, reprinted in *Martin Luther King, Jr.: A Profile*, ed. C. Eric Lincoln (New York: Hill & Wang, 1970), 206–7.

20. For an example of King's publicized criticism of FBI handling of civil rights cases in the South, see the *Atlanta Constitution* and *New York Times* on 19 Nov. 1962. The ongoing sniping between King and FBI director Hoover is related in David J. Garrow, *The FBI and Martin Luther King, Jr.*, hereafter cited as *FBI & MLK* (New York: Penguin Books, 1981).

21. The origins of FBI suspicion of Communist infiltration of SCLC and secret governmental surveillance of King in the early 1960s are described in *FBI & MLK*, ch. 1. Garrow offers an engrossing study of the development of the FBI's subsequent campaign to monitor and discredit King. The extent of Hoover's personal and ideological hostility toward King ran very deep, according to Garrow, to the point of obsession.

22. See *FBI & MLK*, on Kennedy administration efforts to induce King to purge Stanley Levison and another suspect from his organization as well as on King's initial suspension and eventual resumption of contacts with Levison.

23. Ibid., chs. 3 and 4. Although the supposed Communist link through Levison was the original justification for bugging King's hotel rooms and home and office phones, by 1965 the FBI effort to destroy King by collecting

and disseminating compromising data was based not only on the Levison connection but on anything potentially damaging to King. The Communist infiltration charge, which never yielded hard evidence, was displaced by the bureau's subsequent discovery and recording of King's sexual affairs in hotel rooms, which became the chief target of FBI surveillance. Hoover's animosity stemmed from his racist and anti-radical sentiments. By 1966, President Johnson was angry at King's anti-war stance, and both Hoover and Johnson showed keen interest in collecting and seeking to use data about King's extramarital sex life against him. Garrow concludes, however, that in 1967 and 1968 the FBI and White House's main worry about King focused on his political activities and goals. See *FBI & MLK,* 204–8, on the shifting focus of government concern regarding King.

24. Coretta Scott King, *My Life with Martin Luther King, Jr.* (New York: Holt, Rinehart & Winston, 1969), 293–96.

25. Martin Luther King, Jr., *Where Do We Go from Here: Chaos or Community?* (New York: Harper & Row, 1967; Bantam, 1968), 1–4.

26. Ibid., 5–8, 13, 19.

27. Ibid., 80–81.

28. Ibid., 90–92.

29. Ibid., 95.

30. Ibid., 81, 94, 84, 83.

31. Ibid., 85, 93.

32. Ibid., 97–99.

33. Ibid., 177, 59–60, 167, 160, 7.

34. Ibid., 157.

35. Ibid., 198–200, 207–8.

36. Ibid., 203, 212–13.

37. Ibid., 221, 219–20, 215.

38. King, "Beyond Vietnam," address at Riverside Church, New York City, 4 April 1967, printed in *Congressional Record—House,* 113.9, 2 May 1967, 11402–11405. Taped address in Oral History Collection, Schomburg Center.

39. Quotations and information from *FBI & MLK,* 181.

40. For general background on the government's smear campaign against King, and his reaction, see Ibid., chs. 3, 4.

41. In 1967, King told journalist David Halberstam: "For years I labored with the idea of reforming the existing institutions of society, a little here, a little there. Now I feel differently. I think you've got to go to a reconstruction of the entire society, a revolution of values." Halberstam, "Second Coming of Martin Luther King," in Lincoln, *Martin Luther King,* 201–2.

42. C. Scott King, *My Life with Martin Luther King,* 297.

43. Statement by Bernard Lee, quoted in Oates, *Let the Trumpet Sound*, 451.

44. King quoted in Oates, *Let the Trumpet Sound*, 457–58.

45. *FBI & MLK*, 182–87.

46. As a college student, King studied Karl Marx's basic ideas and formed his life-long attitude toward Communism. On the one hand, he found much of Marx's critique of capitalism valid; he generally viewed the phenomena of capitalist exploitation and economic inequality in a Marxian framework. But he also believed that, historically, Communism was a flawed system tending toward oppressive totalitarianism and disregard for the individual. He found its philosophical materialism repugnant, believing that Communism's failure to respect individuals was related to its unwillingness to recognize spiritual realities and, specifically, each person's innate worth as a child of God.

King's social ideal was neither Communism nor capitalism *per se* but "the beloved community," his conception of a commonwealth of love, cooperation, and sharing consonant with Christian values. He typically advocated a social synthesis that avoided the pitfalls and combined the positive aspects of both capitalism and Communism. For an early exposition on this theme, see his sermon, "How Should a Christian View Communism?" in *Strength to Love*, (New York: Harper & Row, 1958), 96–105; original manuscript in Martin Luther King, Jr., Collection, Special Collections Dept., Mugar Library, Boston University, drawer 1. The "revolution of values" that King advocated in *Where Do We Go from Here?* likewise was to "go beyond traditional capitalism and Communism" (216–18).

47. King, "Honoring Dr. Du Bois," Centennial Address at Carnegie Hall, New York City, 23 Feb. 1968; reprinted as introduction in Du Bois, *Dusk of Dawn* (reprint ed., 1968), xiv–xvi, viii, xvi.

48. On friends' concern over King's despondent state of mind, see, e.g., Garrow, *Bearing the Cross*, 611–17.

49. King quoted by C. Scott King, *My Life with Martin Luther King*, 297, and by Hosea Williams, as cited in *FBI & MLK*, 215.

50. King, "Remaining Awake through a Revolution," sermon at Washington National Cathedral, Washington, D.C., 31 March 1968, printed in *Congressional Record—House*, 114.7, "Extension of Remarks," 9 Apr. 1968, 9391, 9395–9397.

51. King, "Mountain Top Speech," Memphis, 3 April 1968, manuscript copy in Schomburg Center, vertical folder file; C. Scott King, *My Life with Martin Luther King*, 317.

52. Andrew Young, "Playboy Interview," *Playboy* Magazine, July 1977, 74.

53. Ralph Abernathy is quoted as claiming that the Poor People's Campaign would have been canceled by King had he lived, in David L. Lewis,

*King: A Critical Biography* (Baltimore: Pelican Books, 1970), 385. When the Washington campaign did take place from May to July 1968, it was a fiasco. On the event, see Adam Fairclough, *To Redeem the Soul of America: The Southern Christian Leadership Conference and Martin Luther King, Jr.* (Athens: Univ. of Georgia Press, 1987), 385–88.

## Conclusion

1. See Sacvan Bercovitch, "Ritual of Consensus," ch. 5, in *The American Jeremiad* (Madison: Univ. of Wisconsin Press, 1978).

2. Even Mary McLeod Bethune, for example, was accused by congressmen of Communist associations in the late forties and was summoned to appear before a congressional investigation committee. See Rackham Holt, *Mary McLeod Bethune* (Garden City, N.Y.: Doubleday, 1964), 247–48.

3. See, for examples, Nancy F. Cott, *The Bonds of Womanhood: "Women's Sphere" in New England, 1780–1835* (New Haven: Yale Univ. Press, 1978), and Eugene Genovese, *Roll, Jordan, Roll: The World the Slaves Made* (New York: Pantheon Books, 1974). Both writers stress the positive uses to which hegemonic ideology has been put by subordinate groups.

4. Leonard Sweet, *Black Images of America, 1784–1870* (New York: W. W. Norton, 1976), 6; Wilson Jeremiah Moses, *Black Messiahs and Uncle Toms: Social and Literary Manipulations of a Religious Myth* (University Park: Pennsylvania State Univ. Press, 1982), ix, 15–16, 233–34, and throughout.

5. A useful Jackson biography is Barbara A. Reynolds, *Jesse Jackson: America's David* (Washington, D.C.: JFJ Associates, 1985), originally published as *Jesse Jackson: The Man, the Movement, the Myth* (1975). An astute although highly critical political analysis of Jackson's 1984 presidential campaign is Adolph L. Reed, Jr., *The Jesse Jackson Phenomenon* (New Haven: Yale Univ. Press, 1986).

6. An invaluable collection of thirty-six important representative speeches by Jackson is Jesse L. Jackson, *Straight from the Heart,* ed. Rodger D. Hatch and Frank E. Watkins (Philadelphia: Fortress Press, 1987), and I quote Jackson extensively from speeches printed therein. Jackson, "Religious Liberty: Civil Disobedience, Conscience, and Survival," Philadelphia, 27 April 1976, printed in *Straight from the Heart* (hereafter cited as *SFH*), 147; "Equity in a New World Order," New Orleans, 16 July 1980, *SFH*, 290; "Save the Family Farm and the Farm Family," Chicago, 26 Jan. 1985, *SFH*, 287; "Equity in a New World Order," *SFH*, 291.

7. Jackson, "In Search of a New Vision and a New Focus," Washington, D.C., 17 May 1980, *SFH*, 97; "Jackson Criticizes Anti-Affirmative

Action Actions," press release, 3 Dec. 1983, Jesse Jackson for President Committee.

8. Jackson as quoted in "Sniping on the Road," *Time*, 19 Dec. 1983, 12; "Jackson Declares Formal Candidacy," *New York Times*, 3 Nov. 1982, 13.

9. Jackson, "An End to Corporate Blackmail," Akron, Ohio, 7 May 1984, *SFH*, 314; "Saving the Family Farm and the Farm Family," *SFH*, 283.

10. Jackson, "Equity in a New World Order," *SFH*, 290; "Political Votes, Economic Oats," Washington, D.C., 20 Jan. 1978, *SFH*, 35.

11. Jackson quotation from the speech "The Rejected Stones: Cornerstones of a New Public Policy," Washington, D.C., 10 May 1983, quoted in *SFH*, xxii.

12. Jackson, "The Quest for a Just Society and a Peaceful World," Washington, D.C., 3 Nov. 1983, quoted in *SFH*, xiv; "The Candidate's Challenge: The Call of Conscience, the Courage of Conviction," Democratic National Convention, San Francisco, 17 July 1984, printed in *SFH*, 3.

13. Jackson, "Liberation and Justice," Chicago, 9 July 1981, *SFH*, 62; "Equity in a New World Order," *SFH*, 306; "Black Americans Seek Economic Equity and Parity," Chicago (?), 16 March 1982, *SFH*, 277.

14. Jackson, "A Case for Continuing Affirmative Action," Chicago, 15 Sept. 1978, quoted in *SFH*, xv; "We Must Act, Not Just React: The Present Challenge of Our Democracy," address to Americans for Democratic Action, 11 June 1978, *SFH*, 38–39, 44; "A Case for Continuing Affirmative Action," quoted in *SFH*, xv.

15. Jackson, "In Search of a New Focus and a New Vision," *SFH*, 99; "The Rejected Stones: Cornerstones of a New Public Policy," quoted in *SFH*, xxiv; "The Candidate's Challenge," *SFH*, 18. Many observers have commented on Jackson's penchant for clothing himself and his movement in messianic rhetoric. See, e.g., Barbara Reynolds, *Jesse Jackson: America's David*, 13.

16. Jackson, "Overcoming New Forms of Denial," Worcester, Mass., 24 May 1981, *SFH*, 101; "Equity in a New World Order," *SFH*, 289.

17. Jackson, "Brown: Twenty-five Years Later," essay in *New York Daily News*, 17 May 1979, reprinted in *SFH*, 87. Jackson purposely presents himself as King's successor by stressing his close personal and organizational ties with the martyred leader, even claiming (inaccurately) that King spoke last to him and died in his arms. See an example of Jackson's summons to realize King's "unfinished agenda" in "Completing the Agenda of Dr. King," *Ebony*, June 1974, 116–18, 120–21. Barbara Reynolds treats Jackson's intense image-making after King's death in order to establish himself as the heir to King's legacy in *Jesse Jackson*, ch. 9.

18. Jackson, "Binding Up the Wounds," Manchester, N.H., 26 Feb. 1984, *SFH*, 132; "Protecting the Legacy of Dr. Martin Luther King, Jr.,"

Atlanta, 15 Jan. 1986, *SFH*, 130–31. For examples of Jackson's charac-
terizing his movement as a spiritual "crusade," see "An End to Corporate
Blackmail," *SFH*, 315, and "Equity in a New World Order," *SFH*, 307.

19. The political enthusiasm for Jackson in 1984 may have arisen as
much from deep contemporary black discontent with American "politics as
usual" as from a reservoir of black hope and optimism. Adolph Reed goes as
far as to identify the highly "dispirited" mood and "uncertain conditions"
prevalent among Afro-Americans as one of the chief factors behind Jackson's national political success in *The Jesse Jackson Phenomenon*, 106.

20. A historic tension in the civil religion between commitment to the
public interest, or civic virtue, and a contrary tradition glorifying the pursuit
of private self-interest—and the danger of the former tradition's eclipse by
the latter—is the major theme of Bellah's book *The Broken Covenant*.
Concern over the strength of "radical individualism" is also pronounced in
Robert N. Bellah, et al., *Habits of the Heart: Individualism and Commitment in American Life* (Berkeley and Los Angeles: Univ. of California Press,
1985).

# INDEX

Abolitionism, 12–13, 15, 18, 22, 32, 35–41, 44, 59, 99–100, 102

Africa, 24–25, 29, 65, 104–5, 127, 130, 135, 143, 175. *See also* African-American colonization plans; Pan-Africanism

African-American colonization plans, to Africa or elsewhere, 14, 24–25, 34, 65

Afro-American Council. *See* National Afro-American Council

Albanese, Catherine, 8–11, 152. *See also* American Revolution; *Communitas*

Alger, Horatio, 66

American Anti-Slavery Society, 18. *See also* Abolitionism

American civil religion, 5–11, 20, 70, 100–4, 131–32, 142–45, 173–74

American Revolution, 6, 8–11, 37, 143, 152–53

American School of Ethnography, 27, 29

Ames, Jessie Daniel, 123

Anglo-Saxonism, 9, 26–27, 30–31, 62–64

Armstrong, General Samuel, 46. *See also* Washington, Booker T.

Association of Southern Women for the Prevention of Lynching, 123

Atlanta Industrial Exposition Address (Atlanta Address or Compromise), 57. *See also* Washington, Booker T.

Atlanta Race Riot of 1906, 95

Atlanta University, 92, 97. *See also* Du Bois, W. E. B.

Auld, Thomas, 17–18

*Autobiography of W. E. B. Du Bois, The* (W. E. B. Du Bois), 132

Barnett, Ferdinand, 74–79

Bellah, Robert N., 194

Bercovitch, Sacvan, 7–8, 67, 186

Bethune, Albertus, 118

Bethune, Mary McLeod, 15–16, 111–26, 143, 193; and Black Cabinet, 111; on black self-help and reform, 116–17; and black women's clubs, 111, 120; on black women's missionary role, 120–21; childhood and youth of, 118; compared with W. E. B. Du Bois, 112, 187; compared with Martin Luther King, Jr., 112, 126, 143; compared with Booker T. Washington, 112, 118–19; compared with Ida B. Wells, 112, conciliatory rhetoric of, toward whites, 112, 118, 121–24; "darky jokes" told by, 123; and Daytona Normal and Industrial School for Negro Girls, 119; as educational administrator and fundraiser, 118–20; and ideology of "true womanhood," 118; and industrial education, 116, 119; on interracial progressive political alliance, 116; as jeremiah, 112–15, 124; and National Youth Admin-